Buddha's Daughters

A SHAMBHALA SUN BOOK

Buddha's Daughters

*Teachings from Women Who Are
Shaping Buddhism in the West*

Edited by Andrea Miller and the editors
of the *Shambhala Sun*

SHAMBHALA · BOSTON & LONDON · 2014

Shambhala Publications, Inc.
Horticultural Hall
300 Massachusetts Avenue
Boston, Massachusetts 02115
www.shambhala.com

9 8 7 6 5 4 3 2 1

First Edition
Printed in the United States of America

⊗ This edition is printed on acid-free paper that meets the
American National Standards Institute z39.48 Standard.
♻ This book is printed on 30% postconsumer recycled paper.
For more information please visit www.shambhala.com.

Distributed in the United States by Penguin Random House LLC
and in Canada by Random House of Canada Ltd

Library of Congress Cataloging-in-Publication Data

Buddha's daughters: teachings from women who are shaping
Buddhism in the West / edited by Andrea Miller and the editors
of the Shambhala Sun.—First Edition.
pages cm
ISBN 978-1-59030-623-9 (pbk.: alk. paper)
1. Buddhism—Doctrines. I. Miller, Andrea, editor of compilation.
BQ4165.B795 2014
294.3′42—dc23
2013017801

Contents

INTRODUCTION · 1

Tsultrim Allione · 5
Meeting the Demon

Jan Chozen Bays · 16
The Joy of Mindful Eating

Charlotte Joko Beck · 24
False Generalizations

Sylvia Boorstein · 30
The Three Marks of Existence
Meeting the Wild World with a Benevolent Heart
Suffering's Not the Only Story

Tara Brach · 42
Befriend Your Fears

Pema Chödrön · 52
When Things Fall Apart
Breathing In Pain, Breathing Out Relief
Practicing Peace in Times of War

CONTENTS

Thubten Chodron · 73
Spiritual Mentor

Darlene Cohen · 83
The Scenery of Cancer

Christina Feldman · 88
Long Journey to a Bow

Carolyn Rose Gimian · 96
I Want to Be Genuine

Joan Halifax · 102
The Way of the Mountain

Blanche Hartman · 119
Just to Be Alive Is Enough

Houn Jiyu-Kennett · 126
Why Study Zen?

Khandro Rinpoche · 137
The Great Impermanence of Death

Ayya Khema · 142
Nothing Special

Sister Chan Khong · 148
Learning True Love
Deep Relaxation

CONTENTS

Anne Carolyn Klein · 158
It's All Good

Judith L. Lief · 165
The Middle Way of Stress

Joanna Macy · 179
Gratitude: Where Healing the Earth Begins

Karen Maezen Miller · 188
Waking Up Alone
Sanitize Option: What Children Do Not Require

Pat Enkyo O'Hara · 204
Include Everything

Toni Packer · 211
What Is the Me?
Images in Relationship

Tenzin Palmo · 223
Vajrayana

Sharon Salzberg · 239
The Journey of Faith
Living Our Love
Don't I Know You?

Maurine Stuart · 262
There Are No Repetitions

CONTENTS

Joan Sutherland · 267
Through the Dharma Gate

Bonnie Myotai Treace · 274
We Cannot Stop the Hail, but We Can Be Awake

CREDITS · 283

ABOUT THE EDITOR · 289

Buddha's Daughters

Introduction

I HAD MY first taste of Buddhism in university when I took a class on Chinese and Japanese religions. Since the presentation was dryly academic, I didn't immediately connect with the Four Noble Truths. Truth be told, I can barely remember taking notes on them, but what did spark my interest was the dissemination of Buddhism. My professor explained that as the Buddha's teachings fanned out across Asia, they took on the flavor of each culture they encountered. And the result—from Tibet to Thailand and beyond— was that Buddhist traditions came to be so varied that early Western colonialists and missionaries were not always aware they embodied a single religion.

My professor did not go on to address modern Buddhism's state of flux—that was beyond the scope of our class. Yet Buddhism is indeed still transforming. Now it's taking root in the West, and decade by decade it's developing into its own Western strain, or strains. Admittedly, the results are mixed. It's uncomfortable, for instance, to see the Western vice of materialism seeping into Buddhist practice. But to date there is one hallmark of Western Buddhism that I believe is cause for unreserved celebration. In the West, women teachers play a prominent role; their wise voices are strong and getting stronger.

Some critics have claimed that to place importance on there being women teachers is to inappropriately genderize the dharma. As I see it, however, it's actually a small step in degenderizing it. Though the Buddha taught that at the ultimate level there is neither male nor female, at the relative level that's far from the case. Beyond just having different bodies, we are socialized differently and accorded different roles and

1

privileges. In a myriad of ways, these factors determine how we experience the world and, by extension, how we experience the spiritual path. So, while both male and female teachers can speak on the universal human experience, women can also have a unique perspective that can be helpful to both male and female students.

Yet Buddhism, like all world religions, has largely been shaped and defined by men. Century after century—right up to the present day—women have been denied teachings and ordinations and have found themselves relegated to monastery kitchens. They've been deemed to be of "lower birth," and in some lineages even the most experienced, aged nun must bow before any monk, even the youngest, least experienced among them. Blocked by such discrimination, women have had limited opportunities to develop into advanced practitioners and teachers. Yet despite the challenges, women have diligently practiced from the beginning—since the days of the Buddha. I hope this anthology serves as an inspiration for contemporary women practitioners.

Buddha's Daughters honors women teachers who are pivotal in shaping Western Buddhism and showcases the incredible diversity of their teachings. The book—organized alphabetically—begins and ends with pieces that introduce us to women ancestors. In "Meeting the Demon," Tsultrim Allione introduces us to Machig Labdron, an innovative eleventh-century yogini who deeply influenced the development of Vajrayana Buddhism. Then in "We Cannot Stop the Hail, but We Can Be Awake," Bonnie Myotai Treace lyrically evokes the poetry and practice of Rengetsu, a Pure Land Buddhist nun who is considered one of the greatest Japanese poets of the nineteenth century.

Between these two bookend pieces, the teachings presented are so broad both stylistically and thematically that it's difficult to tidily pinpoint them as feminine or not. Personally, I prefer not to limit them with labels. These teachings touch on universal truths. Though they're all by women, I believe they are each as universal as any one voice can ever be.

In this anthology, Buddhist concepts and practices are the focus. Sylvia Boorstein, for instance, unpacks her fresh take on the traditional teachings of the three marks of existence, while Pema Chödrön offers a heartfelt teaching on *tonglen,* a practice for developing compassion.

Practices that help bring mind and body into alignment are foundational. For Jan Chozen Bays, what's on our plates is the vehicle. Bite by bite, moment by moment, how do we experience taste, texture, color, scent, sound? Can we be curious and playful as we investigate our responses to food and what really satisfies our deepest hunger? Then Sister Chan Khong leads us through a simple yet powerful meditation on the body. Soften the shoulders, feel the breath, rest the eyes, she says. A relaxed body is a relaxed mind.

In addition to valuing women's voices, Western Buddhism is further characterized by having a large number of lay teachers, and the teachings in this anthology reflect that. Here we see teachings that are both profound and highly practical—fully grounded in lay life, including intimate relationships. Notably, Karen Maezen Miller explores the arc of romance. "Love that lasts allows the *love story* to end," she says. "It isn't laden with romantic fantasies or regret; it's not defined or limited, not stingy or selfish." The love story always ends eventually, but that doesn't necessarily mean a messy breakup. It can, instead, signify the beginning of a real and enduring love.

How to deal with difficulties is addressed in many different ways by the teachers in this collection. In "The Scenery of Cancer," Darlene Cohen teaches by recounting her moving, intensely personal story of practicing with illness. Judith L. Lief, on the other hand, offers us a comprehensive tour de force that explains the source of stress or suffering from the Buddhist perspective.

Leapfrogging from the personal to the global, I am particularly encouraged by the teachings in this anthology that are informed by social awareness. Pat Enkyo O'Hara takes us with her on a street retreat. Sleeping in an alley, eating in soup kitchens, she comes to understand the groundlessness of being homeless. Joanna Macy's passion, in contrast, is for the environment, and she believes that the first step in healing the Earth lies in cultivating gratitude. Capitalism tells us that we need more—more stuff, more entertainment, more comfort. But more only burdens our landfills and feeds our dissatisfaction. So gratitude is liberating, says Macy. It helps us realize that we are sufficient, and that realization frees us.

Publishing *Buddha's Daughters* has involved the effort and support of many people. I would like to thank Beth Frankl, my editor at Shambhala Publications, and her assistant editor, John Golebiewski, as well as colleagues at the *Shambhala Sun* and *Buddhadharma: The Practitioner's Quarterly*, in particular Melvin McLeod. This book was his brainchild and would never have come to be without him. He has also been my mentor for seven years, and I am extremely grateful for everything I have learned from him—and also for his compassion and humor.

Additionally, I would like to thank the women of my blood lineage— my grandmothers, my mother, my aunts. Their fortitude makes me proud; their quirks make me smile. I couldn't be happier that when I look in the mirror, I see snatches of them, and when I look deeper inside myself, I see them there, too.

Tsultrim Allione

As Lama Tsultrim Allione has described it, her first awakening to sexism in Buddhism took place in 1973 while attending a three-month series of empowerments in India given by Dilgo Khyentse Rinpoche. At the time, Tsultrim Allione was a nun, and she and another Western nun were looking for seating when they were told that—being women—they'd have to sit at the back of the temple, behind all the monks, including the squirming, recently ordained six-year-olds who could not yet read.

Seven years later, Tsultrim Allione was living as a lay practitioner in Italy when she lost a child to sudden infant death syndrome. "After Chiara's death," she wrote in the Winter 2010 issue of *Buddhadharma*, "I felt a deep need for the stories of women in my tradition. I needed to know their lives." The biographies of men simply weren't helping her to work through her intense grief.

In 1981, she traveled to India and Nepal in search of the biographies of great Tibetan women practitioners, and this research developed into her first book, *Women of Wisdom*. She says it also gave her strength, inspiration, and a broader awareness of women and women's issues around the world.

In the following teaching, "Meeting the Demon," Tsultrim Allione tells the story of the celebrated eleventh-century Tibetan yogini Machig Labdron. According to Tsultrim Allione, we can learn from this semi-mythical biography how to face and take care of our metaphorical demons, including addiction, stress, trauma, anger, and self-hatred. In so doing, she claims, we can turn these demons into allies. This teaching by Tsultrim Allione is based on the principles of Chöd, a practice found primarily in Tibetan Buddhism, which is meant to cut through the ego. Machig Labdron is known as the Mother of Chöd.

Today Tsultrim Allione is the spiritual director of Tara Mandala, a retreat center she founded in Pagosa Springs, Colorado.

———

Meeting the Demon

MAHATMA GANDHI, one of the greatest peace activists of the twentieth century, changed the course of India's history by quite literally feeding his enemy. Gandhi, the story goes, was told that he would be visited by a British official who would threaten him with prison if he did not give up what the British considered to be the subversive activity of marching in protest of the British salt tax. Gandhi's advisers suggested putting nails in the road to puncture the tires of the official's car.

"You will do nothing of the sort," said Gandhi. "We shall invite him to tea."

Crestfallen, his followers obeyed. When the official arrived, he entered full of pomp and purpose. "Now then, Mr. Gandhi, this so-called salt marching has to stop at once. Otherwise I shall be forced to arrest you."

"Well," said Gandhi, "first let's have some tea."

The Englishman agreed, reluctantly. Then, when he had drained his cup, he said briskly, "Now we must get down to business. About these marches..."

Gandhi smiled. "Not just yet. Have some more tea and biscuits; there are more important things to talk about."

And so it went. The Englishman became increasingly interested in what the Mahatma had to say, drank many more cups of tea and ate many more biscuits until he was completely diverted from his official task, and eventually went away won over to Gandhi's cause. Gandhi used the medium of tea, an English ritual that implies civility and mutual respect, and literally fed this enemy until he became an ally. His tactic of feeding rather than fighting contributed to one of the most extraordinary nonviolent revolutions in history.

This same tactic had been used nearly a millennium earlier, when the great eleventh-century Tibetan yogini Machig Labdron was receiving initiation from her teacher, Sonam Lama, with several of her spiritual sisters. At a key moment in the initiation, Machig magically rose up from where she was sitting until she was suspended in the air about a foot from the ground, and there she danced and spoke in Sanskrit. In a state of profound meditation, she passed through the clay walls of the temple unimpeded and flew into a tree above a small pond outside the monastery.

The pond was the residence of a powerful *naga*, or water spirit. These capricious, mythic beings are believed to cause disruption and disease when disturbed and can also act as treasure holders or protectors when they are propitiated. This particular naga was so terrifying that the local people did not even dare to look at the pond, never mind approach it. But Machig landed in the tree above the pond and stayed there in a state of meditation.

The water spirit considered young Machig's arrival to be a direct confrontation. He approached her threateningly, but she remained in meditation, unafraid. This infuriated him, so he gathered a huge army of nagas from the region in an attempt to overwhelm her. When she saw this mass of terrifying magical apparitions coming, Machig instantly transformed her body into a food offering; however, they could not devour her because she was egoless.

Not only did the aggression of the nagas evaporate, but they committed themselves to Machig, promising not to harm her or other beings, vowing to protect her, and pledging to serve her and anyone who followed her teachings. By meeting the demons and offering her body as food to them with unshakable compassion rather than fighting against them, Machig turned the demons into allies.

While studying Machig's teachings, I began to think about the Western understanding of demons. When I looked up the word in an English dictionary, I discovered that *demon* has not always had such a bad reputation. Derived from the Greek *daemon* or *daimon*, the term originally referred to a person's guiding spirit. The Greek daemon was a divine creature, a guiding spirit to be trusted and relied upon. This early belief in the daemon gradually changed with the advent of the Christian attack on pagan beliefs, so that by the Middle Ages demons were being blamed for every possible disaster, despised and feared as evil. We will see that through the process of meeting and feeding a demon with love and compassion, it can be transformed into a daemon. In this way your demons become your allies, just as the fearsome nagas transformed into protectors when Machig offered them her body as food.

Tales from Western mythology stand in stark contrast to the stories of Machig and Gandhi. The myth of the twelve labors of Hercules is a classic of Western literature, a shining example of the conquering hero's quest, one of the most important personal and political myths to guide Western culture. To absolve himself of the murder of his children, Hercules is given twelve tasks, the second of which sends him to Lema Lake in southern Italy, where a nine-headed, many-legged serpent called Hydra has been attacking innocent passersby. Hercules arrives at the lake accompanied by his nephew and pupil, Iolaus. Upon finding the lair of Hydra, the two men shoot flaming arrows to draw out the beast. But when Hydra emerges and Hercules wades into the water, the angry Hydra wraps its leg around Hercules's ankle, trapping him, and its assistant, a giant crab, drags him to the edge of a bottomless lake. To Hercules's dismay, every time he severs one of Hydra's heads, two grow back in its place.

Ensnared by the monster, Hercules calls to Iolaus for help. Rushing to his uncle's aid, the young man uses a burning branch to cauterize the stub of each of the heads Hercules chops off, preventing the Hydra from growing more. This gives Hercules the upper hand, and eventually only one head remains. This head is immortal, but Hercules realizes he can cut through the mortal neck that supports it. He chops the head off, but it still lies before him, hissing and staring. So he buries the immortal head under a boulder, considering the monster vanquished and his second task completed.

But what kind of victory has Hercules achieved? Has he actually eliminated the enemy or merely suppressed it? Hydra's immortal head, the governing force of its constellated energy, is still seething under the boulder and could reemerge if circumstances permitted. What does this say about Hercules's accomplishment and, more generally, about the monster-slaying heroic mentality that so enthralls and permeates Western literature and society?

Various versions of the myth of the dragon-slaying hero have dominated the Western psyche over the last forty-five hundred years. Although the positive aspect of the myth can lead to heroic battles against truly dangerous demons like Hitler, as well as against disease, poverty, and hunger, it also poses terrible dangers. Among these is inflation of those who identify themselves with the role of the dragon-slaying hero, regardless of their virtue. Another is projecting evil onto our opponents, demonizing them and justifying their murder, while we claim to be wholly identified with good. The tendency to kill rather than to engage the dragon prevents us from knowing our own demons and from turning them into allies.

Evidence that we continue to live out this myth can be seen everywhere, from popular movies to current global events. In today's battles each side identifies itself with the divine good as it struggles against evil. The polarization of good and evil justifies violence as a necessary sacrifice that must be endured to attain victory. Today, perhaps more than ever before, we are trapped by overidentification with the dragon-slaying myth.

Our state of polarization is not only in the outer world; within ourselves we fight demons of addiction, stress, trauma, anger, and self-hatred, to name just a few. We try to dominate everything, inside ourselves and without, including Mother Nature herself. But rather than ever achieving final victory, we become engulfed by the struggle, which holds us captive. As we seek to kill the dragon, we find ourselves in danger of destroying each other and the natural world, making human life on this planet untenable. We can see signs of the ineffectiveness of this myth at every turn. For example:

- Americans spend tens of billions of dollars every year on products and programs to try to lose weight, yet the "battle of the bulge" remains a lost cause. Chronic dieters frequently add five to ten pounds to their weight every time they diet, and eating disorders triggered by the starve-and-binge cycles of diets are killing thousands of us every year.

- Our pursuit of such things as wealth and success is so defined by struggle that even if we finally reach these goals, the ingrained pattern of striving won't allow us to enjoy the fruits of our labor. And once we succeed, we face a draining, never-ending battle to defend what we've gained.

- Experts in addiction tell us that using willpower to fight addiction does not lead to sobriety, and we must stop thinking we can overcome addiction by struggling against it.

- We do not try to understand our illnesses. Instead, whenever we get sick we immediately begin to develop strategies to "fight" the illness. Obituary columns routinely read: "So-and-So died after a long *battle* with cancer."

- Religious fundamentalism is growing in many countries around the world today, emphasizing the chasm between good and evil. Each group staunchly believes it has God on its side. By identifying our own religion with good and others with evil, we are locked in an endless struggle and never get around to facing the evil in ourselves or in our own political systems.

- We have raped the natural world, damming rivers and carelessly using up resources, polluting the atmosphere, and battling the nurturer, Mother Earth. Now nature fights back with a fury of natural disasters: hurricanes, tsunamis, tornadoes, droughts, floods, and global warming. In response we fight climate change, seeking to stop it without addressing the underlying attitude that created the problem to begin with.

- We try to eliminate enemies through war and violence, but violence breeds more violence. For example, a study by U.S. intelligence agencies showed that rather than stemming the growth of terrorism, the war in Iraq invigorated radicalism and worsened the global terrorism threat.

As we live by the myth in which we seek out, battle against, and ultimately destroy the enemy within and without, we also teach this myth to our children. We see this theme in fairy tales, religious stories, and political rhetoric, where heroes like Saint George kill the dragon or vanquish the hidden monster, often with a powerless maiden being "saved" by the hero. We also see it endlessly in films and television programs. Seeking out and destroying "the enemy" may look like the best solution, but in actuality it's creating a more and more dangerous world. Clearly we need to explore the alternative of engaging and communicating with the enemy rather than destroying it.

The approach of feeding rather than fighting our demons provides a way to *pay attention* to the demons within us, avoiding the dangers of repressing what we fear inside ourselves. Facing and feeding our demons avoids the creation of a raging monster that wreaks destruction both in us and in the world.

I propose that we follow Machig's example: the dragon is not slain or even fought against but drawn out and fearlessly nurtured. In this way we bridge the schism between "good" and "evil," and the potential enemy is transformed into an ally. This means that the energy that has been tied up in struggle becomes a positive and potentially protective force, a daemon rather than a demon. Every battle that we have within ourselves is tying up resources that could be put to far better use.

In mythology the dragon often guards a secret treasure. Through feeding our demons and transforming them into allies, we discover our own treasures that have been hidden by our preoccupation with doing battle. As it turns out, when liberated, the energy of the demon that has been locked in struggle *is* the treasure. Feeding our demons also makes us less of a threat in the world. When we become aware of our demons and offer them an elixir of conscious acceptance and compassion, we are much less likely to project them onto others.

Carl G. Jung, the famous Swiss psychologist, described our dark side as "the shadow," which might emerge in dreams or be projected onto others. The shadow he described consists of those parts of ourselves that the conscious mind deems unacceptable. The shadow is the repressed self, the unwelcome aspects of our personality that we disown. It might be our shame, our anger, or our prejudices. It is that which we don't want others to know about us, and it often appears in dreams doing things our conscious self would not consider. When a married person dreams of having an affair, this is the shadow. We are often unaware of the shadow parts of our personality because they are unseen by the conscious mind. The shadow encourages us to finish the whole plate of cookies when we intend not to eat any. The shadow blurts out an insult to someone we are trying to impress.

The process of feeding our demons is a method for bringing our shadow into consciousness and accessing the treasures it holds rather than repressing it. If the shadow is not made conscious and integrated, it operates undercover, becoming the saboteur of our best intentions as well as causing harm to others. Bringing the shadow to awareness reduces its destructive power and releases the life energy stored in it. By befriending that which scares us most, we find our own wisdom. This resolution of inner conflict also lessens the evil produced by the unconscious that contributes to dangerous collective movements.

In the practice of feeding our demons, we offer what is most precious (our own body) to that which is most threatening and frightening (our demons), and in doing so we overcome the root of all suffering, which in Buddhist terms is egocentricity. To give you an idea of how feeding your demons might look in a real-life situation, let me tell you a story of what happened some years ago while I was traveling in Tibet.

My friend Sara and I were traveling by bus on a pilgrimage. By this time I had come to a personal understanding of demons, was teaching the practice of Chöd, and had developed a method of feeding demons. One day we moved to a significantly higher altitude, having driven throughout the night. We had eaten one too many cans of mackerel in tomato sauce as the bus bounced interminably over the dirt track, aggravating our altitude headaches. The dust was so thick that even wrapping my head in a scarf didn't keep it out.

Sara was sitting alone, crying, on a seat ahead of me. I went and sat next to her. She told me about the depression that was attacking her, a demon that she had been battling all of her life, having grown up in a family where she was unwanted. She was desperate, convulsing in sobs. Attempting to help her feed this demon seemed like the best thing I could offer her. So right there, lurching along on the dusty road, we began the process.

I said, "Okay, Sara, let's try an experiment. Let's see what it would look like if you were to give this pain a form."

She closed her eyes and brought her awareness into her body, finding a sensation of nausea and grief she described as dark, reddish purple, heavy, and thick. Then I suggested she allow this to take a living form in front of her. She saw a huge purple monster with a gaping mouth where its stomach should have been. It wanted to consume her.

I said, "Let's see if we can find the real need that lies behind what this demon says it wants."

Sara asked the demon what it needed, and it said it needed her to stop trying to escape, that if she did that, it would feel love and acceptance. Then I suggested that Sara visualize dissolving her body into a nectar of love and feeding the demon until it was completely satisfied.

Slowly Sara stopped sobbing and became quiet. After a while she said, "I fed it, and it got smaller and smaller. I don't understand how it happened, but it's gone."

After enjoying the moment, she said, "My mind has relaxed into a peaceful space I never thought was possible for me. But I still don't know how it happened."

Several months after we returned home, Sara wrote me a letter about this experience. She said, "This trip was the most difficult physical and emotional thing I'd ever done. By nature I am a loner. To be in a large group was difficult, especially since you were the only person I knew before I left on the pilgrimage. That day on the bus when I broke down, I'd reached a point in my life where if I couldn't live with myself, I was going to die. Literally.

"That day all the pain came together. The pain in my head caused by the altitude. The pain in my heart caused by my terrible childhood traumas. The pain of all that I was seeing in Tibet. The pain was too much. When I fed this demon of pain and sadness, it was as if I'd come out the other side as someone completely new. I felt somehow reborn."

The interesting thing about Sara's experience was that it wasn't just a momentary shift. In her letter she said that the pain she had carried all her life never came back. Of course, feeding your demons doesn't always liberate you from long-held pain in one session; usually that requires a series of encounters, but in Sara's case, one was all it took.

In considering the stories of Gandhi, Machig, and Sara, we see a compelling alternative to Hercules's solution of battling against demons. Inspired by their compassion and fearlessness, we can now take a look at how we might meet our demons, feed them, and perhaps even turn them into allies—untapped sources of support and protection.

Jan Chozen Bays

C O-ABBOT OF THE Great Vow Zen monastery in Oregon, Jan Chozen Bays is a pediatrician specializing in child-abuse detection. In 1993, after years of examining small, lifeless bodies, she hit a wall. She was no longer able to let go of the terrible things she was seeing—the bruises, rib fractures, and brain hemorrhages. Then she took part in a *mizuko,* a Buddhist ceremony of remembrance for children who have died, and in this way she found some relief, renewing her ability to continue with her work. Bays's first book, *Jizo Bodhisattva,* was inspired by this experience.

Today she is also the author of *How to Train a Wild Elephant: And Other Adventures in Mindfulness* and *Mindful Eating: A Guide to Rediscovering a Healthy and Joyful Relationship with Food.* In the teaching that follows, we get a taste of Bays's celebratory approach to diet. Mindful eating, we learn, isn't about always eschewing cake in favor of tofu; rather, it's about paying attention to our food so that we can nourish both our bodies and our minds.

In an interview with the *Shambhala Sun,* Bays asserted that "part of being healthy, according to the Buddha, has to do with love, having a good heart and a kind attitude toward everyone. We are healthy when we can be at ease in the body and enjoy arising sensations."

The Joy of Mindful Eating

MINDFUL EATING is an experience that engages all parts of us, our body, our heart, and our mind, in choosing, preparing, and eating food. Mindful eating involves all the senses. It immerses us in the colors, textures, scents, tastes, and even sounds of drinking and eating. It allows us to be curious and even playful as we investigate our responses to food and our inner cues to hunger and satisfaction.

Mindful eating is not directed by charts, tables, pyramids, or scales. It is not dictated by an expert. It is directed by your own inner experiences, moment by moment. Your experience is unique. Therefore you are the expert.

Mindful eating is not based on anxiety about the future but on the actual choices that are in front of you and on your direct experiences of health while eating and drinking.

Mindful eating replaces self-criticism with self-nurturing. It replaces shame with respect for your own inner wisdom.

As an example, let's take a typical experience. On the way home from work Sally thinks with dread about the talk she needs to work on for a big conference. She has to get it done in the next few days to meet the deadline. Before starting to work on the speech, however, she decides to relax and watch a few minutes of TV when she gets home. She sits down with a bag of chips beside her chair. At first she eats only a few, but as the show gets more dramatic, she eats faster and faster. When the show ends she looks down and realizes that she's eaten the entire bag of chips. She scolds herself for wasting time and for eating junk food. "Too much salt and fat! No dinner for you!" Engrossed in the drama on the screen, covering up her anxiety about procrastinating, she ignored what was happening in her mind, heart, mouth, and stomach. She ate unconsciously. She ate to go unconscious. She goes to bed unnourished in body or heart and with her mind still anxious about the talk.

The next time this happens she decides to eat chips but to try eating them mindfully. First she checks in with her mind. She finds that her mind is worried about an article she promised to write. Her mind says that she needs to get started on it tonight. She checks in with her heart and finds that she is feeling a little lonely because her husband is out of town. She checks in with her stomach and body and discovers that she is both hungry and tired. She needs some nurturing. The only one at home to do it is herself.

She decides to treat herself to a small chip party. (Remember, mindful eating gives us permission to play with our food.) She takes twenty chips out of the bag and arranges them on a plate. She looks at their color and shape. She eats one chip, savoring its flavor. She pauses, then eats another. There is no judgment, no right or wrong. She is simply seeing the shades of tan and brown on each curved surface, tasting the tang of salt, hearing the crunch of each bite, feeling the crisp texture melt into softness. She ponders how these chips arrived on her plate, aware of the sun, the soil, the rain, the potato farmer, the workers at the chip factory, the delivery truck driver, the grocer who stocked the shelves and sold them to her.

With little pauses between each chip, it takes ten minutes for the chip party. When she finishes the chips, she checks in with her body to find out if any part of it is still hungry.

She finds that her mouth and cells are thirsty, so she gets a drink of orange juice. Her body is also saying it needs some protein and something green, so she makes a cheese omelet and a spinach salad. After eating she checks in again with her mind, body, and heart. The heart and body feel nourished but the mind is still tired. She decides to go to bed and work on the talk first thing in the morning, when the mind and body will be rested. She is still feeling lonely, although less so within the awareness of all the beings whose life energy brought her the chips, eggs, cheese, and greens. She decides to call her husband to say good night. She goes to bed with body, mind, and heart at ease and sleeps soundly.

Mindfulness Is the Best Flavoring

As I write this I am eating a lemon tart that a friend gave to me. He knows how much I love lemon tarts, and he occasionally brings them to me from a special bakery. After writing for a few hours, I am ready to reward myself with a tart. The first bite is delicious. Creamy, sweet-sour, melting. When I take the second bite, I begin to think about what to write next. The flavor in my mouth decreases. I take another bite and get up to sharpen a pencil. As I walk, I notice that I am chewing, but there is almost no lemon flavor in this third bite. I sit down, get to work, and wait a few minutes.

Then I take a fourth bite, fully focused on the smells, tastes, and touch sensations in my mouth. Delicious again! I discover, all over again (I'm a slow learner), that the only way to keep that "first bite" experience, to honor the gift my friend gave me, is to eat slowly, with long pauses between bites. If I do anything else while I'm eating, if I talk, walk, write, or even think, the flavor diminishes or disappears. The life is drained from my beautiful tart. I could be eating the cardboard box.

Here's the humorous part. I stopped tasting the lemon tart because I was thinking. What was I thinking about? Mindful eating! Discovering that, I have to grin. To be a human being is both pitiful and funny.

Why can't I think, walk, and be fully aware of the taste of the tart at the same time? I can't do all these things at once because the mind has two distinct functions: thinking and awareness. When the thinking function is turned up, the awareness function is turned down. When the thinking function is going full throttle, we can eat an entire meal, an entire cake, an entire carton of ice cream, and not taste more than a bite or two. When we don't taste what we eat, we can end up stuffed to the gills but feeling completely unsatisfied. This is because the mind and mouth weren't present, weren't tasting or enjoying, as we ate. The stomach became full, but the mind and mouth were unfulfilled and continued calling for us to eat.

If we don't feel satisfied, we'll begin to look around for something more or something different to eat. Everyone has had the experience of roaming the kitchen, opening cupboards and doors, looking vainly for something, anything, to satisfy. The only thing that will cure this, a fundamental kind of hunger, is to sit down and be, even for a few minutes, wholly present.

If we eat and stay connected with our own experience and with the people who grew and cooked the food, who served the food, and who eat alongside us, we will feel most satisfied, even with a meager meal. This is the gift of mindful eating, to restore our sense of satisfaction no matter what we are or are not eating.

Common Misperceptions

People get confused about mindfulness. They think that if they just do one thing at a time, like eating without reading, or if they move *veeerrry* slowly and carefully, they are being mindful. We could stop reading, close the book, and then eat slowly but still not be mindful of what we are eating. It depends upon what our mind is doing as we eat. Are we just eating or are we thinking and eating? Is our mind in our mouth, or somewhere else? This is a crucial difference.

As we begin to practice mindfulness, it does help a lot to slow down and to do only one thing at a time. In fact there are two essential aspects of becoming mindful as we eat. They are slowing down and eating without distractions. As we become more skilled in being present, we can be mindful and speedy. In fact we discover that when we are moving quickly, we need to be much more mindful. To be mindful means to have the mind full, completely full, of what is happening *now*. When you're chopping vegetables with a large sharp knife, the faster you slice, the more attentive you have to be, if you want to keep your fingers!

It's also important to understand that mindful eating includes mindless eating. Within the wide field of mindfulness we can become aware of the pull toward mindless eating and notice when and how we slip into it. We can also decide, according to this situation and time, how we're going to approach eating. Part of my work as a doctor involves testifying in court cases as an expert witness. Maybe I'm on the way to court and I haven't had time for lunch. I know it will be hard to stay clear on the witness stand and that court is unpredictable. I may be there for hours. I mindfully decide to undertake mindless eating and order a veggie burger from a fast-food window to eat in the car, trying to at least be mindful about not spilling the special sauce on my one good suit. Mindfulness gives us awareness of what we're doing and, often, why we're doing it.

The Basic Mindful-Eating Meditation

PREPARATION: For this exercise you will need a single raisin. Other foods will also work, such as a dried cranberry, a single strawberry, a cherry tomato, or an unusual type of cracker.

1. Begin by sitting quietly and assessing your baseline hunger: How hungry are you, on a scale of zero to ten? Where do you "look" in your body to decide how hungry you are?

2. Imagine that you are a scientist on a mission to explore a new planet. Your spaceship has landed and found the planet to be quite hospitable. You can breathe the air and walk around without any problem. The surface of the planet seems to be bare dirt and rock, and no one has seen any obvious life-forms yet. The food supplies on your spaceship are running low, however, and everyone is getting hungry. You have been asked to scout out this planet to look for anything that might be edible.

    As you walk around you find a small object lying on the ground, and you pick it up. Place the raisin (or other food item) on your palm. You are going to investigate it with the only tools you have, your five senses. You have no idea what this object is. You have never seen it before.

3. *Eye hunger.* First you investigate this object with your eyes. Look at its color, shape, and surface texture. What does the mind say that it could be? Now rate your eye hunger for this item. On a scale of zero to ten, how much hunger do you have for this object based upon what your eyes see?

4. *Nose hunger.* Now you investigate it with your nose. Smell it, refresh the nose, and sniff it again. Does this change your idea of whether it might be edible? Now rate nose hunger. On a scale of zero to ten, how much hunger do you have for this object based upon what your nose smells?

5. *Mouth hunger.* Now you investigate this object with your mouth. Place it in your mouth but *do not bite* it. You can roll it around and explore it with the tongue. What do you notice?

    Now you can bite this mysterious object, but only once. After biting it once, roll it around again in the mouth and explore it with the tongue. What do you notice?

    Now rate mouth hunger. On a scale of zero to ten, how much hunger do you have for this object based upon what the mouth tastes and feels? In other words, how much does the mouth want to experience more of it?

6. *Stomach hunger.* Now you decide to take a risk and eat this unknown object. You chew it slowly, noticing the changes in the mouth in texture and taste. You swallow it. You notice whether there are still any bits in the mouth. What does the tongue do when you have finished eating it? How long can you detect the flavor?

    Now rate stomach hunger. Is the stomach full or not, satisfied or not? On a scale of zero to ten, rate stomach hunger. In other words, how much does the stomach want more of this food?

7. *Cellular hunger.* Become aware of this food passing into the body. Absorption begins as soon as we begin chewing. Are there any sensations that tell you that this food is being absorbed? How is it being received by the cells in the body?

Now rate cellular hunger. On a scale of zero to ten, how much would the cells like to have more of this food?

8. *Mind hunger.* Can you hear what the mind is saying about this food? (Hint: often the mind talks in "shoulds" or "should nots.") Now rate mind hunger. On a scale of zero to ten, how much would the mind like you to have more of this food?

9. *Heart hunger.* Is the heart saying anything about this food? On a scale of zero to ten, how soothing or comforting is it? Would the heart like you to have more of this food?

You might like to repeat this exercise with liquid. Pick a drink you have never had before, such as an exotic fruit juice. Take your time and assess each kind of thirst separately.

Charlotte Joko Beck

A NATIVE OF New Jersey, Charlotte Joko Beck grew up attending a Methodist church, where—in her words—she "learned a lot of good quotes." She received her education in public schools and at the Oberlin Conservatory of Music, and went on to perform piano professionally. Later, as a single mother with four children, she also worked as a teacher, a secretary, and as an administrator in the chemistry department of the University of California, San Diego.

In an interview with Amy Gross for *Tricycle* magazine, Beck told the story of how she met Maezumi Roshi for the first time when he was giving a talk at a Unitarian Church. She said, "I was out for the evening with a friend, a woman, a sort of hard-boiled business type, and we decided to hear his talk. And as we went in, he bowed to each person and looked right at us. It was absolutely direct contact. When we sat down, my friend said to me, 'What was *that?*' He wasn't doing anything special—except, for once, somebody was paying attention."

Beck was middle-aged before she began practicing Zen, but because of her diligence and natural aptitude, she came to be designated as Maezumi Roshi's third dharma heir. She then went on to establish the Zen Center of San Diego and the Ordinary Mind Zen School, a loosely knit, nonhierarchical organization of her dharma successors.

Today Beck is recognized as having helped to create a sea of change in the world of American Zen. In the early years, there was a tendency among practitioners to dismiss psychological problems and focus on enlightenment. But Beck "had the courage to say that her own teacher's training had done little to curb his alcoholism or deal with his character problems," as Barry Magid wrote in *Buddhadharma: The*

Practitioner's Quarterly. Acknowledging that he was not an unfortunate exception, "she put dealing with anger, anxiety, pride, and sexual exploitation of students into the center of what we must deal with in our practice."

Beck's teachings were firmly grounded in everyday life. Her dharma talks were known for their pragmatism and simplicity, and the practice she taught was disciplined and rigorous yet also in harmony with Western culture. She rarely used robes or her titles, and after moving her practice to San Diego, she stopped shaving her head.

Beck once said, "When the mind becomes clear and balanced and is no longer caught by objects, there can be an opening—and for a second we can realize who we really are. . . . There is no end to the opening up that is possible for a human being."

On June 15, 2011, she passed away at the age of ninety-four.

———

False Generalizations

NASRUDIN, the Sufi sage and fool, was once in his flower garden sprinkling bread crumbs over everything. When a neighbor asked him why, he said, "To keep the tigers away." The neighbor said, "But there aren't any tigers within a thousand miles of here." And Nasrudin said, "Effective, isn't it?"

We laugh because we're sure that the two things—bread crumbs and tigers—have nothing to do with each other. Yet, as with Nasrudin, our practice and our lives are often based upon false generalizations that have little to do with reality. If our lives are based upon generalized concepts, we may be like Nasrudin, spreading bread crumbs to keep away tigers. We say, for example, "I love people, " or "I love my husband. " The truth is that no one loves everyone all the time, and no one loves a spouse all the time. Such generalities obscure the specific, concrete reality of our lives, what is happening for us at this moment.

One may, of course, love one's husband most of the time. Still, the flat generalization leaves out the shifting, changing reality of an actual relationship. Likewise with "I love my work" or "Life is hard on me." When we begin practice, we usually believe and express many generalized opinions. We may think, for instance, "I'm a kind person" or "I'm a terrible person. " But in fact, life is never general. Life is always specific: it's what's happening this very moment. Sitting helps us to cut through the fog of generalizations about our lives. As we practice, we tend to drop our generalized concepts in favor of more specific observations. For example, instead of "I can't stand my husband," we notice "I can't stand my husband when he doesn't pick up after himself" or "I can't stand myself when I do such and such." Instead of generalized concepts, we see more clearly what's going on. We're not covering events with a broad brush.

Our experience of another person or situation isn't just one thing. It can include a thousand minor thoughts and reactions. A parent may say, "I love my daughter," yet this generalization ignores moments such as

"Why is she so immature" or "She's being stupid." As we sit, observing and labeling our thoughts, we become more acquainted with the incessant outpouring of our opinions about anything and everything. Instead of just plastering the whole world with generalizations, we become aware of our specific concepts and judgments. As we become more acquainted with our thinking, we discover that we're shifting, moment by moment, as our thinking shifts.

Let's listen to a young woman. She's been going out with a young man for a little while. She feels that it's going well. If asked, she would say that she really cares about him. Now he has just called her. Let's listen not only to what she says to him but also to what she's thinking to herself:

"Oh, it's so nice to hear from you. You sound great. " ("He could have called me a little sooner.")

"Oh, you took So-and-So out to lunch. Yes, she's a charming person. I know you enjoyed her company. ("I could kill him!")

"You think I don't have much to say? That I'm not a very verbal person? Well, I appreciate your opinion." ("You hardly know me! How dare you make generalizations about me!")

"You did well on your test? I'm glad. Good for you!" ("He's always talking about himself. Does he have any interest in *my* life?")

"You'd like to go out to dinner tomorrow night? I'd love to go. It would be wonderful to see you again!" ("At last, he asked me! I wish he wouldn't wait until the last minute!")

This is a perfectly common interchange between two people, the sort of pretense that passes for communication. These people probably do care for each other. Still, she had one concept after another, about him and about herself. The exchange was a sea of conceptual material; their conversation was like two ships passing in the night—no contact took place.

In Zen practice, we tend to toss around many fancy concepts: "Everything is perfect in being as it is." "We're all doing the best that we can." "Things are all one." "I'm one with him." We can call this Zen bullshit, though other religions have their own versions. It's not that the statements are false. The world *is* one. I *am* you. Everything *is* perfect in being as it is. Every human being on the planet *is* doing the best he or she can at this moment. True enough. But if we stop there, we have turned our practice into an exercise of concepts, and we've lost awareness of what's going on with us right this second.

Good practice always entails moving through our concepts. Concepts are sometimes useful in daily life; we have to use them. But we need to recognize that a concept is just a concept and not reality and that this recognition or knowledge slowly develops as we practice. Gradually, we stop "buying into" our concepts. We no longer make such general judgments: "He's a terrible person" or "I'm a terrible person." We notice our thoughts: "I wish he wouldn't take her out to lunch." Then we have to experience the pain that accompanies the thought. When we can stay with the pain as a pure physical sensation, at some point it will dissolve, and then we move into the truth, which is that everything is perfect in being as it is. Everyone *is* doing the best that he or she can. But we have to move from experience, which is often painful, into truth and not plaster thoughts over our experience. Intellectual people are particularly prone to this error: they think that the rational world of concepts is the real world. The rational world of concepts is not the real world but simply a description of it, a finger pointing at the moon.

Take the experience of having been hurt. When we've been criticized or treated unfairly, it's important to note the thoughts we have and move into the cellular level of being hurt so that our awareness becomes simply raw sensation: our trembling jaw, the contraction in our chest, whatever we may be feeling in the cells of our body. This pure experiencing is *zazen*. As we stay with it, our desire to think comes up again and again: judgments, opinions, blame, retorts. So we label our thoughts and again return to our cellular experience, which is almost indescribable, perhaps just a light shimmering of energy, perhaps something stronger. In that space there is no "me" or "you." When we are this nondual experiencing, we can see our situation more clearly. We can see that "she is doing the best she can." We can see that *we* are doing the best we can. If we say such sentences without the bodily component of experiencing, however, we will not know what true practice is. A calm, cool, rational perspective must be grounded in that pure cellular level. We need to know our thoughts. But that doesn't mean that we must think they're real or that we must act on them. After observing our self-centered thoughts, moment by moment, the emotions tend to even out. This serenity can never be found by plastering some philosophical concept on top of what is actually happening.

Only when we move through the experiential level does life have meaning. This is what Jews and Christians mean by being with God. Experiencing is out of time: it is not the past, not the future, not even the present in the usual sense. We can't say what it is; we can only be it. In traditional Buddhist terms, such a life is being buddha nature itself. Compassion grows from such roots.

We all have our favorite concepts. "I'm sensitive. I'm easily hurt." "I'm a pushy kind of person." "I'm an intellectual." Our concepts may be useful on an everyday level, but we need to see their actual nature. Unexperienced concepts are a source of confusion, anxiety, depression; they tend to produce behavior that is not good for us or for others.

To do the work of practice, we need endless patience, which also means recognizing when we have no patience. So we need to be patient with our lack of patience: to recognize that when we don't want to practice is also part of practice. Our avoidance and resistance are part of the conceptual framework that we're not yet ready to look at. It's okay not to be ready. As we become ready, bit by bit, a space opens up, and we'll be ready to experience a little more and then a little more. Resistance and practice go hand in hand. We all resist our practice, because we all resist our lives. And if we believe in concepts instead of experiencing the moment, we're like Nasrudin: we're sprinkling bread crumbs on the flower beds to keep the tigers away.

Sylvia Boorstein

Acording to Margaret Mead, some people are born with a "teaching gene." If that's true, says Sylvia Boorstein, her father, Harry Schor, had that gene—and she inherited it from him. A math teacher by profession, he loved explaining and demonstrating. He taught her to swim, solve anagrams, and construct crossword puzzles. Boorstein's mother also had a profound effect on her. She was unique amongst the neighborhood mothers, says Boorstein. "She had a job. She drove a car. She had passionately progressive political views and the loudest laugh of anyone I knew. I think I'm just like her."

In 1952, when Boorstein was sixteen years old, she went to a summer camp run by the Jewish National Workers' Alliance. There she caught the eye of Seymour, the camp's chief lifeguard, who was four years her senior. One afternoon, he shyly told her that she had beautiful eyes. Then, three nights later, he proposed and she said yes.

They've now been married for more than half a century, and together they've had a family and have traveled both the world and the spiritual path. That said, claims Boorstein, their motivation for delving into spirituality was different. She quips that while her husband was trying to understand life, she was just trying to *stand* it. In 1976 he attended a vipassana retreat with Joseph Goldstein and came back saying, "Syl, this is it." Yet Boorstein did not initially think so. After her first retreat, her legs ached and her head throbbed. Nonetheless, she was intrigued by an inscription that she'd seen in the retreat house: *Life is so difficult, how can we be anything but kind?* She thought, "If that's what they're teaching in this shul [this synagogue], I need to come back."

By the mid-eighties, Boorstein was a dharma teacher, and it wasn't long after that before she was helping to found Spirit Rock Meditation Center in Woodacre, California. Now she is also a best-selling author, and her books include *It's Easier Than You Think: The Buddhist Way to Happiness* and *That's Funny, You Don't Look Buddhist: On Being a Faithful Jew and a Passionate Buddhist.* Her teachings are characterized by her understanding that the key to suffering less is having warm bonds of emotional connection with others, because it is these that restore our natural state of insight and clarity, especially during difficult times.

In his profile of Boorstein, the journalist Steve Silberman asserts, "She is clearly a doting mother, but she's just as clearly a skillful dharma teacher—a Jewish-American embodiment of the compassion Dogen-zenji called *robai-shin,* 'grandmother mind.'"

The Three Marks of Existence

I WAS WALKING through the airport terminal when my eyes met those of a baby approaching me, strapped into a carrier on his mother's chest, and I *knew* that baby was me. A thrill went through me. I knew in that moment that it did not matter that I was aging, because that baby—*me*, in a newer, fresher guise—was on his way up in life.

I recall laughing, maybe even out loud, as the baby and mother passed by. I knew that the others around me were all me too, and the mother and baby and each other as well, coming and going in this air-line terminal and in life. I felt happy and said to myself, "Thinking about interconnection is one thing, but these moments of direct understand-ing are great." I sat in the boarding lounge feeling tremendous affection for my fellow travelers.

Such an understanding of interconnection comes, in Buddhist prac-tice, from awareness of the three characteristics of experience, also known as the three marks of existence. The first is *impermanence*, or as one teacher put it to me, the idea that "last year's Super Bowl is in the same past as the Revolutionary War." The second is *suffering*, which he described as the result of "the mind unable to accommodate its experience."

These two characteristics, or insights, are fairly easy to make sense of, and when I first began my Buddhist practice, I found I had a basic grasp of them. I thought, "Who doesn't know these things?" But the third characteristic, *emptiness*—the insight that there is no enduring self that separates anything from anything else—seemed more elusive to me and not particularly relevant to my life. I liked the rest of what I was learning and practicing, so I figured I would just let that one alone for now.

The insight about impermanence was, in my early years of practice, what seemed most dramatically evident—although not in a comfort-able way. There were periods, especially on retreat, in which it seemed to me that all I could see was the passing away of everything. I saw, as I hadn't ever before, that sunsets followed every dawn and that the beautiful full moon immediately waned. As I came upon a flower that was newly opening, I simultaneously envisioned the wilted look it would have three days hence. I remember tearfully reporting to my teacher, Joseph Goldstein, "It's so sad! Everything is dying!" He responded, "It's not sad, Sylvia. It's just true." I found that calming at the time, but I would say it differently now. I would say, "It's not sad. But it *is* poignant."

Everything has a life cycle, with beauty in every part of it, and the passing of any part of it evokes a response of either relief or nostalgia. Eighteen-year-olds are usually glad to be finished with adolescence and off to whatever they'll do next. A woman in a class I was teaching recently said her daughter, at that point anticipating her marriage a week hence, was sad that all the excitement of planning and imagining would soon be over forever. An elderly man who once took a seniors' yoga class I was teaching thanked me after the class but said he would not be coming back. "It is too hard for me," he said. "But I would like to tell you that I was a member of the 1918 Olympic rowing team."

I find now that time seems to be speeding up. I've become seventy-five years old in what feels like a brief time. The woman I see when I look in the mirror is my aunt Miriam. It still startles me, but it also inspires me. Knowing that I have limited time left inspires me not to mortgage any time to negative mind states. I am determined not to miss any day waiting for a better one. "Carpe diem!" has never seemed like a more important injunction.

An immediately helpful aspect of my earliest insights into imperma-nence was the increased tolerance and courage I experienced in difficult situations. However much I had known intellectually that things pass, more and more I knew it in the marrow of my bones. I responded better to difficult news. Hearing that my father had been diagnosed with an incurable cancer, I felt both deeply saddened and uncharacteristically confident. I thought, "We'll manage this together. We've run 10K races together. We'll do this too." On a more mundane level, I noticed that I was more relaxed about ordinary unpleasantness. "This painful procedure at the dentist is taking very long, but in another hour I'll be out of here."

From the beginning of my practice, the insight about suffering, especially the extra mental tension that compounds the pain of life's inevitable losses, made sense to me. A melancholy boyfriend I had when I was in high school enjoyed reciting Dylan Thomas poetry to me. I found it romantic, in a Brontë kind of way, but also depressing. I definitely thought it would be wrong to "rage, rage against the dying of the light," and I knew I didn't want to do that. When, years later, I learned about Buddhism's Four Noble Truths, I was particularly inspired by the promise of the fourth noble truth, the path of practice that I thought would assure me a mind that did not rage.

When I first began to teach, I would explain the four truths this way:

Life is challenging because everything is always changing and we continually need to adjust to new circumstances.

Adding struggle to challenge creates suffering. Pain is inevitable, but suffering is optional.

Peace is possible. In the middle of a complicated life, the mind can remain at ease.

The path for developing this kind of mind involves attention to ethical behavior, to disciplining the habits of mind through meditation, and to ardent intention.

I loved the third noble truth, the truth that liberation is possible. I felt that after hearing about the ubiquitous ways that we are challenged—and how heedlessly and habitually we respond to the challenges in unwise ways—it was a great relief to hear "Peace is possible!" I said it with great conviction, and I believed it then and I believe it now. What I've started to add now, out of my own experience, is that however much I know that struggling makes things worse, I still suffer. If I am pained enough or disappointed enough or anxious enough, I still suffer.

Some life experiences bring us to our knees. Someone in a class I was once teaching, after I had talked about the intensity of even terrible experiences modulating with time because "everything passes," said, "In my case I think I am going to pass before the horror of this passes." I was humbled by the anguish I heard in what that person said, and it has kept me more real and more honest.

For a while, in an attempt to be honest but lighthearted, I added what I called the third-and-a half noble truth: that the intention to "surrender to the experience" doesn't necessarily cause it to happen. These days even lightheartedness seems glib to me, so I don't do it anymore. I say, "When the mind is able to surrender to the truth, grieving happens and suffering lessens." But there is no timetable for that to happen, and the only possible response I can have is compassion for myself and for other people. Maybe *that* truth—that we suffer in spite of knowing that peace is possible, and we sense it is true for everyone—contributes to our sense of kinship, that sense of feeling as if I were accompanied that I sometimes experience in a crowd of strangers.

The idea of no separate, enduring self—emptiness—*is* a peculiar idea until we have a direct experience of it. It certainly feels that there is a little "me" living in our bodies that decides what to do, that sees out of our eyes, that realizes it has woken up in the morning. The "me" has thought patterns that are habitual associated with it, so it feels enduring. If I woke up one morning thinking other people's thoughts, it would be deeply disturbing.

So it was a complete surprise to me, some years into my retreat practice, to be practicing walking meditation, sensing physical movements and sights and smells and heat and cool, and realizing that everything was happening all by itself. No one was taking that walk: "I" wasn't there. I *was* there a few seconds later, recovering my balance after the "uh-oh" feeling of "if no one is here, who is holding me up?" I thought, "This is wild! There really *isn't* anyone in here directing the show. It is all just happening." I understood that the arising of intention causes things to happen and that intention arises as a result of circumstances such as hearing the instruction "Do walking meditation." Hearing the instruction was the proximal cause of walking's happening. The habit of following instructions, developed since birth, was another cause.

In years since, the understanding that everything anyone does is a result of karma—of causes and effects—has helped to keep me from

35

labeling people as good or bad. Circumstances and behavior can change, of course, but at any given time no one can be other than the sum of all of his or her contingent causes. A student in a class discussion about this topic once said, "When people ask me, 'How are you?' I always answer, 'I couldn't be better.' Because I couldn't!"

It's true. We couldn't, any of us, be better. In our most out-of-sorts days, we couldn't be better. If we could, we would. Suffering happens, but no "one" decides to suffer.

As a beginning student, I wondered whether hearing about the three characteristics of experience, rather than discovering them for myself, would diminish their impact—that thinking about them wouldn't count as much as discovering them directly. Today I know that thinking, pondering, and reflecting on them count as well as direct moments of experience. Everything counts.

Meditation: Interconnectedness

Here's a practice that directly evokes the truth that there is no separate and enduring self, meditated on in the context of interconnectedness.

Read these instructions and then sit up or lie down with your spine straight and your body relaxed so that breath can flow easily in and out of your body. Close your eyes. Don't do anything at all to manipulate or regulate your breathing. Let your experience be like wide-awake sleeping, with breath coming and going at its own rate.

Probably you'll be aware of your diaphragm moving up and down as your chest expands and contracts. Of course you cannot feel that the exhaling air is rich in carbon dioxide and the inhaling air is rich in oxygen, but you probably know that. You also probably know that the green life in the world—the trees and vines and shrubs and grasses—are breathing in carbon dioxide and releasing oxygen back into the environment. The green world and your lungs, as long as they are both viable, are keeping each other alive.

Without any volition on your part, your body is part of the world happening, and the world is part of your body continuing. Nothing is separate. Your life is part of all life. Where is the self?

———

Meeting the Wild World with a Benevolent Heart

IT'S SEPTEMBER. I am sitting at my computer, working on a book and writing sentences like, "There is no refuge more secure than one's own benevolent heart." Simultaneously, I am thinking murderous thoughts about the redheaded woodpeckers that are diligently drilling holes into the wood siding of my house. I see them, and I hear them: Rat-tat-ta-tat! Rat-tat-ta-tat! They are Acorn Woodpeckers. In the fall, they hide acorns with larval worms inside them. They come back for the acorns in the spring when the worms are large enough to be fed to the woodpeckers' babies. The woodpeckers are supposed to only do this maneuver on the south side of the house, and we have the usual net in place there to dissuade them. But this year they are all over the house. They've made dozens of big holes.

I called the bird store in Santa Rosa. "What should I do?"

"Nothing much you can do. They're supposed to stay on the south."

I called Tom, the man who built this house twenty years ago. "What can we do?"

"I'll come by at the end of the week," he said, "and plug the holes. Otherwise the rains will get in and ruin your inside walls."

Another woodpecker swoops down into view and lands on the house. "Aha," I think. "You'll soon see: I have foiled your plot."

Then I see that instead of resuming drilling, he is carefully inserting an acorn into the wall. I see that he is having some trouble angling the acorn exactly so that it fits through the hole, and I find myself thinking,

"Careful! Don't drop it." The acorn disappears into the wall. Then I think, "Oh, dear! Tom is coming to plug up the holes and when the woodpecker comes back the food won't be available, and then the woodpecker babies . . ."

I have the momentary thought that I might just need to move.

Here's the lesson: It is true that there is no more secure refuge, and no greater happiness, than that of a benevolent heart. And it is also true that it's hard to keep the benevolence going when one's own well-being is threatened. I want my house to remain intact. I want the woodpeckers to thrive. I want to not think murderous thoughts, but they are still one "rat-tat-ta-tat" away.

I tell a friend of mine, also a psychologist, about the woodpeckers. I say, "Maybe feeling furious about the woodpeckers is just a local, convenient substitute for all the other things that frighten me. I'm frightened about the mess the world is in. I'm frightened about the political situation. I'm worried about my grandchildren's future. Sometimes I feel hopeless about making a difference."

He says, "I don't think the woodpeckers are *instead of*. I think they are *in addition to*. Your limbic system is letting you know you are threatened and it can't tell the difference between woodpeckers and war."

I am psychologically validated. I am laughing a little about the whole scene. And I am still "rat-tat-ta-tat!" mad. I have an inner conversation, looking for liberating spiritual wisdom.

"Everything passes," he says.

"Indeed. The structural integrity of my house is also passing."

"You are suffering because you are struggling with what you cannot change."

"This is not helpful news. If I could 'let it be,' I would."

"You and your house and the woodpeckers are all part of the miraculous web of being, all in constant interconnected, interdependent change, all unfolding with marvelous, lawful karmic precision."

"I know that. Knowing is not helping."

The house is quiet. For this moment, the woodpeckers have stopped. I look out at the hole where the newly stored acorn is. I remember my moment of concern lest the acorn drop, and feel relief at reconnecting with my own kind heart. "That was amazing," I think, "the way that bird knew how to jockey that acorn into position so it could fit. I wonder whether woodpeckers just know that in their DNA or whether they watch each other and learn."

I feel the experience of wondering, always pleasant to me, spreading out and soothing my mind. How does that bird figure it out? How does she know it's September? How did Mozart compose music when he was five years old? How come, with a world full of interesting people, we fall in love with some people and not with others?

I needed for it to be quiet for a moment. I needed to remember that my heart really means well and that I feel better when I think with my heart and not my nervous system.

My husband tells me he's just phoned Home Depot and there is a siding that looks like wood but isn't real that we could cover the house with if things get worse. I don't know what we'll do. But whatever it is, I won't do it with anger. The woodpeckers are just doing their thing. And it is amazing.

Suffering's Not the Only Story

At a recent Spirit Rock Meditation Center class, a woman named Nancy, a regular member of the group, told us about coming home the previous evening to hear this message on her answering machine:

"Nancy, this is Randy. I'm calling you from my car. I've just been to the doctor. She had the results of my biopsy. The news is not good. My lymphoma is back. She's already consulted with her colleagues, and no one knows what to try for me next. Oh, my God. There's a flock of turkeys starting to cross the highway. I hope they make it safely to the other side! I'll call you later, okay?"

As Nancy spoke, reciting the message slowly and carefully from memory, I felt several distinct emotions. First, the words *biopsy* and *news is not good* and *lymphoma* aroused tension in my mind—I felt eager to hear more and fearful about what I would learn. Then the improbable image of turkeys marching onto a highway startled me. (Were they single file? Four abreast?) I almost laughed. Finally, Randy's spontaneous wish for the turkeys' survival, in the midst of his need to assimilate dire news about his health, inspired me.

I think the other eighty or so people in the room had similar responses. Although everyone became quite still as Nancy began her story, I noticed that people were smiling as she ended it. I heard some chuckling. Then we talked about our responses to Randy's story.

The fact that Randy, a person known to none of us but Nancy, was able to move beyond the limits of his own story—such a compelling story—to care about others was reassuring. I saw it as a confirmation of the Buddha's third noble truth: liberation from ego-based suffering is possible. One person said it was consoling to know that nothing has to change in our lives in order for the heart to be free to love.

None of us could know, of course, how long Randy's shift of attention from personal anguish to benevolent connection lasted. Perhaps it was just a few minutes, the time it took the turkeys to pass. Indeed, it seems reasonable to imagine that his shift away from grief and dismay and confusion ought to have been brief. We are programmed by instinct, as emotionally healthy animals, to respond vigorously to challenges to our own survival and to the survival of our kin. Not to think "I might be dying soon. How can I possibly handle this? Will I be able to deal with the pain? What can I do for my family? What if I cannot bear this grief?" would be a form of denial. That Randy's attention shifted at all, even for a brief moment, was inspiring assurance of the mind's essential freedom.

The group heard Randy's story and responded first of all with wishes for his wellness. Indeed, we prayed for him. Later, the discussion became general. People remembered their own experiences of incidents that dramatically shifted the mind away from turmoil. Someone remembered how, at a family gathering just after the funeral of a dearly loved relative, the mention and recollection of a playful afternoon many years past caused everyone to laugh; how odd it had seemed—and what a relief it had been—to find that grief is permeable.

"Everything is permeable" is, I think, a useful alternative phrasing of "Everything is impermanent." Impermanence is the first of the three characteristics of experience that the Buddha taught as liberating insights. Even "Everything is insubstantial," which may be the closest correct translation, does not console the grieving mind. The pain of loss feels substantial. Reminding a person who is grieving, "This too shall pass," a cliché that trivializes a person's pain and creates distance rather than connection, exacerbates suffering. What is reassuring are moments when we are aware of the absence of suffering, within the acknowledged context of great pain. Surcease—rather than peace—is possible always.

Tara Brach

THE AUTHOR of *Radical Acceptance* and *True Refuge*, Tara Brach is a clinical psychologist and the founder of and senior teacher at the Insight Meditation Community of Washington, D.C. When asked what she views as the essential common ground between Western psychology and Buddhism, Brach claims it's their understanding that suffering comes from the parts of our being that are not recognized and embraced in the light of awareness.

Facing challenging emotions, many of us turn to what Brach calls false refuges. That is, we try to lose ourselves in stopgap measures, such as alcohol or television, overeating or shopping. But, she teaches, true refuge is possible. It's the awakened heart that allows us to embrace the world just as it is—with all of its ups and downs, joys and sorrows—and it's true because it doesn't depend on anything outside ourselves, be it a situation, person, or emotion.

According to Brach, true refuge has three gateways: truth, love, and awareness. This is her secularized articulation of the three jewels of Buddhism, and she opts for this nonreligious language because the search for true refuge and the three gateways to it are not limited to Buddhist practitioners but are, rather, universal. In the context of Buddhism, truth is dharma; love is sangha; and awareness is Buddha. But in Christian terms, for example, "the Father is awareness," Brach claims, "the Son is the living truth of this moment-to-moment experience, and when awareness and moment-to-moment experience are in relationship, there is love, which is the Holy Ghost."

"Truth," explains Brach, "is the understanding that comes out of being present with the life that's right here and now. Love is bringing presence to the domain of the heart, to the domain of relationships, and the realization that arises out of that is interconnectedness. Then awareness is when we bring presence to the formless awakeness that is right here. When we discover the refuge of our own formless being, that's awareness waking up to itself."

In the following teaching, Brach explores how we can find healing and freedom by shining a light of compassion on what scares us.

————

Befriend Your Fears

MARIA DESCRIBED herself, during our first therapy session, as a "prisoner of fear." Her slight frame was tense, and her dark eyes had an apprehensive look. From the outside, she said, her life appeared to be going very well. As a social worker, she was a strong advocate for her clients. She had good friends, and she had been living with her partner, Jeff, for three years. Yet her incessant worrying about how things might go wrong clouded every experience.

When stuck in morning traffic, Maria was gripped with fear about being late for work. She was perpetually anxious about disappointing her clients or saying the wrong thing at staff lunches. Any hint of making a mistake spiraled into a fear of being fired. At home, if Jeff spoke in a sharp tone, Maria's heart pounded and her stomach knotted up. "This morning he complained that I'd left the gas tank near empty, and I thought, 'He's going to walk out and never come back,'" she said. Maria could never shake the feeling that, just around the corner, things were going to fall apart.

Maria was living in what I call the trance of fear. When you are in this trance, fearful thoughts and emotions take over and obscure the larger truths of life. You forget the love between you and your dear ones; you forget the beauty of the natural world; you forget your essential goodness and wholeness. You expect trouble and are unable to live in the present moment.

Brain chemistry and genetics may predispose a person to excessive fearfulness, and it can be fueled by societal circumstances, such as the perception of a terrorist threat. Traumatic childhood experiences may also give rise to the trance of fear.

For Maria, the fear took hold in elementary school, when her mother was holding down two jobs and going to night school, leaving Maria to care for her two younger siblings. Her father worked erratically, drank too much, and had an unpredictable temper. "He would barge in at dinnertime, red faced and angry, yell at me, and then disappear into his room," she told me. "I had no idea what I'd done wrong." When Maria was thirteen, her father vanished without a word, and she always felt that she had driven him away.

It is understandable that Maria's fear of her father's anger became linked with a belief that her "badness" made him leave. But even if your personal history is not so distressing, you might spend a part of your life worrying about the ways in which you aren't good enough.

Necessary Fears

Fear itself is a natural and necessary part of being alive. All living beings experience themselves as separate, with a sense of "me in here" and "the world out there." And that sense of separateness leads you to recognize that you can be injured by others and that, eventually, the "me in here" will die. At the same time, you are genetically programmed to keep yourself alive and free from harm, and it is fear that signals you to respond when threats arise. It lets you know to hit the brakes when the car in front of you suddenly stops or to call 911 if you are having chest pain.

The problem is that fear often works overtime. Mark Twain said it well when he quipped: "I have been through some terrible things in my life, some of which actually happened." Think for just a minute about all of the time you've spent fearful and worrying. Looking back, you might see that much of what you fearfully anticipated turned out fine. Precious moments in life—moments that could have been full of love, creativity, and presence—were taken over by habitual fear.

Here's the good news: When you bring what I call *unconditional presence* to the trance of fear, you create the foundation for true spiritual awakening. In other words, as you learn to face your fears with courage and kindness, you discover the loving awareness that is your true nature. This awakening is the essence of all healing, and its fruition is the freedom to live and love fully.

Unsafe Havens

While the basic experience of fear is that "something is wrong," many people turn that feeling into "there must be something wrong with me." This is especially true in Western culture, where one's sense of belonging to family, community, and the natural world is often weak and the pressure to achieve is so strong. You may feel as though you must live up to certain standards in order to be loved, so you constantly monitor yourself, trying to see if you're falling short.

When you live in this trance of fear, you instinctively develop strategies to protect yourself. I call these attempts to find safety and relief "false refuges," since they work, at best, only for the time being.

One such strategy is physical contraction. When you stay trapped in fear, you begin to feel tight and guarded, even when there is no immediate threat. Your shoulders may become permanently knotted and raised, your head thrust forward, your back hunched, your belly tense. Chronic fear can generate a permanent suit of armor. In such a state, we become, as the Tibetan teacher Chögyam Trungpa taught, a bundle of tense muscles defending our very existence.

The trance of fear traps the mind in rigid patterns too. The mind obsesses and produces endless stories, reminding you of the bad things that might happen and creating strategies to avoid them.

In addition to physical armoring and mental obsession, there are many well-worn behavioral strategies for reducing or avoiding fear. You might run from fear by staying busy, trying to accomplish a lot, or judging others critically to boost your ego. Or maybe you take the popular approach of numbing yourself by indulging in too much food, drugs, or alcohol. Yet no amount of doing or numbing can erase the undercurrents of feeling fearful and unworthy. In fact, the efforts you make to avoid fear and prove yourself worthy only reinforce the deep sense of being separate and inadequate. When you run from fear and take false refuge, you miss being in the very place where genuine healing and peace are possible.

Bringing compassion and mindfulness directly to the experience of fear will help dissolve the trance, taking you inside to the real refuge of unconditional presence. Compassion is the spacious quality of heart that allows and holds with tenderness whatever you are experiencing. It seeks to answer the question, "Can I meet this moment, this experience, with kindness?" Mindfulness is the clear recognition of your moment-to-moment experience. Here the inquiry to use is "What is happening inside me right now?" Being mindfully attentive means that you are aware of the stories you are telling yourself and the feelings and sensations in your body. You can initially emphasize either compassion or mindfulness in meditation; both are essential when facing fear.

Unexamined Beliefs

One evening, Maria arrived at my office distraught and unnerved. A coworker was sick, and Maria's boss had asked her to step in as supervisor for their team of social workers. Sitting rigidly with her eyes downcast, she said bleakly, "Tara, I am really scared."

I invited her to pause—to breathe and simply be aware of the two of us sitting together. "I'm here with you right now," I said. "Would it be all right if we paid attention to the fear together?" Looking up at me, she nodded. "Good," I said, and went on. "You might begin by asking yourself, 'What am I believing right now?'" Maria responded without hesitation. "I'm going to let everyone down," she said. "They'll see that it was a mistake to ever hire me. They'll want to get rid of me."

When you are emotionally stuck, becoming mindful of what you believe at that moment can be a powerful part of awakening from trance. When you bring your stories and limiting beliefs to light, they gradually have less hold on your psyche. I encouraged Maria simply to acknowledge the thoughts as a story she was telling herself and then to sense the feelings of vulnerability in her body. I assured her that if the process felt like more than she could handle, we could shift our attention—it's not helpful to feel overwhelmed or possessed by fear. After a few moments, she reported in a shaky voice, "The fear is big. My stomach is clenched, and my heart is banging. Mostly there is a gripping, aching, empty feeling in my heart."

I invited her to check in with the fear, to ask it what it wanted from her. Maria sat quietly for a few moments and then began speaking slowly: "It wants to know that it's okay that it's here . . . that I accept it. And . . ." At this point she became quiet for some long moments. "And that I pay attention, keep it company." Then, in a barely audible voice she whispered, "I will try. I want to keep you company." This was one of Maria's first moments of being truly compassionate with herself. Instead of pushing away her feelings, she was able to gently acknowledge and accept them.

Love Lessons

What Maria and all of us need is to feel that we are loved and understood. This is the essence of unconditional presence, the true refuge that can heal the trance of fear. As the Buddha taught, our fear is great, but greater yet is the truth of our essential connectedness.

If you've been wounded in a relationship, the love and understanding of friends are essential components in bringing a healing presence to your fears. You need the gift of this caring presence from others, and through meditations that cultivate compassion and mindfulness, you can learn to offer it to yourself.

And if you've been traumatized, I think it's important to seek the help of a therapist as well as an experienced meditation teacher as you begin deepening your presence with fear. Otherwise, when you allow yourself to reexperience the fear, you may find it to be traumatic rather than healing. In Maria's case, we spent several weeks working with meditative practices that develop unconditional presence. I acted as her guide, and when she became aware of fear, I encouraged her first to pause, because pausing creates a space for you to arrive in the present moment. Then she would begin mindfully naming out loud what she was noticing: the thoughts she was believing, the shakiness and tightness in her belly, the squeeze in her heart.

With whatever was arising, Maria's practice was to notice it, breathe with it, and with gentle, nonjudging attention, allow it to unfold naturally. If it felt overwhelming, she would open her eyes and reconnect to the sense of being with me, to the songs of the birds, to the trees and sky outside my office window.

Abandoning False Refuges

The challenge in facing fear is to overcome the initial reflex to dissociate from the body and take false refuge in racing thoughts. To combat this tendency to pull away from fear, you awaken mindfulness by intentionally leaning in. This means shifting your attention away from the stories—the planning, judging, worrying—and fully connecting with your feelings and the sensations in your body. By gently leaning in instead of pulling away, you discover the compassionate presence that releases you from the grip of fear.

My meditation student Phil got an opportunity to lean in to fear the first night his sixteen-year-old son borrowed the car. Josh had promised to return home by midnight. But midnight came and went. As the minutes passed, Phil became increasingly agitated. Had Josh been drinking? Had he had an accident? By 12:30 Phil was furious, trying his son's cell phone every few minutes.

Then he remembered the instructions on mindfulness from the weekly meditation class he attended. He sat down, desperate to ease his agitation. "Okay, I'm pausing," he began. "Now, what's going on inside me?" Immediately he felt the rising pressure in his chest. Noting "anger, anger," he experienced the sensations filling his body. Then, under the anger, Phil felt the painful clutch of fear. His mind was imagining the police calling with the news that is a parent's worst nightmare. He leaned in, breathing with the fear, feeling its crushing weight at his chest. The story kept arising, and each time, Phil returned to his body, bringing his breath and attention directly to the place of churning, pressing fear.

As he leaned in to the fear, he found buried within it the hollow ache of grief. Then, drawing on a traditional Buddhist compassion practice, Phil began gently offering himself the message "I care about this suffering," repeating the phrase over and over as his eyes filled with tears. Phil was holding his grief with compassion, and as he did so, he could feel how much he cherished his son. While the fear remained, leaning in had connected him with unconditional presence.

A short while later, he heard the car rolling into the driveway. Josh barged into the living room and launched into his defense: He had lost track of time. The cell phone had run out of juice. Instead of reacting, Phil listened quietly. Then, with his eyes glistening, he told his son, "This last hour was one of the worst I've gone through. I love you and . . ." He was silent for some moments and then continued softly, "I was afraid something terrible had happened. Please, Josh, don't do this again." The boy's armor instantly melted, and apologizing, he sank onto the couch next to his dad.

If Phil had not met his fears with unconditional presence, they would have possessed him and fueled angry reactivity. Instead, he opened to the full truth of his experience and was able to meet his son from a place of honesty and wholeness rather than blame.

Fear's Gift

Several months after we had started therapy, Maria arrived for our session with her own story of healing. Two nights before, she and Jeff had been arguing about an upcoming visit from his parents. Tired from a difficult day at work, he suggested they figure things out the next evening. Without their usual goodnight kiss, he just rolled over and fell asleep.

Filled with agitation, Maria got up, went into her office, and sat down on her meditation cushion. As she had done so often with me, she became still, pausing to check in and find out what was going on. There was a familiar swirl of thoughts: "He's ashamed of me. He doesn't really want to be with me." Then she had an image of her father, drunk and angry, walking out the front door, and she heard a familiar inner voice saying, "No matter how hard I try, he's going to leave me." She felt as if icy claws were gripping her heart. Her whole body was shaking.

Taking a few deep breaths, Maria began whispering a prayer: "Please, may I feel held in love." She called to mind her spirit allies—her grandmother, a close friend, and me—and visualized us circling around her, a presence that could help keep her company as she experienced the quaking in her heart. Placing her hand gently on her heart, she sensed compassion pouring through her hand directly into the core of her vulnerability.

She decided to let go of any resistance to the fear and let it be as big as it was. Breathing with it, she felt something shift: "The fear was storming through me, but it felt like a violent current moving through a sea of love." She heard a gentle whisper arise from her heart: "When I trust I'm the ocean, I'm not afraid of the waves." This homecoming to the fullness of our being is the gift of fear, and it frees us to be genuinely intimate with our world. The next evening when Maria and Jeff met to talk, she felt at peace. "For the first time ever," she told me, "I could let in the truth that he loved me."

As long as you are alive, you will feel fear. It is an intrinsic part of your world, as natural as a bitter cold winter day or the winds that rip branches off trees. If you resist it or push it aside, you miss a powerful opportunity for healing and freedom. When you face your fears with mindfulness and compassion, you begin to realize the loving and luminous awareness that, like the ocean, can hold the moving waves. This boundless presence is your true refuge—you are coming home to the vastness of your own awakened heart.

Pema Chödrön

IN AN EFFORT to cope with the painful dissolution of her second marriage, Pema Chödrön explored different therapies and spiritual traditions, but nothing helped. Then she read an article by Chögyam Trungpa Rinpoche that advised working with emotions rather than trying to get rid of them. At the time, Pema Chödrön wasn't aware that Chögyam Trungpa was Buddhist, but what he said in the article struck a chord, and he eventually became her root guru. He had the ability, she has said, to show her how she was stuck in habitual patterns.

In 1974, Pema Chödrön ordained as a novice nun under the Sixteenth Gyalwa Karmapa, head of the Tibetan Kagyu lineage. Because full ordination is denied to women in the Tibetan tradition, Pema Chödrön didn't think she would ever take the *bhikshuni* vows that would make her a fully ordained nun. Yet in 1977 the Karmapa encouraged her to seek someone authorized and willing to perform the ceremony. This search took several years and finally brought her to Hong Kong, where in July 1981 she became the first American in the Vajrayana tradition to undergo bhikshuni ordination.

The next big step in Pema Chödrön's life was to help Chögyam Trungpa establish Gampo Abbey in Nova Scotia. The abbey, completed in 1985, was the first Tibetan Buddhist monastery in North America for Western men and women, and she took on its directorship. But as Pema Chödrön reveals in "When Things Fall Apart," her early years at the abbey were extremely challenging because there were no distractions there, and she was forced to face aspects of herself that she'd long denied. In this teaching, Pema Chödrön unflinchingly unpacks her human foibles and personal tragedies. This level of openness is a hallmark of her teaching style in general and has contributed greatly to her becoming one of the most sought-after Buddhist teachers in America. People can relate to her.

Pema Chödrön is also celebrated as a specialist in *lojong,* a Mahayana form of mind training that utilizes pithy aphorisms. She was instructed personally in this training method by Chögyam Trungpa, which, she has said, "is why I took off with it." In the second teaching presented here, "Breathing In Pain, Breathing Out Relief," Pema Chödrön presents tonglen, the meditation practice traditionally associated with lojong. This practice encourages a radical shift. With tonglen we reverse our impulse to avoid suffering and seek pleasure, and in the process we find a larger view of reality.

"Practicing Peace in Times of War" is the final teaching by Pema Chödrön featured in this book. Prejudice, hatred, war—their origins are in our hearts and minds, she says. To create a culture of peace and compassion, we must begin by addressing how we as individuals respond to the challenges in our daily lives.

———

When Things Fall Apart

GAMPO ABBEY is a vast place where the sea and the sky melt into each other. The horizon extends infinitely, and in this vast space float seagulls and ravens. The setting is like a huge mirror that exaggerates the sense of there being nowhere to hide. Also, since it is a monastery, there are very few means of escape—no lying, no stealing, no alcohol, no sex, no exit.

Gampo Abbey was a place to which I had been longing to go. Trungpa Rinpoche asked me to be the director of the abbey, so finally I found myself there. Being there was an invitation to test my love of a good challenge, because in the first years it was like being boiled alive.

What happened to me when I got to the abbey was that everything fell apart. All the ways I shield myself, all the ways I delude myself, all the ways I maintain my well-polished self-image—all of it fell apart. No matter how hard I tried, I couldn't manipulate the situation. My style was driving everyone else crazy, and I couldn't find anywhere to hide.

I had always thought of myself as a flexible, obliging person who was well liked by almost everyone. I'd been able to carry this illusion throughout most of my life. During my early years at the abbey, I discovered that I had been living in some kind of misunderstanding. It wasn't that I didn't have good qualities; it was just that I was not the ultimate golden girl. I had so much invested in that image of myself, and it just wasn't holding together anymore. All of my unfinished business was exposed vividly and accurately in living Technicolor, not only to me, but to everyone else as well.

Everything that I had not been able to see about myself before was suddenly dramatized. As if that weren't enough, others were free with their feedback about me and what I was doing. It was so painful that I wondered if I would ever be happy again. I felt that bombs were being dropped on me almost continuously, with self-deceptions exploding all around. In a place where there was so much practice and study going on, I could not get lost in trying to justify myself and blame others. That kind of exit was not available.

A teacher visited during this time, and I remember her saying to me, "When you have made good friends with yourself, your situation will be more friendly too."

I had learned this lesson before, and I knew that it was the only way to go. I used to have a sign pinned up on my wall that read: "Only to the extent that we expose ourselves over and over to annihilation can that which is indestructible be found in us." Somehow, even before I heard the Buddhist teachings, I knew that this was the spirit of true awakening. It was all about letting go of everything.

Nevertheless, when the bottom falls out and we can't find anything to grasp, it hurts a lot. It's like the Naropa Institute motto: "Love of the truth puts you on the spot." We might have some romantic view of what that means, but when we are nailed with the truth, we suffer. We look in the bathroom mirror, and there we are with our pimples, our aging face, our lack of kindness, our aggression and timidity—all that stuff.

This is where tenderness comes in. When things are shaky and nothing is working, we might realize that we are on the verge of something. We might realize that this is a very vulnerable and tender place, and that tenderness can go either way. We can shut down and feel resentful or we can touch in on that throbbing quality. There is definitely something tender and throbbing about groundlessness.

It's a kind of testing, the kind of testing that spiritual warriors need in order to awaken their hearts. Sometimes it's because of illness or death that we find ourselves in this place. We experience a sense of loss—loss of our loved ones, loss of our youth, loss of our life.

I have a friend dying of AIDS. Before I was leaving for a trip, we were talking. He said, "I didn't want this, and I hated this, and I was terrified of this. But it turns out that this illness has been my greatest gift." He said, "Now every moment is so precious to me. All the people in my life are so precious to me. My whole life means so much to me." Something had really changed, and he felt ready for his death. Something that was horrifying and scary had turned into a gift.

Things falling apart is a kind of testing and also a kind of healing. We think that the point is to pass the test or to overcome the problem, but the truth is that things don't really get solved. They come together and they fall apart. Then they come together again and fall apart again. It's just like that. The healing comes from letting there be room for all of this to happen—room for grief, for relief, for misery, for joy.

When we think that something is going to bring us pleasure, we don't know what's really going to happen. When we think something is going to give us misery, we don't know. Letting there be room for not knowing is the most important thing of all. We try to do what we think is going to help. But we don't know. We never know if we're going to fall flat or sit up tall. When there's a big disappointment, we don't know if that's the end of the story. It may be just the beginning of a great adventure.

I read somewhere about a family who had only one son. They were very poor. This son was extremely precious to them, and the only thing that mattered to his family was that he bring them some financial support and prestige. Then he was thrown from a horse and crippled. It seemed like the end of their lives. Two weeks after that, the army came into the village and took away all the healthy, strong men to fight in the war, and this young man was allowed to stay behind and take care of his family.

Life is like that. We don't know anything. We call something bad; we call it good. But really we just don't know.

When things fall apart and we're on the verge of we know not what, the test for each of us is to stay on that brink and not concretize. The spiritual journey is not about heaven and finally getting to a place that's really swell. In fact, that way of looking at things is what keeps us miserable. Thinking that we can find some lasting pleasure and avoid pain is what in Buddhism is called samsara, a hopeless cycle that goes round and round endlessly and causes us to suffer greatly. The very first noble truth of the Buddha points out that suffering is inevitable for human beings as long as we believe that things last—that they don't disintegrate, that they can be counted on to satisfy our hunger for security. From this point of view, the only time we ever know what's really going on is when the rug's been pulled out and we can't find anywhere to land.

We use these situations either to wake ourselves up or to put ourselves to sleep. Right now—in the very instant of groundlessness—is the seed of taking care of those who need our care and of discovering our goodness.

I remember so vividly a day in early spring when my whole reality gave out on me. Although it was before I had heard any Buddhist teachings, it was what some would call a genuine spiritual experience. It happened when my husband told me he was having an affair. We lived in northern New Mexico. I was standing in front of our adobe house drinking a cup of tea. I heard the car drive up and the door bang shut. Then he walked around the corner, and without warning he told me that he was having an affair and he wanted a divorce.

I remember the sky and how huge it was. I remember the sound of the river and the steam rising up from my tea. There was no time, no thought, there was nothing—just the light and a profound, limitless stillness. Then I regrouped and picked up a stone and threw it at him.

When anyone asks me how I got involved in Buddhism, I always say it was because I was so angry with my husband. The truth is that he saved my life. When that marriage fell apart, I tried hard—very, very hard—to go back to some kind of comfort, some kind of security, some kind of familiar resting place. Fortunately for me, I could never pull it off. Instinctively, I knew that annihilation of my old dependent, clinging self was the only way to go. That's when I pinned that sign up on my wall.

Life is a good teacher and a good friend. Things are always in transition, if we could only realize it. Nothing ever sums itself up in the way that we like to dream about. The off-center, in-between state is an ideal situation, a situation in which we don't get caught and we can open our hearts and minds beyond limit. It's a very tender, nonaggressive, open-ended state of affairs.

To stay with that shakiness—to stay with a broken heart, with a rumbling stomach, with the feeling of hopelessness and wanting to get revenge—that is the path of true awakening. Sticking with that uncertainty, getting the knack of relaxing in the midst of chaos, learning not to panic—this is the spiritual path. Getting the knack of catching ourselves, of gently and compassionately catching ourselves, is the path of the warrior. We catch ourselves one zillion times as once again, whether we like it or not, we harden into resentment, bitterness, righteous indignation—harden in any way, even into a sense of relief, a sense of inspiration.

Every day we could think about the aggression in the world, in New York, Los Angeles, Halifax, Taiwan, Beirut, Kuwait, Somalia, Iraq, everywhere. All over the world, everybody always strikes out at the enemy, and the pain escalates forever. Every day we could reflect on this and ask ourselves, "Am I going to add to the aggression in the world?" Every day, at the moment when things get edgy, we can just ask ourselves, "Am I going to practice peace, or am I going to war?"

Breathing In Pain, Breathing Out Relief

ON SEPTEMBER 11, 2001, the bottom fell out for millions of people. When the two planes flew into the Twin Towers of the World Trade Center, life as many of us knew it changed forever. There was a societal experience of groundlessness. The truth of uncertainty and change was very immediate for those living in New York City, for those living all over the United States, and for many people around the world.

In the days that followed, in this all-pervasive atmosphere of not knowing what was happening or what to do, large groups gathered in cities and towns throughout America to do a practice called *tonglen*. The instruction was to breathe in as deeply as possible the pain and fear of all of those who had been in the burning towers, all of those who had jumped to their death, all of those in the airplanes, and all the millions traumatized by this event. And also to breathe in the anger of the hijackers and those who had planned the attack. And then to breathe out, sending relief to them all.

Some sent love and care to all who were suffering. Some sent coolness and an escape from the scorching heat of the flames to those who had been trapped in the towers and planes. Some sent fearlessness. Some sent the aspiration that no one would hold feelings of hatred or rage. Breathing in, all of them did the only thing they could to support those who hadn't survived. Breathing out, they found a way to put into practice a deep longing to be of help, whatever that might mean. Of course, thousands of people in New York City and elsewhere immediately volunteered their support. In fact, there was such a flood of volunteers that many had to be turned away. But no one was turned away from the tonglen gatherings, and people who could not help in any other way joined with many others whose intention was to ease the suffering of those who had died in unimaginable pain and those they had left behind.

Tonglen is a core practice for warriors in training, the most effective tool for developing courage and arousing our sense of oneness with others. It's a practice for staying in the middle of the river. It gives us the strength to let go of the shore.

There are various ways that tonglen is taught, but the essence of it is breathing in that which is unpleasant and unwanted, and breathing out—sending out—that which is pleasing, relieving, enjoyable. In other words, we breathe in the things we usually try to avoid, such as our sadness and anger, and we send out the things we usually cling to, such as our happiness and good health. We breathe in pain and send out pleasure. We breathe in disgrace and send out good reputation. We breathe in loss and send out gain. This is an exceedingly counterhabitual practice. It helps us overcome our fear of suffering and tap into the compassion that's inherent in us all.

The word *tonglen* is Tibetan for "sending and receiving." It refers to our willingness to take on the pain of others we know are hurting and extend to them whatever we feel will ease their pain, whatever will enable them to stay present with the sorrows and losses and disappointments of life.

Practicing tonglen awakens our natural empathy, our innate ability to put ourselves in others' shoes. Caring about people when they're scared or sad or angry or arrogant can be a challenge; it confronts us with our own pain and fear, with the places where we're stuck. But if we can stay with those unwanted feelings, we can use them as stepping-stones to understanding the pain and fear of others. Tonglen allows us to acknowledge where we are in the moment and, at the same time, cultivate a sense of kinship with others. When painful feelings arise, we breathe them in, opening to our own suffering and the suffering of everyone else who is feeling the same way. Then we send relief to us all.

This is the style of tonglen that has been the most liberating for me. It uses the very immediate and unsettling rawness of our own discomfort as a link to others. It allows us to understand in an experiential, nonconceptual way that our suffering is not unique but is shared by millions and trillions of other beings, animal as well as human. We find out that we have cancer, and we breathe in the fear, the disbelief, the pain of all cancer patients, and send relief to all. We lose someone dear to us, and it connects us to everyone who is overcome with grief. We lie awake with insomnia, and it links us to countless others who are lying awake. On the spot, we breathe in our sleeplessness and the sleeplessness of others, breathe in our anxiety, our agitation, and the same discomfort felt by others. On the spot, we send out restfulness, peace of mind, contentment—even a visualization of all of us sleeping soundly.

Tonglen is a practice for thinking bigger, for touching into our sameness with all beings. Instead of withdrawing into ourselves, we can use the grittiness, the harshness of the human condition, as a way to rouse our natural ability to love, to care, to understand our interconnectedness. With tonglen our misfortunes become a means to awaken our heart, enabling us to work wholeheartedly for the sake of others and at the same time be a true friend to ourselves.

Tonglen isn't just a practice to do on the meditation cushion. It's particularly useful right in the midst of our life, wherever we are as we go about the day. Maybe a letter or an e-mail arrives from a friend who's having a hard time, who's depressed, who's grieving an upsetting loss. Right then, you can start breathing in your friend's pain, connecting with his sadness or despair and wishing for his suffering to lift. Then, as you exhale, you can send him relief—joy, caring, peace of mind, or whatever seems most appropriate.

Perhaps you're out on the street and see someone abusing a dog, beating it or yelling at it or yanking on its leash. You can breathe in the pain you assume the dog is feeling, then send out relief. It might be a wish for the dog to experience kindness and safety, even a nice, juicy bone. You can also breathe in what the abuser is likely to be feeling—the rage and confusion that are causing her to strike out so cruelly. Breathe in her anger and, on the out breath, send her anything you think would allow her heart to soften. It could be feeling loved, feeling okay about herself, feeling more space in her mind and more tenderness in her heart.

Tonglen is especially useful when we get into a conflict with someone and feel our own pain and confusion rising. Let's say you walk into a room and someone says something you don't like or gives you a nasty look. Ordinarily you might shut down or go blank or obsess about getting even, or whatever you do to exit when you don't want to deal with painful feelings. With tonglen, however, you can work with the emotions right then. Maybe you're feeling fear. You can open yourself completely to it—the smell of it, the texture of it, the tension in your body—and breathe it all in. As you continue to breathe in fear, you can open to include everyone everywhere who's afraid. You can even stretch your limit and include the person who triggered your fear, with the wish that he or she be free of suffering. Then, as you breathe out, you can send out an aspiration for all beings who are feeling fear, yourself included, to be free of it.

Right on the spot, you own your feelings completely. Instead of pushing the emotions away, you're completely in touch with them. This isn't the same as being self-absorbed, caught up only in your own distress. Far from it. Tonglen puts us in touch with all the others who are just like us, who feel the way we do. We all experience pain and pleasure. We all gravitate to what's comfortable and have an aversion to what's not.

Often people ask me, "But how do I know that other people are feeling the same thing I am?" I think it's safe to say that there's almost nothing we feel that millions of other people aren't also feeling—or haven't felt at some time. Our story lines are different, but when it comes to pain and pleasure and our reaction to them, people everywhere are the same.

Tonglen goes against the grain of how we usually deal with the world: wanting life on our own terms, wanting things to work out for our own benefit, no matter what happens to others. The practice begins to break down the walls we've built around ourselves, begins to liberate us from the prison of self. As this protective shield starts to come apart, we naturally feel a wish to reach out. People need help, and we can provide it—both literally and at the level of aspiration for their well-being.

Tonglen reverses the usual logic of avoiding suffering and seeking pleasure. To the degree that we can open to our own pain, we can open to the pain of others. To the degree that we can stay present with our own pain, we can hang in with someone who's provoking us. We come to see pain as something that can transform us, not as something to escape at any cost. As we continue to practice tonglen, our compassion is bound to grow. We'll find ourselves increasingly more able to be there for others, even in what used to seem like impossible situations.

Not that there won't be times when we simply can't do the practice. It may be that when we're confronted with suffering, our own or someone else's, we can't face it, so we go numb. Or we may have no problem getting in touch with pain, but we can't send out relief. The situation may seem so overwhelming that we can't think of any form of relief that would make a dent in what we're witnessing or feeling. But whatever the reason we can't do tonglen, it isn't grounds for self-criticism or despair. Life is full of opportunities for us to try again.

Resistance of any sort points to how important it is to bring a sense of spaciousness to this practice. One way to do this is to imagine that you're breathing into a space as vast as the sky. If you sense your body as boundless, transparent, and big enough to accommodate any amount of suffering, you can breathe in knowing that there is nowhere for the pain to get stuck. Then, as you breathe out, you can send out that same feeling of openness and freedom, the feeling that there's lots of room, unlimited room, enough room to accommodate anything—misery, delight, the whole gamut of human emotions.

As a formal meditation practice, tonglen has four stages. The first stage is a pause, a moment of stillness and space, a brief gap. If you need an image for this, you can reflect on any experience of wide-open space, such as gazing out at the ocean or looking up into a cloudless sky.

The second stage is a visualization, working with texture. As you inhale, breathe in hot, heavy, thick energy—a feeling of claustrophobia. Breathe it in completely, through all the pores of your body. Then, as you exhale, breathe out a sense of freshness, of cool, light, bright energy. Radiate it outward 360 degrees. Continue for a few minutes, or until the imagery is in sync with the in and out breaths.

The third stage involves breathing in a specific painful situation, opening to it as fully as possible, then breathing out spaciousness and relief. Traditionally we begin tonglen for a person or animal we wish to help, but we can also begin with our personal experience in the moment—a feeling of hopelessness or anger, for example—and use that as a stepping-stone for connecting us with the painful feelings of others.

In the fourth stage, we extend tonglen further. If we're doing it for a friend with AIDS, we extend it to all of those with AIDS. If we're doing it for our alcoholic sister, we extend it to all alcoholics, to all of those suffering from addiction. If we're already doing tonglen for all of those experiencing the same pain that we are, we can extend it to all of those, all over the world, who are suffering in any way, mentally or physically. And we can extend it still further to include all of us caught up in self-absorption, all of us tormented by our fixated minds and our inability to let go of hope and fear.

As a general guideline, we start tonglen practice with a situation that is immediate and real, not something vague or impersonal. Then we extend it to include more and more beings who are suffering in a similar way, as well as to all of us suffering from ego clinging, all of us suffering from resistance to uncertainty and impermanence.

If we ourselves have had even a glimmer of what egolessness feels like, of what awakening feels like, of what freedom feels like, then we want that for others too. When we see that they're hooked, instead of being critical and judgmental, we can empathize with what they're going through—we've been there and know exactly how they feel. Our wish for other people is the same as our wish for ourselves: to appreciate ourselves, to recognize when we're caught and disentangle ourselves from those feelings, to stop reinforcing the dysfunctional patterns that prolong our suffering, to reach out to others, to experience the goodness of being human.

Whether we do tonglen as a formal practice or on the spot, does it take time to get used to? Yes, it does. Does it take getting accustomed to the rawness of pain? Does it take patience and gentleness? Yes, it does. There's no need to get discouraged when the practice seems too hard. Allow yourself to ease into it slowly, at your own pace, working first with situations that are easy for you right now. I always remember what Chögyam Trungpa used to say when I was losing my confidence and wanted to give up. He'd sit up tall and smile broadly and proclaim, "You can do it!" Somehow his confidence was contagious, and when I heard those words, I knew I could.

I once read a poem about practicing tonglen in a time of war. The imagery was of breathing in bombs falling, violence, despair, losing your legs and coming home with your face burned and disfigured, and then sending out the beauty of the earth and sky, the goodness of people, safety, and peace. In the same spirit, we can breathe in hatred and jealousy, envy and addiction—all the sorrow of the human drama— using our personal experience of that pain and extending tonglen to all others caught in the same way. Then we can breathe out flexibility, lightheartedness, nonaggression, strength—whatever we feel will bring comfort and upliftedness and relief. The pain of the world pierces us to the heart, but we never forget the goodness of being alive.

Chögyam Trungpa once said, "The problem with most people is that they are always trying to give out the bad and take in the good. That has been the problem of society in general and the world altogether."

The time has come for us to try the opposite approach: to take in the bad and give out the good. Compassion is not a matter of pity or of the strong helping the weak; it's a relationship between equals, one of mutual support. Practicing tonglen, we come to realize that other people's welfare is just as important as our own. In helping them, we help ourselves. In helping ourselves, we help the world.

Practicing Peace in Times of War

WAR AND PEACE start in the hearts of individuals. Strangely enough, even though all beings would like to live in peace, our method for obtaining peace over the generations seems not to be very effective: we seek peace and happiness by going to war. This can occur at the level of our domestic situation, in our relationships with those close to us. Maybe we come home from work and we're tired and we just want some peace, but at home all hell is breaking loose for one reason or another, and so we start yelling at people. What is our motivation? We want some happiness and ease and peace, but what we do is get even more worked up, and we get everyone else worked up too. This is a familiar scenario in our homes, in our workplaces, in our communities, even when we're just driving our cars. We're just driving along and someone cuts in front of us and then what? Well, we don't like it, so we roll down the window and scream at the person.

War begins when we harden our hearts, and we harden them easily—in minor ways and then in quite serious, major ways, such as hatred and prejudice—whenever we feel uncomfortable. It's so sad, really, because our motivation in hardening our hearts is to find some kind of ease, some kind of freedom from the distress that we're feeling.

Someone once gave me a poem with a line in it that offers a good definition of peace: "Softening what is rigid in our hearts." We can talk about ending war and we can march for ending war, we can do everything in our power, but war is never going to end as long as our hearts are hardened against each other.

What happens is a chain reaction, and I'd be surprised if you didn't know what I'm talking about. Something occurs—it can be as small as a mosquito buzzing—and you tighten. If it's more than a mosquito—or maybe a mosquito is enough for you— something starts to shut down in you, and the next thing you know, imperceptibly the chain reaction of misery begins: you begin to fan the grievance with your thoughts. These thoughts become the fuel that ignites war. War could be that you smash that little teensy-weensy mosquito. But I'm also talking about war within the family, war at the office, war on the streets, and also war between nations, war in the world.

We often complain about other people's fundamentalism. But whenever we harden our hearts, what is going on with us? There's an uneasiness and then a tightening, a shutting down, and then the next thing we know, the chain reaction begins and we become very righteous about our right to kill the mosquito or yell at the person in the car or whatever it might be. We ourselves become fundamentalists, which is to say we become very self-righteous about our personal point of view.

Jarvis Masters, who is a prisoner on death row, has written one of my favorite spiritual books, called *Finding Freedom*. In a chapter called "Angry Faces," Jarvis has his TV on in his cell but he doesn't have the sound on because he's using the light of the TV to read. And every once in a while he looks up at the screen, then yells to people down the cell block to ask what's happening.

The first time, someone yells back, "It's the Ku Klux Klan, Jarvis, and they're all yelling and complaining about how it's the blacks and the Jews who are responsible for all these problems." About half an hour later, he yells again, "Hey, what's happening now?" And a voice calls back, "That's the Greenpeace folks. They're demonstrating about the fact that the rivers are being polluted and the trees are being cut down and the animals are being hurt and our Earth is being destroyed." Some time later, he calls out again, "Now what's going on?" And someone says, "Oh, Jarvis, that's the U.S. Senate, and that guy who's up there now talking, he's blaming the other guys, the other side, the other political party, for all the financial difficulty this country's in."

Jarvis starts laughing, and he calls down, "I've learned something here tonight. Sometimes they're wearing Klan outfits, sometimes they're wearing Greenpeace outfits, sometimes they're wearing suits and ties, but they all have the same angry faces."

I remember reading once about a peace march. When one group was coming back from the march, some pro-war people started cutting them off and blocking them; everyone started screaming and hitting each other. I thought, "Wait a minute, is there something wrong with this picture? Clobbering people with your peace sign?" The next time you get angry, check out your righteous indignation, check out your fundamentalism that supports your hatred of this person because this one really is bad—this politician, that leader, those heads of big companies. Or maybe it's rage at an individual who has harmed you personally or harmed your loved ones. A fundamentalist mind is a mind that has become rigid. First the heart closes, then the mind becomes hardened into a view, then you can justify your hatred of another human being because of what that person represents and what he or she says and does.

If you look back at history or you look at any place in the world where religious groups or ethnic groups or racial groups or political groups are killing each other, or families have been feuding for years and years, you can see—because you're not particularly invested in that particular argument—that there will never be peace until somebody softens what is rigid in his or her heart. So it's necessary to take a big perspective on your own righteousness and your own fundamentalism when it begins to kick in and you think your own aggression and prejudice are reasonable.

I try to practice what I preach; I'm not always that good at it, but I really do try. The other night I was getting hard-hearted, closed-minded, and fundamentalist about somebody else, and I remembered this expression that you can never hate somebody if you stand in their shoes. I was angry at him because he was holding such a rigid view. In that instant, I was able to put myself in his shoes and I realized, "I'm just as riled up and self-righteous and closed-minded about this as he is. We're in exactly the same place!" And I saw that the more I held on to my view, the more polarized we would become, and the more we'd be just mirror images of each other—two people with closed minds and hard hearts who both think they're right, screaming at each other. It changed for me when I saw it from his side and I was able to see my own aggression and ridiculousness.

If you could have a bird's-eye perspective on the Earth and could look down at all the conflicts that are happening, all you'd see are two sides of a story where both sides think they're right. So the solutions have to come from a change of heart, from softening what is rigid in our hearts and minds.

One of the most inspiring modern examples we have of this is the civil rights movement. I was recently rereading the writings of Martin Luther King Jr., and I understood once again that the whole movement was based on love—love that doesn't exclude anybody. This is also the Buddhist idea of love. In this view, you want everybody to be healed.

Now, some political activists might say, "Okay, but nothing will ever change just by holding that all-inclusive, loving view." But the truth is, when you take that view and you begin to live by it, at the level of your own heart in your own everyday life, something begins to shift very dramatically, and you begin to see things in a different way. You begin to have the clarity to see injustice happening, but you can also see that injustice, by its very definition, is harming everybody involved. It's harming the people who are being oppressed or abused, and it's harming those who are oppressing and abusing.

And from a Buddhist point of view, those who are being oppressed have a chance—just as people did in the civil rights movement—to be purified by what is happening to them. They have the opportunity to let hatred be replaced by love and compassion and to try to bring about change by nonviolence and nonaggression. Instead of sinking into self-absorption, they have a chance to let their suffering link them with the suffering of all beings—those harming, those helping, and those feeling neutral. In other words, they have a chance to soften what is rigid in their hearts and still hold the view that injustice is being done and work toward unwinding that injustice or that cruelty.

But those who are oppressing may be so prejudiced and rigid in their minds that there's very little opportunity for them to grow and learn. So they're the ones who ultimately suffer the most, because their own hatred and anger and prejudice continue to grow. There is nothing that causes more pain and suffering than to be consumed by bigotry, to be consumed by cruelty and anger.

So war and peace start in the human heart. Whether that heart is open or whether that heart closes has global implications.

Recently I was teaching from a Buddhist text called *The Way of the Bodhisattva,* which offers guidance to those who wish to dedicate their lives to alleviating suffering and to bringing benefit to all sentient beings. This was composed in the eighth century in India by a Buddhist master named Shantideva. In it he has an interesting point to make about peace. He says something along the lines of "If these long-lived, ancient, aggressive patterns of mine that are the wellspring only of unceasing woe, that lead to my own suffering as well as the suffering of others, if these patterns still find their lodging safe within my heart, how can joy and peace in this world ever be found?"

Shantideva is saying that as long as we justify our own hard-heartedness and our own self-righteousness, joy and peace will always elude us. We point our fingers at the wrongdoers, but we ourselves are mirror images; everyone is outraged at everyone else's wrongness.

And then Shantideva makes another thought-provoking point. He says that the people whom we get so upset at, they eventually move away or they die. And likewise, with nations that fight each other, time passes and either the nations no longer exist or they shift alliances and enemies become allies. He reminds us how everything changes with time. But the negative seeds that are left in our mind stream, the impact of our hatred and our prejudice, are very long-lived. Why so? Because as long as we keep strengthening our anger and self-righteousness with our thoughts and our words and our actions, they will never go away.

Instead, we become expert at perfecting our habits of hard-heartedness, our own particular brand of rigid heart and closed mind.

So what I'm advocating here is something that requires courage— the courage to have a change of heart. The reason this requires courage is that when we don't do the habitual thing, hardening our heart and holding tightly to certain views, then we're left with the underlying uneasiness that we were trying to get away from. Whenever there's a sense of threat, we harden. And so if we don't harden, what happens? We're left with that uneasiness, that feeling of threat. That's when the real journey of courage begins. This is the real work of the peacemaker, to find the soft spot and the tenderness in that very uneasy place and stay with it. If we can stay with the soft spot and stay with the tender heart, then we are cultivating the seeds of peace.

I think to do this kind of work it's very helpful to take some kind of personal vow. You make it clear in your own mind what you wish for and then you make a vow. For instance, let's say you hit your children and it's habitual, but then you make a vow to yourself: "Whatever happens, I'm not going to hit them." You seek help and you look everywhere for ways to help you not hit them when that uneasiness arises and everything in you wants to close your heart and mind and go on automatic pilot and do the thing that you always hate yourself for doing. You vow that to the best of your ability—knowing that sometimes there's going to be backsliding, but nevertheless, to the best of your ability—you vow not to cause harm to yourself or to anybody else and to actually help yourself and your children.

This kind of vow should be put in words that are meaningful and true to you so they aren't somebody else's good thoughts but actually your own highest, heartfelt wish for yourself. Your motivation behind the vow is that you equate it with the ultimate kindness for yourself, not the ultimate punishment or the ultimate shaping up, like "I'm bad, I need to shape up." No, the basic view is that there's nothing wrong with you or me or anybody else.

It's like what the Zen master Suzuki Roshi once said. He looked out at his students and said, "All of you are perfect just as you are *and* you

70

could use a little improvement." That's how it is. You don't start from the view of "I'm fundamentally messed up and I'm bad and therefore I have to get myself into shape." Rather, the basic situation is good, it's sound and healthy and noble, *and* there's work that we need to do because we have ancient habits that we've been strengthening for a long time and it's going to take a while to unwind them.

Living by a vow is very helpful, and actually it's Jarvis Masters who caused me to think about this. His Tibetan teacher, Chagdud Tulku Rinpoche, went to San Quentin prison and, through the glass, talking through a telephone, did an empowerment ceremony in which Jarvis took the vow never to cause harm and to the best of his ability to try to help. He has lived by these vows so earnestly, and when I read his book sometimes I laugh out loud at the extremes to which he has to go not to cause harm in a place like San Quentin.

To prevent some hostile, disrespectful guards from being killed, for instance, he had to talk some angry inmates into flooding their cells because they needed a way to express their rage. He knew that if he didn't come up with something, they were planning to retaliate by stabbing the guards. So instead he said, "Listen, the thing is, you don't need to kill them. These guys are wanting to get out of here to go to a party, so you just need to ruin their day by making them work late cleaning up the mess we'll make." And everyone bought it, so they just flooded the tier.

One of my favorite stories about Jarvis was when he unintentionally helped some other inmates connect with the absolute, vast quality of their own minds. There is a teaching that says that behind all hardening and tightening and rigidity of the heart, there's always fear. But if you touch fear, behind fear there is a soft spot. And if you touch that soft spot, you find the vast blue sky. You find that which is ineffable, ungraspable, and unbiased, that which can support and awaken us at any time. And somehow Jarvis, in this story of trying to avert harm, conveyed this fundamental openness to the other inmates.

One day there was a seagull out on the yard in San Quentin. It had been raining, and the seagull was there paddling around in a puddle. One of the inmates picked up something in the yard and was about to throw it at the bird. Jarvis didn't even think about it—he automatically put out his hand to stop the man. Of course this escalated the man's aggression, and he started yelling. Who the hell did Jarvis think he was? And why did Jarvis care so much about some blankety-blank bird?

Everyone started circling around, just waiting for the fight. The other inmate was screaming at Jarvis, "Why'd you do that?" And out of Jarvis's mouth came the words, "I did that because that bird's got my wings."

Everyone got it. It simply stopped their minds, softened their hearts, and then there was silence. Then they all started laughing and joking with him. Even years later, they still tease him, "What did you mean, Jarvis, 'That bird's got my wings'?" But at that moment, everyone understood.

If we begin to take responsibility for our own self-righteousness, it leads to empathy. Here's one more Jarvis story to illustrate this. Many of the prison guards in San Quentin are very kind and helpful, but some of them get mean and unreasonable and take their frustrations out on the prisoners. That day there had been plenty of that happening, and tempers were short. An inmate came up to Jarvis in the yard and asked, "Is it your Buddhism that keeps you so calm, Jarvis? How can you stand it when these guards are giving you such shit?"

And Jarvis said, "Oh, it has nothing to do with Buddhism. I just think that if I retaliate, they'll go home and beat their kids. I don't want that to happen to any of those little kids." The other man got it completely. Our empathy and wisdom begin to come forward when we're not clouded by our rigid views or our closed heart. It's common sense. "If I retaliate, then they'll go home and beat their kids, and I don't want that happening."

There are many stories, but the basic message I'm trying to convey is that to the degree that each of us is dedicated to wanting there to be peace in the world, then we have to take responsibility when our own hearts and minds harden and close. We have to be brave enough to soften what is rigid, to find the soft spot and stay with it. We have to have that kind of courage and take that kind of responsibility. That's true spiritual warriorship. That's the true practice of peace.

Thubten Chodron

THUBTEN CHODRON is an American-born nun in the Tibetan Buddhist tradition whose teachers have included the Dalai Lama, Tsenzhap Serkong Rinpoche, and Kyabje Zopa Rinpoche. In 1977, she was ordained in India, and in 1986 she received full ordination in Taiwan.

"The ordination connected me not only to all the nuns of the past but also to all the nuns that are yet to come," she has said. "I realized that I had to take responsibility for future generations of nuns. I could no longer stay in my childlike state and complain, 'Why do nuns face difficult conditions? Why doesn't anyone help the nuns?' I had to grow up and take responsibility for improving not only my own situation but also that of future generations. I came to see that practicing dharma is not simply doing my own personal studies and practice; it is preserving something very precious so that others can have access to it."

Thubten Chodron was a coorganizer of "Life as a Western Buddhist Nun," a conference held in 1996 so that nuns could broaden their community beyond their own abbeys and support one another on their quest to achieve greater equality with men in liturgical matters, particularly ordination. Material from this conference became the anthology *Blossoms of the Dharma: Living as a Buddhist Nun,* which Thubten Chodron edited.

For two years Thubten Chodron directed the spiritual program at Lama Tzong Khapa Institute in Italy, and for ten years she was resident teacher at Dharma Friendship Foundation in Seattle. Then in 2003 she founded Sravasti Abbey, a Buddhist monastic community in Washington State, where she currently serves as abbess.

Her books include *How to Free Your Mind: Tara the Liberator* and *Don't Believe Everything You Think: Living with Wisdom and Compassion.* She has also edited several books for her teachers, including *A Chat about Heruka* and *A Chat about Yamantaka* by Zopa Rinpoche.

Spiritual Mentor

SOME PEOPLE wonder if it's necessary to have a spiritual master. Can we teach ourselves and discover the path alone? Can't we learn from books? To learn worldly skills—for example, reading, carpentry, surgery, or even driving a car—we need to be taught. It's difficult to learn on our own, and it could even be dangerous. Imagine trying to teach ourselves to pilot a plane! If we depend upon teachers to learn ordinary skills, then certainly we'll need the guidance of qualified teachers for spiritual matters, which are more profound and which influence not only this life but many future lives as well.

A living teacher can do what a book cannot do: answer our questions, act as an example of how to practice the teachings in daily life, encourage and inspire us on the path, and correct our behavior. Books can enrich and expand what we learn from our teachers, but they can't replace the spiritual relationship we form with a few wise people on the path.

The Sanskrit term for teacher, spiritual master, and spiritual mentor—all of which are synonymous—is *guru*. This refers to someone who is "weighty in good qualities." The Tibetan term *lama* means "unsurpassable."

There isn't an examination to pass to become a teacher. Rather, when others request someone for teaching and guidance, that person becomes his or her mentor. Some people are commonly referred to as "lama" or "master." This is because they have many students. However, whether they become *our* teacher is up to us. Similarly, other people may not generally be known as "lama" or "teacher," but if we choose them as our teachers, then they become our spiritual mentors.

When we're first learning about Buddhism, we may not have a specific spiritual master. That's fine. We can learn from a variety of teachers and practice accordingly. People who have only a general interest in Buddhism probably won't select a master. However, after a while, people who are serious in their practice will feel the need to establish a teacher-student relationship with spiritual masters so they can receive closer guidance.

Choosing Our Spiritual Mentors

Because our spiritual mentors will have a great influence on us, it's important to choose them carefully. For example, we don't marry just any person. We first look at the other's qualities and weaknesses, see if our dispositions are similar, and check if we feel we can care for that person through thick and thin. Similarly, it's advisable to examine a person well before taking him or her as our spiritual mentor.

Nowadays, we're faced with a spiritual supermarket: there are many teachers from which to choose. Anyone can teach one philosophy or another, put on a good show, and win over followers. But sincere seekers aren't interested in charisma; they look for substance.

It may take time to find and identify our masters. To start, we can attend talks and learn from people without accepting them as our masters. This enables us to examine both their character and our ability to relate to them well. We can take our time in deciding whether to accept someone as our master: the great Indian sage Atisha examined the renowned master Serlingpa for twelve years before taking him as his spiritual mentor.

It's not advantageous to select people as our spiritual mentors simply because they have many titles, sit on high seats, or wear impressive robes or hats. We shouldn't look for pomp, fame, or charisma but instead seek out teachers who have excellent spiritual attributes. Also, we shouldn't select someone just because he or she is our friend's teacher. We must choose ourselves, according to the teacher's qualities and our experience with him or her.

In the *Mahayanasutralamkara,* Maitreya outlined ten qualities of excellent masters. He advised us to look for people who have the following qualities:

1. Pure ethical discipline. Our teachers set an example for us. Because

we need to modify our unruly actions of body, speech, and mind, it's wise for us to choose teachers who have done so. They will instruct us how to improve ourselves and will be good examples for us to follow.

2. Experience in meditative concentration.

3. Deep understanding of the teachings on wisdom. These first three qualities show that someone is well trained in the three higher trainings that lead to liberation—ethical discipline, concentration, and wisdom.

4. More knowledge and a deeper realization of the subject to be taught than we have.

5. Enthusiastic perseverance to teach and guide their students. If we choose a person who doesn't enjoy teaching or is reluctant to guide others, we won't be able to learn very much.

6. Extensive learning from competent teachers. We want to learn from those who know the scriptures well and will teach according to them. People who make up their own teachings or misunderstand the Buddha's teachings can't show us the path to enlightenment.

7. Correct conceptual understanding or direct meditative insight into emptiness.

8. Skill to articulate the dharma clearly so we'll understand it correctly.

9. Motivation of loving-kindness and compassion. This is a very important point. We can't trust someone who teaches in order to receive offerings, respect, or a large following. There is a danger that we'll be led astray by such a person, thereby wasting our lives and potentially engaging in negative activities. Therefore, it's extremely important to select as our masters people who have a pure and genuine wish to benefit their students and lead them on the path to enlightenment.

10. Patience and willingness to teach people of all levels of intelligence. We aren't perfect and will make mistakes because of our afflictions of anger and attachment. We need teachers who won't abandon us but will instead be patient and forgive us. In addition, we want teachers who won't be discouraged when we don't understand what they teach.

It may be difficult to find teachers with all of these qualities. In that case, these are the most important attributes they should have:

1. They have more good qualities than faults.

2. They regard creating the ethical causes for happiness in future lives more important than enjoying the pleasures of this life.

3. They cherish others more than themselves.

To learn what qualities teachers have, we can examine their behavior, their understanding of dharma, and how they treat their students. It's not wise to ask dharma teachers, "Are you enlightened?" for even if they were, they wouldn't tell us. The Buddha forbade his disciples to declare publicly what attainments they have. He wanted his followers to be humble, sincere, and unpretentious. Worldly people love to brag about their accomplishments; spiritual people are not like that. Their goal is to subdue the ego, not to enhance it.

We choose our spiritual mentors. When we decide that we would like someone to be our master, we can ask him or her personally to accept us as students. However, this isn't necessary; some masters are very busy with many students, so it's difficult to see them privately. In this case, we can make a strong mental decision that someone is our spiritual master. After that, when we again hear teachings from that person, he or she becomes our teacher. Also, if we take refuge, precepts, or empowerment (initiation) from someone, he or she automatically becomes our spiritual mentor.

We may have several spiritual masters, yet one remains the most important to us and is the one to whom we refer all serious matters.

This master is called our "root spiritual master." This person is the one either who first made the dharma touch our hearts and firmly set us on the path or with whom we feel the closest connection.

Following Our Mentor's Instructions, but Not Blindly

Having chosen a person as our spiritual mentor, we then follow that person's dharma instructions to the best of our ability. In that way, we'll progress on the path.

Some people are fickle in their relationships with their masters and run from one master to another until they find one who tells them what they want to hear. Such students make little progress because of their own lack of commitment and respect.

We should care for our teachers, offering both our service and the requisites they need to live. When we appreciate the kindness of our teachers in showing us the path to happiness, we'll happily want to help them. As our teachers are working for the benefit of others and for the spread of the dharma, our offerings will be put to good use.

Our dharma practice is the best offering to make to our teachers. If we have material possessions, talents, and time, we can offer those. However, we don't neglect our practice, for that is what our teacher cares about most. When we follow the dharma instructions we've received and keep whatever precepts we've taken, that pleases our teacher more than anything else.

When we notice what appear to be faults in our masters, it's counterproductive to criticize them angrily. Often we see faults in others simply because we're projecting onto their actions the motivation we would have if we acted like that. But that may not be our teacher's motivation; he or she may do things for completely different reasons than we've supposed. In fact, our master may behave in a certain way to show us what we look like when we act like that.

It's easy for us to find faults in anyone and everyone, but doing so isn't advantageous if we're spiritual practitioners striving to develop tolerance and love. If we angrily criticize and reject our masters, we close the door to benefiting from all of their good qualities. That is a great loss.

However, if our master does something that seems contrary to the Buddha's teachings, we can ask him or her to explain that action. Alternatively, we can simply keep a respectful distance, not take that behavior as an example of how we should act, and cultivate relationships with other teachers whose behavior corresponds to the Buddha's teachings.

We relate to spiritual teachers to increase our wisdom and self-responsibility. Blindly following someone because "that person is my master so whatever he does is perfect" isn't acting intelligently. If our spiritual master asks us to do something that we're not able to do or that we feel isn't correct, we can respectfully tell him or her that we're unable to do that.

Being Honest

Our spiritual mentors are our best friends, and it's to our advantage to speak and act honestly with them. Some students are two-faced: they act well in the presence of their teachers, but at other times they gossip, lose their temper, and mistreat others. This is counterproductive.

Nor should we try to win our teacher's favor by pretentious sweet talk. Who are we fooling? Our master cares about the state of our minds, not about superficial appearances.

It's hypocritical to be kind to our teachers and rude to others. Our teachers want all beings to be happy, and thus we contradict our teachers' advice when we're belligerent and mean to others. If we hold our teachers in high esteem and other beings in contempt, we haven't understood the true meaning of the dharma. To progress on the path, we need to treat both our teachers and other people with respect.

Let's think deeply about the meaning of respect. Some people confuse respect with fear and are then painfully shy and afraid of doing something wrong near a religious practitioner. There's no need to be emotionally immobilized like this. Interestingly, it may be our selfish mind that is afraid to look bad or foolish in front of someone else.

On the other hand, we shouldn't treat our masters like casual friends. A balance is required: let's endeavor to have a good motivation and act well both when we're around our mentors and when we're not. But at the same time, let's not be afraid to admit our bad qualities to them. We can be honest with our teachers and seek their advice on how to improve.

Cherishing Our Teachers versus Being Attached to Them

Some people confuse attachment to their teachers with commitment to them. This can be very painful, for if our teachers don't give us as much attention as we want, we then feel rejected. Attachment causes us to cling to our masters for emotional security, praise, and attention. But as we develop true appreciation of our teachers, we'll recognize their qualities and will be grateful for their kindness.

Attachment is self-oriented, while cherishing our teachers is based on sincere spiritual aspirations. Of course we may miss our teachers when we're separated from them for a long time, but we must ask ourselves if we're missing them because we want dharma teachings and guidance or because we want to feel loved.

The purpose of having a dharma teacher isn't to please our egos but to destroy our ignorance and selfishness by practicing the teachings. Our teacher's job is not to meet our emotional needs but to lead us on the path to enlightenment. When our teachers point out our faults, we can be happy that they care for us enough to do this. They trust we'll welcome their advice rather than be offended. One time I saw a master tell a student his mistakes at a large gathering. I thought, "That must be a close disciple. The master knows that person wants to eliminate his egotistical pride and won't mind being publicly reprimanded." In fact, when I got to know the disciple, I discovered he was indeed a good practitioner.

Our relationships with our teachers will grow and develop over time. They can be very rewarding relationships, because by depending on wise and compassionate spiritual guides, we'll enhance our good qualities and eliminate our unwholesome ones. The closeness we feel with our spiritual mentors, who are genuinely concerned with our welfare and progress, is unlike the relationships we have with others. Our teachers will never stop helping us, no matter what we do. While this isn't a license for us to act recklessly, we needn't feel insecure that our teachers will cut off the relationship when we make mistakes. Our spiritual mentors are forgiving and compassionate, and we can therefore trust them.

As our understanding of the path to enlightenment deepens, so will our feeling of closeness with our teachers. This occurs because our minds become more similar to theirs. As our determination to be free increases and our altruistic motivation develops, we'll feel naturally close with our teachers, for we'll have the same interests and goals. Truly understanding emptiness diminishes the feeling of separation that is caused by grasping at inherent existence. Eventually, when we become buddhas, our realizations will be the same as those of our teachers.

Darlene Cohen

ALTHOUGH SHE WAS ordained as a Zen priest in 1999, Darlene Cohen always described herself as being less interested in practice in a monastic setting than in seeing what happens when we get off our cushions and face our everyday work and family challenges.

In the 1970s, while living at San Francisco Zen Center's Green Gulch Farm, Cohen developed rheumatoid arthritis, and this agonizing and crippling disease led her to explore how meditation helps us find ease in the midst of chronic pain and catastrophic situations. She then went on to write *Arthritis: Stop Suffering, Start Moving; Turning Suffering Inside Out;* and *Finding a Joyful Life in the Heart of Pain*. Much of what she taught was grounded in the idea that pain and pleasure are interconnected and that our ability to experience one is dependent on our understanding of the other. When we push away our pain, we likewise push away our pleasure, so relief actually lies in paying closer attention.

In the following piece, Cohen chronicled her personal story of facing cancer. Sometimes in life you don't get to choose, she discovered, but sometimes—even when the path is hard—that can be a good thing.

In January 2011, at the age of sixty-eight, Cohen passed away from ovarian cancer. She was survived by her husband, Tony Patchell, also a Zen priest, and their son, Ethan.

The Scenery of Cancer

IN *Opening the Hand of Thought,* Uchiyama Roshi talks about experience as "the scenery of life." Experience simply presents itself, one minute after another, the way scenery rolls by a window on a road trip. Such experience is fully engaging if we allow it to be our whole world, moment after moment, without preference. Rinzai put it this way: "Even if all the buddhas in the ten directions were to appear before me, I would not rejoice. Even if the three hells were to appear before me, I would have no fear. Why is this so? Because there is nothing to dislike." Oh, really? I have often thought. That's not always been my experience.

The three hells appeared before me last September, when I went to the doctor with a distended belly (I had tolerated that distended belly for almost two months because it matched a lifelong worry: Am I getting fat?) and was diagnosed with ovarian cancer.

The word *cancer* carries with it some very scary baggage, such as death, debilitating illness, and the removal of much-loved body parts. But the baggage of cancer has been most conspicuous in the people around me. I have become a finite resource: some people have started attending every class and lecture I give; long-distance students have canceled our phone appointments and flown in to see me; I don't have holes in my *dokusan* schedule now. For me, though, the idea of an imminent leave-taking is too abstract. I don't feel like I'm going anywhere. When I asked my acupuncturist if he thought I was in denial, he said, "Most people, when they get cancer, have some life-altering experience. They become aware of their lives for the first time and reorganize their priorities to make room for some kind of spiritual life. But isn't that already your job?"

I had six treatments of chemotherapy. I was put in the hospital for the first two-day rounds so they could monitor me. They shot my belly full of toxic drugs until I labored just to take in air. I felt pregnant but not with any child of this world. I couldn't lie down or sit with that enormous belly on top of me; I could only walk. For hours I staggered up and down the hospital corridors, pushing the IV stand ahead of me and occasionally stumbling against the wall with exhaustion. Finally, in the middle of the night, a nurse with tears in her eyes cut me loose from the IV and I walked free. The next morning I thought, Dear God, what do you have to do to bring tears to the eyes of an oncology nurse?

I went home on the third day, and chemo hell continued. I couldn't breathe deeply, eat, or drink. I lived in a primal animal realm in which I was a creature without thought patterns or discriminative judgment, experiencing sensations and emotions that passed through in a constant stream. For twelve days I lay on my couch, laboriously breathing in and out, enveloped in a gestalt of pain and fear.

Yet simultaneous to that misery was the most beautiful autumn I'd ever seen in my life, happening right outside my room in a grove of maples and redwoods. The slanting light, characteristic of northern California autumns, dramatically showcased the reds, golds, apricots, and browns of the evolving plants. As dawn broke each morning, sunbeams penetrated the windows along my eastern wall, progressively highlighting the dark wood of my chair and table, the threads of my blanket, the reds and blues of my rug —and my waiting body. At such ecstatic times I felt as if I were being lifted and carried right through the windows into the air on a heavy linen sheet borne by the sweet-faced angels that used to illustrate the turn-of-the-century hymn sheets. My world was full, lush, and compelling.

Since then I have wondered what grounded my willingness to sink into pain and fear and ecstasy as they manifested in turn. What enabled me to patiently observe the "scenery" of my illness as it unrolled?

In my animal realm, more attuned to the pulses of the Earth than I ever was before, I began to be palpably aware of the well-being ceremonies that people were doing for me all over the country. Whole sanghas were chanting every day for me with all the psychic vitality at their command.

I had immediately felt the benefits when I woke up from the surgery to remove the tumor: As the anesthetic let me go and I moved toward consciousness, I became aware of a path of stepping-stones spread out before me in the dark. I put a cautious foot on one, and it held me utterly. I stepped on the next with my other foot. It held me absolutely. The stones were immovable, supportive, reliable. I stepped confidently until the light flooded in and I saw the faces of my husband, Tony, and my good friend Keith smiling down at me in my bed.

When I had my hip replaced two decades ago, life before and after the surgery was completely different. Life before was one flowing whole, but until I healed, life after surgery felt mismatched. This time, however, there has been no rent in the fabric of my life. The days before the tumor surgery and the days after continue to be all of a piece: I see students, I write lectures, I get cut open, I eat Jell-O, I receive visitors, I feel as sick as a barfing dog, I pace the corridors, I ride home with the passenger seat all the way down, and so on, to the experience of golden apricot colors, helplessness, dread, and being borne on a sheet carried by angels.

Next to this kind of unbidden adventure, a life of preference becomes not only self-indulgent but also deadened. When my son was a child, I refused to see the stupid Muppet movies popular then or to go to Disneyland or to color Easter eggs. He had to do all of that with his friends' parents. Now I wonder what kind of narrow-minded twit chooses her aesthetic tastes over spending exuberant time with her child! When you insist on having only particular kinds of experiences, nothing can deeply touch you. You're too busy judging. On the other hand, a life lived openly without filters includes pain, heartbreak, Disneyland, and unpleasant occurrences. But you do have a satisfying feeling of being infinitely approachable; the universe gets through to you, whatever scenery it's hauling.

For many years now, I have been consciously practicing not always choosing what I prefer. The first time I ever did this, I was in an ice cream parlor. I was surveying the flavors, trying to determine which would be the most intense chocolate experience. Suddenly it occurred to me to just step away, close my eyes, and pick a flavor. I did so and, much to my horror, I picked orange sherbet. I thought, should I go through with this? Yes, I decided. And you know what? Orange sherbet is great! Sherbet melts faster on the tongue than ice cream, and though I'm not a fruit-flavor fan, the taste of intense citrus was delicious—unexpectedly delightful and refreshing. And to think, if it weren't for that little experiment, I would have gone to my grave without ever having tasted orange sherbet.

Most of our preferences don't make much difference, like whether to choose chocolate or orange, but if you always go with your preference in every matter, then it's harder when it does matter—like preferring health to cancer. The statistical weight of your always choosing what you prefer becomes enormous, and your flexibility sags under it. It's much harder to see everything as scenery.

Now I regularly practice nonpreference. I wear whatever underwear comes up in my hand from reaching into the drawer. I randomly choose the third item down on a menu. And I watch with enthusiasm every movie my grandson chooses.

Christina Feldman

FOR THE FIRST few years that Christina Feldman practiced Buddhism, she assumed gender was not an issue, so it came as a shock when she undertook practice in a monastic setting and experienced what she describes as "an institutionalized rejection of women." Her unease with the discrimination came to a head when she was invited to give a discourse, only to discover that it was deemed inappropriate for her to take the seat traditionally occupied by the speaker. That, after all, would place her—a woman—physically higher than the monks. Alternatives were proposed: she could sit in the abbot's hut and speak through the public address system or she could deliver her speech from the back of the hall or a man could deliver her speech for her, if she wrote it down for him. Finally it was reluctantly decreed that she could take the traditional seat, but this caused many monks to decline attendance.

"A woman embarking on a spiritual journey travels a path on which there are few sure guides to inspire and affirm her," Feldman writes in the introduction to her book *Woman Awake: Women Practicing Buddhism*. "Established religions have repeatedly armored themselves against women, seeking to silence their voices. Our blind acceptance of models and expectations, and the inner denial and division they represent, can only serve to suffocate the inner spiritual vision from which our freedom is born. We need to be willing to risk the loss of external affirmation and approval if we are to know ourselves deeply. We need to be willing to risk listening to ourselves as well as others. The validity of our spiritual path can only be qualified by our own experience and understanding."

Today Feldman coteaches Women in Meditation, an annual retreat at Spirit Rock Meditation Center in California. She is a guiding teacher of the Insight Meditation Society in Barre, Massachusetts, and a guiding teacher and cofounder of Gaia House, a retreat center in England. Her books include *Compassion: Listening to the Cries of the World* and *The Quest of the Warrior Woman: Women as Mystics, Healers, and Guides.*

In the following teaching, she addresses overcoming the last great obstacle to awakening: the conceit of self.

———————

Long Journey to a Bow

When news of the impending death of a beloved and esteemed teacher swept through the village, well-wishers gathered to pay their last respects and honor him. Standing around the master's bedside, one by one they sang his praises and extolled his virtues as he listened and smiled weakly. "Such kindness you have shown us," said one devotee. Another extolled his depth of knowledge; another lamented that never again would they find a teacher with such eloquence. The tributes to his wisdom, compassion, and nobility continued until the master's wife noticed signs of restlessness and kindly asked his devotees to leave. Turning to her husband, she asked why he was disturbed, remarking upon all the wonderful tributes that had showered him. "Yes, it was all wonderful," he whispered. "But did you notice that no one mentioned my humility?"

The conceit of self (*mana*, in Pali) is said to be the last of the great obstacles to full awakening. Conceit is an ingenious creature, at times masquerading as humility, empathy, or virtue. Conceit manifests in the feelings of being better than, worse than, and equal to another. Within these three dimensions of conceit are held the whole tormented world of comparing, evaluating, and judging that afflicts our hearts. Jealousy, resentment, fear, and low self-esteem spring from this deeply embedded pattern. Conceit perpetuates the dualities of "self" and "other"— the schisms that are the root of the enormous alienation and suffering in our world. Our commitment to awakening asks us to honestly explore the ways in which conceit manifests in our lives and to find the way to its end. The cessation of conceit allows the fruition of empathy, kindness, compassion, and awakening. The Buddha taught that "one who has truly penetrated this threefold conceit of superiority, inferiority, and equality is said to have put an end to suffering."

Although I didn't recognize it at the time, my first significant encounter with conceit happened in the very beginning of my practice in the Tibetan tradition, a serious bowing culture. I'm not talking about a tradition that just inclines the head slightly but a culture in which Tibetans undertake pilgrimages of hundreds of miles doing full prostrations the entire way. In Tibetan communities the serious bowers can be spotted by the callus in the center of their forehead. Walking into my teacher's room in the Himalayan foothills for the first time, I found myself shocked to see people prostrating themselves at his feet. My reaction was visceral; I saw their bowing as an act of self-abasement, and I determined never to do the same. My conceit appeared in the thoughts that questioned what this plump, unsmiling man swaddled in robes had done to merit this attention. The recurrent words *I, me, better, worse, higher, lower, worthy,* and *unworthy* provided fuel for plenty of storytelling and resistance.

Over the years, as my respect and appreciation for this teacher's generosity, kindness, and wisdom grew, I found myself inching toward a bow, often a token bow with just a slight bob of my head. Occasionally I would engage in a more heartfelt bow born of deeper gratitude, but still an element of tension and withholding remained. I continued to practice in other bowing cultures. In Asia I witnessed the tradition of elderly nuns with many years of practice and wisdom kneeling before teenage monks who had yet to find the way to sit still for five minutes. In Korea I saw a practice environment where everyone bowed to everyone and everything with respect and a smile. It dawned on me that bowing was not, for me, just a physical gesture but also an object for investigation and a pathway to understanding conceit. The bow, I came to understand, was a metaphor for understanding many aspects of the teaching—pride, conceit, discriminating wisdom, and self-image.

My first challenge on this journey was to distinguish the difference between a bow as an act of letting go of conceit and a bow that reflected belief in unworthiness. As Kate Wheeler once wrote in *Tricycle,* "A true bow is not a scrape." Many on this path—both men and women—carry a legacy of too many years of scraping, cowering, and self-belittlement, rooted in a belief in their own unworthiness. The path to renouncing scraping can be long and liberating, a reclaiming of dignity and a letting go of patterns of fear. Discriminating wisdom, which we are never encouraged to renounce, clearly understands the difference between a bow and a scrape. A true bow can be a radical act of love and freedom. As Suzuki Roshi put it, "When you bow there is no Buddha and there is no you. One complete bow takes place. That is all. This is nirvana."

Conceit manifests in the ways we contract around a sense of "self" and "other"; it lies at the core of the identities and beliefs we construct, and it enables those beliefs to be the source of our acts, words, thoughts, and relationships. Superiority conceit is the belief in being better or worthier than another. It is a kind of conceit that builds itself upon our appearance, body, mind, intelligence, attainments, stature, and achievements. It can even gather around our meditative superiority. We see someone shuffling and restless on his or her meditation cushion and then congratulate ourselves for sitting so solidly. We might go through life hypercritical, quick to spot the flaws and imperfections in others, sure we would never behave in such unacceptable ways.

Superiority conceit is easily spotted when it manifests in arrogance, bragging, or proclaiming our excellence to the world. On retreat we may find ourselves rehearsing the conversations we will have with our partner, recounting our trials and triumphs, but especially our heroism in completing the retreat where others failed. We can feel remarkably deflated when our partner's only interest is in when we're going to take out the garbage. It can be subtle in our inner beliefs in our specialness, rightness, or invulnerability. Superiority conceit looks like a safer refuge than inferiority conceit (thoughts of being worse than another), but in truth both cause the same suffering. Feelings of superiority have the power to distort compassion into its near enemy, pity, and to stifle the capacity to listen deeply. Superiority conceit disables our receptivity to criticism because we become so convinced of the truth of our views and opinions.

A traditional Buddhist story tells of the time after the Buddha's death when he descended into the hell realms to liberate all the tormented beings imprisoned there. Mara (the personification of delusion) wept and mourned, for he thought he would get no more sinners for hell. The Buddha said to him, "Do not weep, for I shall send you all of those who are self-righteous in their condemnation of sinners, and hell shall fill up again quickly."

Inferiority conceit is more familiar territory for many of us, probably because a chronic sense of unworthiness is so endemic in our culture. The torment of feeling worse than others and not good enough is the daily diet of inferiority conceit. A student on retreat came in distress to report that none of her more familiar dramas and agitation were appearing, and she was convinced she was doing something wrong. The teacher suggested that this odd experience could actually be one of calmness and was surprised when the suggestion was met with even more distress and denial, with the student's exclaiming, "Calm is not something I can do." Another student experiencing rapture in her practice continued to assert that it was menopausal flashes, unable to accept that she could experience deep meditative states. Inferiority conceit gathers in the same places as superiority conceit—in the body, mind, and appearance, as well as in the long list of mistakes we have made throughout our lives.

Inferiority conceit is fertile in its production of envy, resentment, judgment, and blame, which go round and round in a vicious circle of storytelling, serving only to solidify our belief in an imperfect self. This belief is often the forerunner of scraping as we create heroes and heroines occupying a landscape of success and perfection we believe to be impossible for us.

Governed by inferiority conceit, we may be adept at bowing to others yet find it impossible to bow to ourselves, to acknowledge the wholesomeness and sincerity that keep us persevering on this path. Learning to make that first bow to ourselves is perhaps a step to realizing that a bow is just a bow, a simple gesture where all ideas of "self" and "other," "worthy" and "unworthy," fall away. It is a step of confidently committing ourselves to realizing the same freedom and compassion that all buddhas throughout time have discovered; it is acknowledging that we practice to be liberated. We practice because it seems impossible; we practice to reclaim that sense of possibility. We learn to bow to each moment, knowing it is an invitation to understand what it means to liberate just one moment from the burden of self-judgment, blame, envy, and fear. Letting go of inferiority conceit awakens our capacity for appreciative joy and reclaims the confidence so necessary to travel this path of awakening.

Seeing the suffering of superiority and inferiority conceit, we might be tempted to think that equality conceit is the middle path; however, a closer look shows us that it is more a conceit of mediocrity and minimal expectations. Equality conceit is when we tell ourselves that we all share in the same delusion, self-centeredness, and greed, that we all swim in the same cesspool of suffering. We see someone falling asleep on his or her cushion and feel reassured. We observe a teacher dropping a salad in the lunch line, and it confirms our view that people are essentially and hopelessly mindless. Sameness can seem both comforting and reassuring. Thinking that others are also struggling on the path can make us feel relieved of the responsibility to hold aspirations that ask for effort and commitment.

Equality conceit can express disillusionment with human possibility. When we look at those who appear happier or more enlightened than we and primarily see their flaws, we are caught in equality conceit. We see those who seem more confused or deluded than we, and we know we have been there. We see our own delusions and struggles reflected in the lives of others and think that we are relieved of the task of bowing. The offspring of equality conceit can be a terminal sense of disappointment, resignation, and cynicism. After Al Gore's documentary, *An Inconvenient Truth,* was released, several newspapers responded by publishing the electric bill of his home. What wasn't mentioned was how the home's electricity was generated by solar power. It seemed there was a driving need to reduce his message and show that we're all hopeless carbon emitters.

All forms of conceit give rise to the endless thoughts and storytelling that solidify the beliefs we hold about ourselves and others. Liberating ourselves from conceit and the agitation it brings begins with our willingness to sensitize ourselves to the subtle and obvious manifestations of conceit as they appear. The clues lie in our judgments and comparisons, the views we construct about ourselves and others. Suffering, evaluating, envy, and fear are all signals asking us to pause and listen more deeply. We learn to bow to those moments, knowing they are moments when we can either solidify conceit or liberate it. Instead of feeding the story, we can nurture our capacities for mindfulness, restraint, and letting go. Instead of volunteering for suffering, we may be able to volunteer for freedom. It is not an easy undertaking, yet each moment that we are present and compassionate in the process of conceit building is a moment of learning to bow and take a step on the path of freedom.

Life is a powerful ally because it offers us the opportunities to let go of the conceit of self. There are times when our world crumbles. Unpredictable illness and other hardships come into our lives, and we face the reality once more that we are not in control. Sometimes there is simply no more that "I" can do. In those moments, we can become agitated or we can acknowledge that we are meeting the first noble truth: at times there is unsatisfactoriness and suffering in life. When we face the limitations of our power and control, all we can skillfully do is bow to that moment. The conceit of self is challenged and eroded not only by the circumstances of our lives but also by our willingness to meet those circumstances with grace rather than with fear.

A teacher was asked, "What is the secret to your happiness and equanimity?" She answered, "A wholehearted, unrestricted cooperation with the unavoidable." This is the secret and the essence of a bow. It is the heart of mindfulness and compassion. To bow is to no longer hold ourselves apart from the unpredictable nature of our lives; it is to cultivate a heart that can unconditionally welcome all things. We bow to what is, to all of life. By liberating our minds from ideas of "better than," "worse than," or "the same as," we liberate ourselves from all views of "self" and "other." The bow is a way to the end of suffering, to an awakened heart.

Carolyn Rose Gimian

CAROLYN ROSE GIMIAN is a senior editor of the works of the late Chögyam Trungpa Rinpoche, including *The Collected Works of Chögyam Trungpa* and *Smile at Fear: Awakening the True Heart of Bravery*. She is also the founding director of the Shambhala Archives, the archival repository for Chögyam Trungpa's work in Halifax, Nova Scotia.

"Humor. Anyone who meditates knows about it," Gimian has written. "*Natural funniness* is the term that Chögyam Trungpa used. It's natural cheerfulness, light touch, appreciation, and joy. Sometimes in the meditation hall, someone giggles, amazed by a toe wiggling in front of them. You pick up the giggle and soon everyone is laughing, trying not to laugh, laughter exploding. How naughty. Back to the breath."

Infused with this humorous light touch, Gimian's teachings are totally accessible. In the one presented here, she takes a look at the path that great meditators before us have laid out. How can we be sure we're following it genuinely? There are no guarantees, but there are some keys for keeping it real.

"When you are there, just there, without trying to hold everything solidly together, you begin to find that you don't need to sustain a story line about yourself and your life," says Gimian. "Who is it for anyway? You can afford to relax with yourself, get to know yourself. You don't have to put on makeup for yourself; you don't have to put on a smile. You can leave the mental toupee on the shelf and like yourself just as you are."

I Want to Be Genuine

WHEN I WAS ASKED to write an article about how to make meditation practice genuine and real, I wasn't sure whether to be proud or insulted. Maybe I was being asked because it was obvious what a fraud I am on the meditation cushion, because it was obvious I'd be able to write honestly about failure.

Well, guilty as charged. Failure to be peaceful, failure to be mindful, failure to be aware, failure to be kind, failure to think big, failure to be generous (or insert your favorite virtue/accomplishment I've failed at). On the other hand, sitting on the cushion for a lot of years (if I tell you how many, it will be *really* embarrassing) has yielded *some* results. I have witnessed a whole circus of bizarre fantasies, emotions, and extreme mental states, starring anger, lust, hatred, delusion, arrogance, pride, depression, anxiety, and a host of other amazing performers. I've made friends with Speedy, Distracted, and Lazy, three of the seven dwarfs of meditation for small-minded people. However, I do have one genuine accomplishment: I have gotten completely and totally bored.

Boredom is my great achievement. Isn't that what you aspire to in your meditation practice? To be totally, fully bored with yourself, your practice, your life, your fantasies, etc., etc., etc.? No?

My topic, the actual topic I was asked to write about, is genuineness. *Genuine* is a term that is bandied about quite a lot these days, and it can mean many things, depending on the context. Through my search engine, I found that a lot of advertising companies use the word *genuine* in the title of their companies and Web sites. Suspicious. I also noticed that popular searches with *genuine* as the first word were mainly for car parts. If you're going to drive an automobile, you would like it to have genuine parts, I'm sure. But this is not what I associate with genuineness in spiritual practice.

On the other hand, my word processor tells me that synonyms for *genuine* include *real, authentic, indisputable, true, unadulterated, actual, legitimate,* and *valid.* As far as the practice of meditation is concerned, these sound pretty good. I would definitely like my meditation to be real, authentic, indisputable, true, unadulterated, actual, legitimate, and valid.

Okay, so how are we going to achieve that? And what are the pitfalls? Simple. To be genuine, you have to be honest with yourself first and then with others. Don't make anything up. Just do it. Just be it. It's pretty straightforward. But being honest with yourself is not so easy. There's a little thing called self-deception that gets in the way.

Now that we've introduced that scary word *self-deception*, we have our work cut out for us. In the realm of overcoming self-deception, it's probably better to have no goal in your practice, but that's a very difficult thing. Since meditation actually works, it's hard not to have a goal. It actually does make you kinder, more aware, less speedy, happier, more mindful, more efficient, more peaceful, more in the moment, and so on. I'm not belittling these. They are important and valid outcomes of meditation. There are many studies and self-reports that support this. I'm a fan, a true believer. But this doesn't specifically address genuineness.

In fact, when it comes to being genuine, it may be better to have one of those definite but perhaps limited purposes and let genuineness, which is all-pervasive, take care of itself. Indeed, unwittingly, you do manifest genuineness through the practice of meditation. You become more transparent and available to yourself, your thoughts are less fixed, you discover both natural strength and natural gentleness, and you're able to see through preconceptions.

I presume you're all waiting for the but, the pitfall. Here it comes, and it's a big one: largely, it's attachment to credentials.

Sometimes experience comes blessedly, with no connection to credentials. If out of nowhere you have an experience of openness, joy, compassion, or awareness, an experience that doesn't seem causally connected to anything particular in your life, then it is largely free from credentials. It's a gift. It's just what it is. Enjoy it for what it is, while it lasts.

But as soon as you become a "meditator," whether you have been meditating for one hour, one week, one retreat, or twenty years, you may begin to feel the need to label your meditation experiences and to communicate them to others. That's the beginning of gaining your spiritual credentials. You've just done your first meditation retreat. You go home and tell your family and friends about it: "Oh, it was fantastic. I had a really hard time for a few days, and my body hurt and I couldn't control my thoughts, but then I had the most amazing (or insert other adjective) experience." Whatever it was. Well, what else are you going to say? "Nothing happened. It was a complete waste of time, but I want to keep doing this." Huh? We have positive experiences, and we want to share them with others. That's an ordinary and acceptable thing to do. Pretty benign.

A little less benign is that, internally, we are looking for confirmation, signs that something is happening in our practice. We are looking for results, progress on the path. That also may be natural, but it's a little more dangerous because after a while we may tend to manufacture results or jump on things in our practice. If we have a "good" (that is, peaceful) meditation session, we are pleased and we try to repeat that. Another time we are frustrated when our mind is a roaring freight train of thoughts and emotions. Or we are experiencing huge upheavals in our life, yet nothing is coming up when we're on the cushion. Shouldn't they manifest in our meditation? We may try to manufacture emotionality and crisis in our practice. There are many other examples of how our expectations manifest in our meditation practice.

All of these concerns about our practice and our various meditation experiences are genuine signs of—wait for it—*confusion*. Actually, the recognition of confusion is quite helpful. Seeing our confusion is an important and, dare we say, genuine discovery. If we look into our experience, we see that we are very, very confused in some fundamental way. That may be the most authentic realization that comes up over and over in our meditation practice. If we are willing to acknowledge confusion, at the beginning, in the middle, and at the end, then the path and the teachings are real, even if we may not seem to be getting anywhere.

Give up any hope of fruition. This slogan from the *lojong* (mind-training) tradition is another way of putting it. This is the idea of our practice being anticredential, or free from credentials—through and through, start to finish. That is why boredom, our starting point, is so helpful. It's really not a very good credential. If someone asks what you have achieved after three days or three years or three decades of meditating, it's not that impressive to say, "I'm thoroughly bored." To prepare for writing this article, I looked at ads for spiritual paths and retreats, and not one of them said, "Come sit with us. We'll make you completely bored."

But boredom is actually a great sign, if it is genuine, complete boredom that includes being bored with your confusion, your anger, your arrogance, your everything, your you. I'm probably letting the cat out of the bag a bit, but if you commit yourself fully to your practice and discipline, you eventually wear out a lot of things—they begin to seem quite unnecessary and quite boring.

Boredom is genuinely helpful in ventilating our minds. The point of meditation is obviously not to encourage or enshrine our confusion, so getting really bored with our story lines, positive and negative, helps us clarify our confusion immensely. Of course, the path of meditation is not designed to deter us from commitment, confidence, and positive achievements in life. Meditation is not a nihilistic enterprise. But the approach of collecting credentials rather than wearing them out is problematic. It is very dangerous to try to con buddha mind, hoping to find a shortcut. It's not dangerous to buddha mind itself, but it may lead to self-deception, the opposite of being genuine.

This is often a problem the longer you have been practicing, especially if you become an instructor or a spiritual model of some kind for others. Then you *really* feel that you have to demonstrate some accomplishment, and you may begin to panic if you don't find anything in yourself that qualifies. People are looking to you for advice. They may be watching your every move, or so you think. They may ask you, "What was it like when you were just a beginner like me?" "How did you become so wise, kind, open, generous, blah blah blah?" And you start to think, "Well, I must have accomplished something. Yes, I am wiser, kinder, more open, more generous, more blah blah blah." You may try to fulfill people's expectations because you actually want to help them. But you also want to avoid embarrassment.

The interesting thing is that people actually see right through one another, so really we could relax about the whole thing. It's an open secret. Or as Leonard Cohen wrote, "Everybody knows." Everybody really does know his or her own and others' little secrets. We know, that is, if we admit to ourselves what we see, what we really know. That perception sees what is truly genuine.

Unfortunately, it's not so easy to relax with that in ourselves. We have a lot of resistance to simply being ourselves, without pretense or adornment, with all of our warts and wrinkles. It is quite uncomfortable. So often we put on a little show for ourselves and others, thinking that's what is required. We try to give the people what they want. We try to give ourselves what we think we want. It's actually very sad, and in the long run it doesn't help us or others. But in the short run, it's a pretty good con.

But while everybody may know, that's not a license for telling other people what's wrong with them or what's good for them. To do that, you'd have to *really* know. You'd have to be able to see others not just as schmucks or charlatans, devils or angels, but also as the immaculately genuine human beings they are. That has to start in one's own practice. Sitting with ourselves without expectation, viewing practice as *practice*, as life's work rather than a race to the finish line. In that way, we leave space so that buddha mind, genuine mind, can shine through at the most unexpected moments.

Genuineness *is* actually that simple. But I have to confess that I fall short most of the time, failure that I am.

A little voice pops up: Give it up. Abandon any hope of fruition.

I yield to the little voice.

Joan Halifax

I'M A KIND OF 'plain rice' Buddhist," Roshi Joan Halifax has said. "I've seen some really amazing things, but they haven't amazed me." As she defines it, "plain rice" Buddhism is the meditation of everyday life: "When it's time to meditate, you meditate, and when it's time to make a bed, you make a bed. Not very exciting but, actually, exciting. The fierce kind of excitement. Excitement without excitation. It's about being alive."

A Zen priest and anthropologist, Halifax is the founder, abbot, and head teacher of Upaya Zen Center, a Buddhist monastery in Santa Fe, New Mexico, as well as a founding teacher of the Zen Peacemaker Order. For more than three decades, her work and practice have focused on Engaged Buddhism, especially in the area of terminal illness.

Growing up, Halifax saw her grandmother providing comfort to her dying friends. Yet her grandmother's own death was difficult and lonely. At the funeral, when Halifax saw the body in the open casket, she realized that much of her grandmother's suffering had been rooted in the family's fear of death. "At that moment," Halifax writes in her book *Being with Dying*, "I made the commitment to practice being there for others as they died." Today she is the founder and director of a professional training program that teaches contemplative end-of-life care.

The environment is the other major thread in Halifax's Engaged Buddhist focus. In the piece that follows, "The Way of the Mountain," we can see how her environmentalism is based on a deep appreciation of nature, of geographies.

The Way of the Mountain

EVERYBODY HAS A geography that can be used for change. That is why we travel to far-off places. Whether we know it or not, we need to renew ourselves in territories that are fresh and wild. We need to come home through the body of alien lands. For some, these journeys of change are taken intentionally and mindfully. They are pilgrimages, occasions when Earth heals us directly.

Pilgrimage has been, for me and many others, a form of inquiry in action. Although there is usually a particular destination to go to when on pilgrimage, it is the journey itself that is the thing. Once in *dokusan* (Zen interview) with Richard Baker Roshi, I asked the following question: "'Going to the temple, you take the path. Entering the temple you leave the path.' What does this mean?" Without a pause, his response was "Joan, the path is the temple."

People have traveled over this Earth with a heart of inquiry for millennia. They have sung through the land as a living being, offered themselves, their steps, their voices and prayers as acts of purification that opened them to an experience of connectedness. Whether it is Huichol peoples of Mexico who annually journey to Wirikúta; or Australian aborigines, whose song-lines connect dreamings across thousands of miles; or Hindu pilgrims who make their way to the Mother Ganges, or Shiva's Abode; or Buddhist pilgrims who reconstitute the life of the Buddha by visiting the groves and mountains, towns and villages where his birth, realizations, teachings, and passing occurred, pilgrimage is a remembering in the passing through of sacred time and sacred space.

Mountains have long been a geography for pilgrimage, places where peoples have been humbled and strengthened. They are symbols of the Sacred Center. Many have traveled to them in order to find the concentrated energy of Earth and to realize the strength of unimpeded space. Viewing a mountain at a distance or walking around its body, we can see its shape, know its profile, survey its surrounds. The closer you come to the mountain, the more it disappears. The mountain begins to lose its shape as you near it. Its body begins to spread out over the landscape, losing itself to itself. On climbing the mountain, the mountain continues to vanish. It vanishes in the detail of each step. Its crown is buried in space. Its body is buried in the breath.

On reaching the mountain's summit, we can ask, What has been attained? The top of the mountain? Big view? But the mountain has already disappeared. Going down the mountain, we can ask, What has been attained? Going down the mountain? The closer we are to the mountain, the more the mountain disappears. The closer we are to the mountain, the more the mountain is realized.

Mountain's realization comes through the details of the breath. Mountain appears in each step. Mountain then lives inside our bones, inside our heartdrum. It stands like a huge mother in the atmosphere of our minds. Mountain draws ancestors together in the form of clouds. Heaven, Earth, and Human meet in the raining of the past. Heaven, Earth, and Human meet in the winds of the future. Mountain Mother is a birth gate that joins the above and below. She is a prayer house. She is a mountain. Mountain is a mountain.

Mountains are extolled not only for their qualities but also for their effect on those who relate to them. Taking refuge in them, pilgrimaging to them, and walking around or ascending them has long been a way for the shaman and the Buddhist to purify and realize the mind of the mountain. The surface of inner and outer landscape, of the above and below, meet in the mountain body. The sense of place is confirmed in the mountain body. The spirit of place is confirmed when the mountain disappears into the landscape of the mind. Thus one reveres mountains.

Some of us are drawn to mountains the way the moon draws the tide. Both the great forests and the mountains live in my bones. They have taught me, humbled me, purified me, and changed me: Mount Fuji, Mount Shasta, Mount Kailash, the Schreckhorn, Kanchenjunga. Mountains are abodes for ancestor and deity. They are places where energy is discovered, made, acquired, and spent. Mountains are symbols, as well, of enduring truth and of the human quest for spirit.

As a student of Buddhism and a mountain wanderer, I have been deeply affected by the writings of Zen Master Dogen (1200–1253), the ancestor and founder of the Soto school of Japan. Dogen Zenji wrote a remarkable vernacular text, the *Shobogenzo* (*The Treasury of the True Dharma Eye*), which includes the Mountains and Rivers Sutra. Reading it, I learned something about mountains and something about mind.

Dogen says that mountains and rivers at this very moment are a revelation of Truth. Mountains are conditioned, relative, and connecting Beings and are perfect exactly as they are. Mountains and rivers, in their relative and absolute nature, have no identity that is separate or distinct from anything else. Mountains express rivers, and rivers express mountains. Mountains are hidden in rivers, and rivers are hidden in mountains. Mountains and rivers are mandalas that have all qualities as potentials within them.

Dogen realized that the activity of mountains and rivers, like Buddhist spiritual life, was not in the world but of the world itself. From this perspective, mountains and rivers are not only Buddha's true nature but share in the great body of all true nature.

Several months before he wrote the Mountains and Rivers Sutra, Dogen composed the *Keisei sanshohu* (Sound of the valley, form of the mountain), a work based on this verse by the poet Su Tung-p'o:

The sound of the valley stream is his long, broad tongue,
The mountain, his Pure Body.
This evening's eighty-four thousand verses—
How will I tell them tomorrow?

Dogen tells us,

Mountains and rivers at this very moment are the actualization of the word of the ancient Buddhas. Each, abiding in its phenomenal expression, realizes completeness. Because mountains and rivers have been active since before the Empty Aeon, they are alive in this present moment. Because they have been the self since before form arose, they are the realization of freedom. . . . We must carefully investigate the walking of the blue mountains, the walking of the self.

And he goes on:

Thus, the accumulated virtues [of the mountain] represent its name and form, its very lifeblood. There is a mountain walk and a mountain flow, and there is a time when the mountain gives birth to a mountain child. The mountains become the Buddhas and Ancestors, and it is for this reason that the Buddhas and Ancestors have thus appeared

Dogen ends the sutra with the advice that

there are mountains hidden in jewels; there are mountains hidden in marshes, mountains hidden in the sky; there are mountains hidden in mountains. There are mountains hidden in hiddenness. An ancient Buddha has said, "Mountains are mountains and rivers are rivers." The meaning of these words is not that mountains are mountains but that mountains are mountains. Investigate mountains thoroughly. When you investigate mountains thoroughly, this is the work of the mountains. Such mountains and rivers of themselves become wise persons and sages.

In Dogen's world of mountains and rivers, of plum blossoms and bright moons, everything is the body of the Buddha, everything has the sound of Truth in it. Hidden within each thing is every other thing, like Indra's Net of Jewels. Dogen sought to convey all the basic activity of the world as mutual and enlightened. The mountains are the buddhas and ancestors, writes Dogen: "The blue mountains devote themselves to the investigation of walking; the East Mountain devotes itself to the study of 'moving over the water.' Hence, this study is the mountain's own study. The mountains, unchanged in body and mind, maintaining their own mountain countenance, have always been traveling about studying themselves."

Before Dogen and after Dogen, in Tibet, China, and Japan, wilderness, and most particularly the greatness of mountains, has called rustic ascetics to their strength and stillness. The ideograph for Chinese *hsien* and Japanese *sen* is made up of two parts, one meaning person, the other meaning mountain. In Taoism and in Ch'an Buddhism, the hsien was a spiritual practitioner who used the mountain as a birth gate to awakening. Japan, like China, had a number of spiritual schools inspired by mountain mind. The tradition of Taoist naturalism and Esoteric Buddhist cosmology and rituals combined in the background of Shinto asceticism to give rise to Shugendo. The ascetic practitioners of the Shugendo sect are called *yamabushi,* or "those who lie down in the mountains."

In the Esoteric Buddhist schools of Tendai and Shingon, with which Shugendo sects were affiliated, ceremony and extreme, intensive practices are a means for the mountain to be realized. These mountain bodies are worshipped through the activities of pilgrimage, fasting, running, prayer, and solitude, yet it is the mountains themselves that do the true teaching. Here the teachings are directly incorporated, completely embodied. Although the modern world has turned some of the old Tendai pilgrimage running paths into asphalt roads, marathon monks still ply their way down these routes at predawn hours in their purificatory practices. In the Shugendo sect, practice life is focused on pilgrimage to and ascent of sacred mountains and ceremonial activities in which the mountain is the ground and space for practice.

In Asia, mountains have called pilgrims to them for thousands of years. In the summer of 1987, I hitchhiked across Tibet in order to walk around such a mountain. This mountain you could not climb, and not because of physical obstacles; rather, there are sacred laws that have kept its crown free from trespass. For many, many years, pilgrims have made their way to this holy place. They have come from the south, from the dry and wet heat of India. They have come from the east, from the high plains, barley fields, and villages of Tibet. They have come from the grasslands of the north and the deserts of the west as well. They have walked with and against the sun around this mountain.

They have been brought as babies to be carried around this mountain, and as elders they have made their way to this place to die.

Some circle this great body in a day. Others seem to take a lifetime to make the circuit. Some ride on yaks, and others ride the earth around this holy giant as they prostrate with dust clinging to their bellies. With three friends I walked, just simply walked, one step at a time, around the big four-sided body of this Mountain Being.

In the beginning I thought I was walking around Mount Kailash. I was convinced of it. I looked constantly to my right, and there was its snowy pyramidal crown. Mount Kailash. At the end of the walk, it seemed as though I had circumambulated myself. I was somehow standing outside myself and walking around myself. It was not until some years after the journey that the mountain would disappear into me. But I would have to dream it many times, the joy and suffering of this walk. After this, the mountain would appear inside the atmosphere of my mind.

I had known for twenty-five years about this mountain that I was to encounter and in whose body I was to be given a new body. What took me to Tibet was Buddhist practice, learning from shamans, a profound concern for tribal peoples and the environments in which they live, and the passion I have for wilderness. I was also sent there by one of my Native American teachers, who had told me to go to complete a rite of purification, to offer myself to this place. The pilgrimage had been set in my bones for many years.

In the summer of 1987 three traveling companions and I sat around a small pink Formica table in an apartment in Kathmandu. We were guests of Daku Tenzing Norgay. It was tea time, and a visit with Daku had been long overdue. She and I had hiked to the base camp of Kanchenjunga years before, and during that journey we had developed a strong friendship. One night, after a severe snowstorm in the high altitudes of Sikkim, I told her of my commitment to make the Kailash *perikerama* (circumambulation). Now that promise was going to be fulfilled. Daku wanted to leave her husband's ashes on the Dolma La Pass of Kailash and wished to join our party but was not able to because she could not obtain a visa. Her husband, Tenzing Norgay, was the first man to attain the summit of Mount Everest. His life from that moment had taken on superhuman as well as problematic aspects as he suffered both from fame and from alcohol. To take his ashes to Kailash would ensure him an auspicious rebirth.

In the middle of the small, pink, shiny table beside the teapot were two *tsa-tsa*, miniature stupas made of Tenzing's ashes. Such objects represent the enlightened form of the Buddha. Would I take them to Kailash on her behalf? I carefully wrapped the tsa-tsa in red cloth and put them in my pack with the promise that her request would be fulfilled. So began the two months of travel through rain and mud, across great and spacious landscapes, through lifeways of soldiers, lamas, and nomads that brought our little party of four to the Mountain of the Four Directions.

We left Kathmandu Valley at the beginning of August and traveled north to the end of the road destroyed by the monsoon. We were lightly geared for two months of travel—food, shelter, and clothing, no more than forty pounds apiece. The point was not to take the West with us but to leave behind as much as possible.

Because of the wild rains, roads had vanished along the winding river's course, cutting off the flow of vehicular traffic between Nepal and Tibet. It took four days of foot travel to make our way into Tibet. We struggled through living mud slides, dodged falling rocks as cliffs were blasted to open a new road, and made our way with a stream of humanity northward. This was the summer of 1987, and people of every description were drawn to Tibet for a taste of liberation that was to last for only an instant.

Even before we had departed Nepal, as we with great difficulty made our way toward the border, I had begun to question my sanity in undertaking this endeavor. I noticed that those few Westerners who were on the trail were in their twenties, and I began to think that I had exceeded the age limit. But the ashes in my pack would become a companion for me, urging me on when my will weakened. Finally we crossed the border and caught rides in jeeps, trucks, and buses to an army post in the high, purple-and-tan central valley of Tibet.

In the freezing predawn, still aching and confused with altitude sickness, I squeezed into a bus and hoped that the sun would soon rise to reveal the expanse of the country through which we were passing. We had climbed by foot and vehicle close to ten thousand feet in these past few days, and the world of familiar sights and sounds, the world of Western things and thoughts, was just beginning to fade from my consciousness.

North we went to Shigatse, the seat of the Panchen Lama. Carefully avoiding the jaws of hungry dogs, we circled the great monastery of the Panchen Lama and on the full moon of August witnessed the most spectacular display of lightning I have ever seen. It was symbolic of the nature of central and western Tibet. Nothing is mediated. Everything seems to strike directly—the penetrating and pervasive light, the relentless wind, the sand from her high deserts that blasts away skin, the great rivers sourced in her that feed and flood the plains of India and China, the directness and humor of the people of the far west that sweeps away one's disquietude, the slap of monks' hands as they triumph in debate, and even the odd and cold cruelty of many of the Chinese colonists who regard Tibet as a savage hell.

I could see why the shamans of the high altitudes had invented a book of the dead that then became a map for the Buddhists who were to arrive later. I discovered why oracles and trance mediums found fertile ground in this barren land. I understood why the Mountain of Kailash was holy not only to those who practice the religion of Bon, the indigenous shamanism of Tibet, but also to Hindus, Jains, and Buddhists. For even in the days before the Chinese army made entry and exit to this land difficult, only those with will and good fortune made it through the obstacles impeding access to this aspect of Earth and the mind that it evokes.

Traveling to Lhasa and then south again, I often thought I would just keep on going south back to Nepal, so difficult was the journey. But the ashes in my pack seemed to have a voice of their own, and so I turned west at Lhatse and did the long, hard stretch toward Kailash. After two weeks of riding in truck, bus, and jeep, I finally saw the mountain rise behind boiling clouds.

The old bus we were in stopped its tortured movement and disgorged almost all of us. There we stood on the wrinkled ground of a dry riverbed to see the white head of the mountain appear. One could never confuse Kailash with any other mountain. Shaped like a pyramid, its flanks shimmering with snow, it looks from certain angles like a sphinx, silent and mysterious. From its north side, faces appear on its flanks, like guardians, old men, or ancestors. Its west face asks one in, and the eastern face is hidden.

Finally we arrived in Tarchen (altitude 15,100 feet), a small settlement on the south side of Kailash, whose altitude reaches 22,028 feet. We began to set up camp amid cold, chaotic winds coming from every direction. The atmosphere was filled with charged particles, and each thought, each action felt amplified. An argument broke out between me and one of my companions; the tension that had been building between the two of us over these months in Asia blew up in this wild and restless wind. I was exhausted from the journey. My backbone was rubbed raw from hard travel, my psychic spine was also painfully exposed. When my companion attacked me, I broke. All of the unexpressed fears about survival rushed to the surface, and suddenly I felt like a Tibetan being beaten by the Chinese. In the midst of this, I thought, I am in Tibet. Who are the Chinese anyway? Who is the enemy anyway? Nearby were lama and Bonpo priest, herder and mother, soldier and pilgrim. Who are we anyway? What's the big deal? We seem so small in this landscape: a dark blue sky above and an endless horizon.

I stayed alone in my tent by the river. Upriver, laundry was being washed and animals' guts cleaned out. The freezing water rushing past my tent seemed pure despite the filth it carried along. Yaks were circling my sleeping place. I remembered the tales of bandits in this region, but one is so exposed here that any protection other than the spiritual kind is useless. Kailash, Shiva's birthplace, Buddha's final resting place, was sheltering all of us who were sleeping and waking in the shadow of a mountain.

It was too early to begin our journey around the mountain. Full moon was several weeks away. Spiritual athletes of every color were doing *nyingkor,* one-day shots around the mountain. The more circumambulations of the mountain, the more merit is generated, according to local tradition. It's a long, hard way to Kailash, so a few heartier and more spiritually ambitious pilgrims did their high-speed, seventeen-hour, high-altitude walks with a frequency that daunted this feeble observer.

Most were going in the "Dalai Lama" direction, clockwise. But some went in the "Bon" direction, counterclockwise. Judging by the number of Tibetans going counterclockwise, I have a hunch that the old Bonpo tradition is gaining in strength. Bonpo would make it possible for a believer to work with the difficult circumstances in Tibet through the spirit realm, through magic. Although Tibetan Buddhism is probably one of the most interesting traditions for working with negative forces, the Bon tradition has old, old roots, much older than Buddhism. These years of suffering and oppression that Tibetan people have had to endure under Chinese rule may be fertilizing the roots of the Bon tradition. Certainly, there is evidence of increasing strength in the Bon tradition among Tibetans living in Kathmandu.

South of Kailash is Lake Manasarovar, fifty-five miles in circumference. Its name means "lake born from the mind of Brahma." Although we had thought only about the mountain, something moved us south to the lake to await the waxing of the moon. We arrived at Chiu Gompa (Bird Monastery), past the gold mines on the Ganga Chu that connects the waters of Manasarovar with Lake Raksas Tal. The latter is the dark lunar brother to Manasarovar's sun body. The waters of Lake Manasarovar seemed to cleanse whatever was offered to them—clothes, dinner dishes, or us, inside and out. They say that immersion in its waters ensures one an incarnation as a god.

I finally went into partial seclusion in a meditation cave high up a cliff on the north side of the lake. From my perch, I watched storms making and unmaking themselves. Light and darkness moved in and out of each other as day passed into night. The great massif Gurla Mandhata glistened like a huge, white crouching animal on the opposite shore of the lake. Ravens floated below my cave as I hung in the air on the tiny stone terrace made years ago by the hands of some brave pilgrim. On the blackened ceiling of my cell were the constellations daubed in *tsampa*, roasted barley flour. A stone box lined with freshwater seaweed was my bed. The small altar above my head held a picture of His Holiness the Dalai Lama.

The lake, like Kailash, is a place where circumambulation is made. We had intended to do this, but I was too weak from loss of weight and the strains of the journey to make the trip. We were also almost out of food. A lama who had lived in a nearby cave for three years gave us tsampa, wheat flour, and rice to help tide us over. We supplemented this with nettles collected for soup. The Tibetan diet, at this level anyway, is simple, and I related to the ascetic Milarepa's cave practice without too much difficulty.

At last I seemed to be out of earshot of the neurobabble of Western culture. I was convinced that it was the altitude, but one morning I recognized that my receiver was down, and sitting in the cave, I at last knew what it was to be literally stoned, to move at a rate of speed like that of rocks, stones, and mountains. Things were going very slowly. I now understand how a place can shape the human psyche. This vast, clear lake with its wild and barren shore mirrored the ever-changing weather and light of the region. In the stillness of dawn, I looked into the face of Manasarovar and discovered that my face was also still and empty of "weather." The spirit of this place is big and free. I was caught by its emptiness.

Full moon was less than a week away, and so we left Manasarovar for Kailash. Back in Tarchen, we wandered among the camped nomads, buying a bit of very rancid yak butter, freshly ground tsampa, and sweets. Then one morning, early, before leaving for the perikerama, I prepared forty-four chapatis, eleven for each of us along the way. Cooking the tsampa-and-flour chapatis one by one in the tiny pan top brought me completely into the present moment. This done, we departed with a minimum of gear.

Within a few steps, it was clear to me that I needed to find my own way and my own stride. At first I was behind the others. Then with a burst of energy, I flowed along the trail, leaving behind the sense of the personal. Suddenly, I was at the first Chakstel Gang, one of four prostration stations at the four corners of the mountain. Turning the southwest corner to enter the west valley, I once more looked south and saw Gurla Mandhata and Raksas Tal in the distance and was reminded of the purifying days at the lake. I turned my back on this scene, and walking past piles of carved *mani* stones and yak skulls, prayer flags beating in the wind, I headed north along Kailash's west flank.

The lush green valley, called the Valley of the River of the Gods, has a fine stream meandering through thick mounds of grassy earth. Cushion for at least a dozen pilgrim families, the valley has long been a place of transit for trader and pilgrim alike. Old men and women, newborns, and large families lazed in the warm summer sun, having tea, laughing, and celebrating the commencement of the formal part of the *kora,* the circumambulation. I was invited as I moved along to join this one and that for the inevitable cup of yak-butter tea.

Warmed by good company and nourishment, I moved down the trail like a spirit with no sense of hindrance. The great Tarboche (flagpole) that is dedicated to the Buddha drew me. Pointing toward the heavens, it was woven round with flags in the colors of the five Buddha families. Yak hair and clothing were tied to the stringers that anchor the pole to earth. At a distance, I saw three old women dressed in black yak-wool *chubas* moving in a circle around the pole. I followed their footsteps as my gaze was drawn to the center pole and then toward the heavens, where the sky showed itself an intense, deep blue. Each year, a great *mela* is held when the flagpole is dug out and raised in the early morning of the May full moon, the day of Buddha's birth, enlightenment, and death. As I left the well-trodden path around the pole, I turned toward it one more time and saw it as an exclamation point that marked change.

My companions did not appear, and so on I flew. A wild sense of joy beat on the ground as each step took me northward. The sky was turning darker, and I decided to spend the night alone. I watched the ridges of the western range etch themselves in black on Kailash's west face. The evening light was penetrating, and I walked on to see where I would sleep for the night.

At dark I came upon a most unusual boulder. It was blackened with soot and shiny with yak butter; many offerings of mani stones were on the ground around it. These offering stones, carved with the mantra Om Mani Padme Hum (the jewel in the lotus), had been left by the devout. The great rock, called the Saddle of Faith, is a place to pray for an auspicious rebirth, an opportunity I had not anticipated. I carefully laid out my sleeping bag so my head was toward the huge stone and the holy mountain was guarding my feet. Later that night the moon would rise almost full over this place, and I stayed awake and followed its light until dawn.

As it turned out, I had bedded down on the trail. All through the night pilgrims passed by me, and I mentally went with them on their night kora. Goats, sheep, and yaks wandered past me. Again the utter joy of being in this place sent me shaking. Before the moon came, the sky was washed with stars. After the moon came, the sky was washed with light. At dawn I moved on.

Although the altitude was sixteen thousand feet, I felt no shortness of breath. When I reached the north end of the west valley, the sun greeted me. Time for a bath in the creek. The ground was thawing, and so was I. Off came the jeans and long underwear, and in I went. What an ecstasy! This was beyond cold.

The walk continued. But shortly I was in the company of two Khampas who kept me flying along the north side of Kailash, where I gestured that I would not go with them over the pass that night. Full moon was the next day. Something needed to be done beneath Kailash's core in the glacial melt. So my Khampa friends and I passed three hours in the making and drinking of tea, and then they disappeared into the afternoon.

I, on the other hand, walked, one breath, one step, toward the core and the north face of Kailash. Near the top, birds were landing on my shoulders and riding me for steps at a time. I had never been this high before. The next day, two of my companions and I would make this climb again. We bathed the tsa-tsa of Tenzing's ashes in the milky glacial waters, purification for Tenzing Norgay's remains. At the core, we left offerings that we had carried for others to this high place and then descended in a snowstorm. That night the sky blazed white with the moon.

Is the point of the pilgrimage the pass, I wondered? And so the four of us, reunited, began the climb, but now our gear was being carried by yaks and we walked in the company of a large Drogpa family, nomads of the region who were also doing the perikerama. Halfway to Dolma La Pass (the Pass of the Noble Mother Tara), we crossed through Shiwa Tsai, the "Place of Yama," the Lord of Death. Old clothing, human and yak hair, and other offerings were scattered across the rocky landscape. This is the realm of death before rebirth on the pass. The sense of the journey as initiation deepened here when I saw a pilgrim lying as if dead among the scattered offerings. I myself stopped and sat quietly in the midst of old clothing and hair and gazed up at the final ascent to the pass. Birth and rebirth require sacrifice. What is to be sacrificed? What is to be saved?

I stood up and began to walk up the Hill of Salvation one step at a time. Just before we arrived at the pass, a wild snowstorm hit the mountain with relentless energy. The Drogpas, their yaks, and our gear disappeared into flying snow as we neared the summit, and as I arrived at the summit's great stone shrine, wind was howling through its prayer flags and the clothing and yak-hair offerings. I remembered that another name for the pass is "the Mother Who Helps One Cross Over." It was time to leave Tenzing's ashes at Tara's great stone shrine.

The feeling of wolf was in the air. Not only was a snowstorm besieging the pass, but one of our party had fallen into a rage. The energy of such places amplifies whatever is in the air. In the midst of atmospheric and psychological changes, I climbed the great icy black shrine, the

Dolma Stone, and left the tsa-tsa of Tenzing Norgay's ashes on its summit. According to legend, the Noble Mother Tara disappeared beneath this great stone in the form of twenty-one wolves after she helped the monk Gotsangpa get to the top of the pass. The icy stone was carved with mantras, dotted with offerings of frozen yak butter and tsampa, and adorned with stringers on which flags, hair, and clothing were flying. All around the frozen, glistening rock were offerings of garments, tea bowls, bags, and sacred stones.

Suddenly, the sky cleared, and we raced through the snow down the other side of the pass. There was no trail, no path. Also there was no warm and dry place to stay in the rainy valley below, so we sang for our supper in the warm tent of our Drogpa companions. This was the east side of Kailash, whose face was now hidden.

The next day the wind took off our skin as we pushed against it toward Tarchen and the end of the kora. One discovers during pilgrimage that there is no place to escape from oneself. Whatever the mountain gives you, earth and sky give you, you cannot refuse. Pilgrimage is not the mountain nor the pass. The mountain is a mirror that accurately reflects the minds of those who come to it. Like the circle, which is a sign of nonduality, the walk around Mount Kailash is about the perfection of our true nature in all of its displays.

Although I can say little to nothing about my own true nature, I can say that Kailash took me down and into its depths even as I crossed over its pass. Little was left of me psychically or physically after circling it. Leaving Kailash, the way back to Nepal along the Brahmaputra River across the southern deserts of Tibet was no easier. Whatever I had lost on Kailash, I lost the rest on the journey home.

Mountain pilgrimages bring the quality of firmness into the life of an individual, a firmness of place and vision that is hard earned. The firmness arises out of the complete physical involvement the mountain demands of the pilgrim. It also confirms the sense of the continuity of things it brings to the journeyer. Born and reborn again, as cloud and river, rock and clay, mountains bring us into the experience of returning to the origins of peoples and of place.

The true nature of mountains is that they are mountains. They practice both stillness holding their place and moving with change. Men and women can be reborn through mountains. Ancestors abide in mountains. And mountains disappear the closer you are to them. As Dogen wrote in the *Shobogenzo:* "They passed aeons living alone in the mountains and forests; only then did they unite with the Way and use mountains and rivers for words, raise the wind and rain for a tongue, and explain the great void." Realizing fully the true nature of place is to talk its language and hold its silence.

Blanche Hartman

I<small>N</small> *Zen Master Who?* James Ishmael Ford describes Zenkei Blanche Hartman as "one of the premier teachers that the San Francisco Zen Center has produced," and as "a quiet and yet compelling leader exercising her authority through her simple and pure presence, a true heir to Suzuki's Dharma."

Hartman is known as a dedicated social-justice activist, a proponent of interfaith dialogue, and a leader in the ancient spiritual art of sewing the priest's robe (*kesa*) and the lay precept holder's garment (*rakusu*). In her younger years, Hartman studied at the University of California and worked as a chemist for the state of California. In 1947, she married Lou Hartman and three decades later they were ordained by Richard Baker. Then she went on to receive dharma transmission from Mel Weitsman and to become the first woman to serve as a co-abbot of the SFZC. In both the United States and Japan, she has led retreats for women.

There is no greater gift than to be grateful for our lives, Hartman tells us in the following teaching. And gratitude, she asserts, leads naturally to generosity, because we want to share this gift with others.

———

Just to Be Alive Is Enough

THERE ARE two related practices that guide my life these days: cultivating gratitude and cultivating generosity. Generosity, *dana paramita,* is the first of the perfections of the heart of a bodhisattva. It is deeply supported by the experience of gratitude.

Gratitude as an experience, and not just a sentiment, came into my life most vividly during a vacation in Connecticut sixteen years ago. I had gone with my niece to an exhibition of vintage automobiles, an old hobby of mine. At one point I was having some chest pain, and she said, "Aunt Blanche, you look horrible; I'm going to call an ambulance."

Her prompt action, and the skill of paramedics, doctors, and nurses, made it possible for me to go home ten days later. As I was walking away from the hospital with my husband, I thought, "Wow! I'm alive! I could be dead. The rest of my life is just a free gift!" After a couple more steps, I thought, "Gee, it *always* has been a free gift, from the beginning." I was flooded with gratitude just to be alive and understood what Suzuki Roshi meant when he once said, "Just to be alive is enough." Even though there may be difficulties and disappointments, and sometimes real pain and hardship, I really do like being alive.

This was one of those moments of practice that give rise to spontaneous gratitude. It was not at all like that when I came close to dying twenty years earlier, before I ever heard of Zen or meditation practice. At that time, my primary response was fear—terror, actually—at realizing my own mortality. Up until then I had known that everyone dies eventually, but it was impersonal. Now I knew that I, *personally,* was going to die and that it could happen at any moment. I understood firsthand the teaching "Death is certain. The time of death is uncertain."

The great ancestor Nagarjuna said, "To see into impermanence *is* bodhichitta [the altruistic aspiration to awaken for the benefit of all beings]." As a result of that experience, I began a frantic search to understand how you live a life that you know is going to end. That search finally led me to Suzuki Roshi and practice. It is clear to me that my dharma practice in the years between my first and second brushes with death caused the dramatic change in my response. So you can understand why I feel that one of the greatest gifts of practice is gratitude.

But I need to be careful not to suggest that anyone should practice expecting some particular result. Suzuki Roshi often cautioned: "No gaining idea! No goal-seeking mind!" He said, "The most important point in our practice is to have right or perfect effort. Right effort directed in the right direction is necessary. If your effort is headed in the wrong direction, especially if you are not aware of this, it is deluded effort. Our effort in our practice should be directed from achievement to nonachievement. . . . When you are involved in some dualistic practice, it means your practice is not pure. We do not mean to polish something, trying to make some impure thing pure. By purity we just mean things as they are."

All the teachers I know have emphasized that we practice for the sake of practice—just to express and actualize our intrinsic buddha nature for the benefit of all beings. There is nothing we need to get that is not already right here, right now, in this very body and mind as it is.

The Heart Sutra says there is "no attainment because there is nothing to attain." Sawaki Kodo Roshi said, "Zazen is good for nothing. And until you get it through your thick skull that it's good for nothing, it's *really* good for nothing!" In my first *zazen* instruction, Katagiri Dainin Roshi said, "We sit to settle the self on the self and let the flower of our life force bloom," again suggesting that everything we need is right here.

To seek for something other than "just this" implies that something is missing, that we are not complete somehow. The first time I heard Suzuki Roshi speak, he said, "You are perfect just as you are." I thought, "He doesn't know me. I'm new here." But again and again he would keep pointing in that direction, saying, "You have everything you need," "You are already complete," "Just to be alive is enough." I finally had to assume that I was not the sole exception to these assertions, but I was still dubious. And as I continued to practice and to talk with other students of the buddha dharma, I found that many people share the conditioning that leads us to think that there's something wrong with us. If we could only *get, do,* or *be* something more, *then* we would be all right.

The Zen teacher Cheri Huber also addressed this common source of distress with her book entitled *There Is Nothing Wrong with You: Going Beyond Self-Hate.* I found the book very helpful and have recommended it to many people, including my daughter, who has recommended it to many of her friends. For me, coming to accept that there is nothing wrong with me has been a very important part of growing up. (I understand that Chögyam Trungpa Rinpoche once said, "Our mantra should be 'OM grow up svaha!'") I have had a lot of help in this from practicing with the three treasures: my teachers, the dharma, and my friends in the sangha, including a psychotherapist.

It's so easy for us to get the idea that there's something wrong with us. And it's so hard to let go of that and just appreciate this one life, as it is, as a gift. My first spontaneous experience of gratitude came more than thirty years ago as I was preparing to enter Tassajara Zen Mountain monastery. I was sitting *tangaryo,* a practice in which new monastics sit continuously (with brief breaks) for a number of days (five at Tassajara) to settle themselves and clarify for themselves and others that they are ready to immerse themselves in monastic practice.

I had had to wait several years before I could go to Tassajara because I still had teenage children at home and I also needed to work. So I was really glad to finally be there, but it was also very difficult. I had sat weeklong *sesshins* before, but in tangaryo we didn't have walking meditation between periods of zazen; we just sat all day. And it was hot, and there were flies, and our knees hurt, and so on. On about the fourth day, I became more aware of what was going on around me. I heard the sounds of the students working outside. I became aware of the cooks preparing food for us, and the servers serving us, and I began to feel grateful that they were all working *so that I could sit!* Then I began to feel grateful that Suzuki Roshi had come to this country to teach us and establish the monastery *so that I could sit!* And then, like a line of dominoes falling, my gratitude went racing back through the whole lineage, from Suzuki Roshi to the Buddha—if any of them hadn't kept this practice alive, I wouldn't have the opportunity to sit today. So instead of being miserable, hot, hurting, and tired of flies, I experienced overwhelming gratitude for everyone who had made it possible for me to practice the buddha dharma.

In fact, not only is life a gift, and practice a gift, *everything* we have, without exception, has come to us through the kindness of others. Years ago Tara Tulku Rinpoche, a wonderful Vajrayana teacher, visited us at Green Gulch Farm, where I then lived. He taught us a traditional meditation to cultivate gratitude. He asked us to think of everything that we thought was ours and consider how it came to us. Our food, clothing, houses, books, tools, toys, health: anything we can think of comes to us through the kindness of others. Even something we have made with our own hands depends on the tools and materials we used to make it. And we, through the activities of our life, are also offering gifts to others. This dance of offering and receiving is going on continually. Gratitude and generosity generate each other.

For me, this gift of gratitude has been a great delight, so naturally I wish it for everyone. When the Buddha made the first turning of the wheel of dharma, he spoke to his friends with whom he had practiced asceticism before he accepted the bowl of rice and milk and sat down under the Bodhi Tree. The first thing he said was, "Friends, there is *dukkha* [suffering]." What better antidote to suffering can there be than gratitude? And with this experience of gratitude there is a natural response—wanting to give something back, to share with others this gift of life and the opportunity to practice. How can we do this?

The Zen teacher Kobun Chino Roshi, who came here from Japan as a young monk to help Suzuki Roshi start the monastery at Tassajara, once said, "You don't use the precepts for accomplishing your own personality or fulfilling your dream of your highest image. You don't use the precepts that way. The precepts are the reflected light-world of one precept, which is Buddha's mind itself, which is the presence of Buddha. Zazen is the first formulation of the accomplishing of Buddha existing.... The more you sense the rareness and value of your own life, the more you realize that how you use it, how you manifest it, is all your responsibility. We face such a big task, so naturally such a person sits down for a while. It's not an intended action; it's a natural action." How shall we use this life, how manifest it so as to share this gift?

Dogen Zenji, the founder of the Soto school, said of zazen, "Put aside the intellectual practice of investigating words and chasing phrases and learn to take the backward step that turns the light and shines it inward. Body and mind of themselves will drop away and your original face will manifest." He also said, "To study Buddhism is to study the self. To study the self is to forget the self. To forget the self is to be awakened by everything. And this awakening continues endlessly." This waking up is the aspiration of bodhichitta. If we really want to benefit beings, we must wake up, see reality as it actually is. Then we will know how to benefit beings.

Going back to what I mentioned in the beginning, in addition to assuring us that we are perfect as we are, Suzuki Roshi also said, "There's always room for improvement." He said, "Zen is making your best effort on each moment . . . *forever.*" And the question arose in me, "What is it to make effort with no gaining idea? What kind of effort is that?" In his poem "Zazenshin," Dogen Zenji said, "Realization is effort without desire." That was a real puzzle to me, because as far as I could recall, my effort had always been directed toward accomplishing some goal or being good or at least looking good. This question became my koan. I could not put it down. I have wrestled with it for years. This koan has served me well, and I offer it to you.

There are teachings in the Abhidharma, the basic Buddhist description of mind, about right effort: to relinquish unskillful mind states that have arisen, not to give rise to unskillful mind states that have not yet arisen, to cultivate skillful mind states that have not yet arisen, and to maintain skillful mind states that have arisen. But that didn't satisfy me as an answer to my koan. There seemed to be something more that I needed to understand about making constant effort while accepting and embracing *just this,* as it is.

One spring at Tassajara I walked to the *zendo* along the same path every day. One day I noticed a few green shoots pushing their way up through the soil. Every day there were more and they were higher. And one day there were some buds. And then one day there were suddenly many golden daffodils! And my koan broke open. Here was effort without desire right in front of me all the time! Just letting the flower of the life force bloom right here, right now, wholeheartedly and with nothing held back—giving ourselves completely to whatever arises right in front of us moment after moment.

Someone once asked Suzuki Roshi, "Roshi, what's the most important thing?" and he answered, "To find out what's the most important thing."

I think this question of how we live our life, how we actually live this life—not what we think about it, not what we say about it, but how we actually live it—may be the most important thing. Dogen Zenji said, "To expound the dharma with this body is foremost. Its virtue returns to the ocean of reality. It is unfathomable; we just accept it with respect and gratitude."

How can we expound the truth of existence—the interdependence, interpenetration, and interbeing of all existence—with this body, in how we live our lives day by day, with all the beings with whom we share our lives?

Houn Jiyu-Kennett

BORN IN 1924, Rev. Master Houn Jiyu-Kennett was baptized Peggy Teresa Nancy Kennett. Her childhood was shadowed by her parents' unhappy marriage, and then her youth was shadowed by the loss of her father to a long illness and the terror of World War II. Her hometown—Sussex, England—was badly bombed, and Jiyu-Kennett was deeply affected by the sound of explosions, the sight of red skies at night, and the death of her best friend, who drowned, caught in barbed wire that had been strung along the coast for defense.

Why did such death and cruelty exist? This was the question that Jiyu-Kennett believed drove her to Zen. But as her teacher was eventually to tell her, all questions exist on three levels. There is the question that is actually asked; the question in the back of the questioner's mind; and the true question, usually subconscious. Another facet of Jiyu-Kennett's question was: *Why am I alive when so many of my friends are dead?* But the real heart of her question was: *Why am I as I am?*

"Death and cruelty were in me just as much as they had been in Hitler's S.S. troops," Jiyu-Kennett explained later in life. "The real reason for my going to the East was because I wanted to do something about myself and I knew that I was willing to put up with anything in order to change."

Jiyu-Kennett began her priest training in 1962 when she was ordained in Malaysia. She then continued her training in Japan under Koho Zenji, who was the chief abbot of Dai Hon Zan Sojiji, one of the head temples of Soto Zen Buddhism in Japan. Koho Zenji encouraged Jiyu-Kennett to help establish Zen in the West, and a couple of years after his death, she relocated to the United States. In 1970 she founded Shasta Abbey, located in northern California, and until she passed away in 1996, she served as its abbess and spiritual director.

Jiyu-Kennet was one of the first Western women to become a Zen master.

———————

Why Study Zen?

I WOULD LIKE to talk to you about why one comes to study Zen in the first place. You have to start off on the "me" side, on the greed side. You see, somebody comes to religion not because he or she really wants to but because the person has nowhere else to go. You go to religion when psychology, psychiatry, and everything else breaks down, and you say, "Oops, where do we go from here?" Then you start saying, "Well, maybe there is something that I don't know very much about," and you start looking for a priest or a teacher. And if you're lucky, you find one who knows his or her job.

So, what is it that primarily drives people to do this? A lot of people say that it is fear of death, but it isn't: it's fear of life. Far more people are scared of living than are scared of dying; they are terrified of living. They can put up with death: they know that it is going to come sometime, and there's always a doctor to put it off as long as possible, and then, with any luck, there are nice drugs that will make it easy. But tomorrow you've got to go and face the boss; you've got to go to work; you've got to drive on the freeway, and there may be a maniac driving beside you: what do you do? The fear of life is what drives people to religion, what drives them to psychiatrists, what drives them to psychologists: "How do I act?" "How do I interact with people?" And when questions at that level don't give me the answer, I stop and I say, "All right, I must have a look deep within me." And then you come to the most important thought of all, "Maybe it's not life or death that's the problem: maybe the problem is me."

The fact that most people fear life a lot more than they fear death is one of the reasons that so many young people are attracted to Zen Buddhism. Given what the world is like outside, I must confess I don't blame them. I probably would have done something totally different in life if I had not been a teenager during World War II, and at the age of twenty-one, after having had all the bombings and the like in England, I came to the conclusion that any life I had left was a bonus and that I'd better do something about using the bonus sensibly. I've never told people that, but that's the reason I went into religion. When you know truly what it is to have unborn and undying buddha nature within you, then you do not fear life. The older person usually comes to religion because, although he or she may not fear death, it is a very difficult thing and the person wants some help in dealing with it. Therefore, you find the young and the older person, and you usually do not find too many in the middle. They are usually "too busy doing other things" to look inside themselves.

This actually means that they have allowed themselves to lose sight of what is really important in life. And, indeed, most of us at any age are so self-satisfied that we are content with just being able to "get by," which is usually about as far as the average psychologist hopes to get you: so that you don't have problems with the world in general, so that you just get by without infringing on anybody. When you say, "That isn't enough, I want to go further than this," then you come to religion. When you say, "I'm not satisfied; there must be something more," and there is nowhere else to turn, where do you look? *Inside you.*

But before you are willing to do that, you've got to be really "fed up" with you. Which is why so very few people do it: there is much too much self-satisfaction. The most difficult person to teach Zen to is someone who's complacent. So, complacency is the enemy, and you should know that it is the enemy. You should not be afraid of the word *enemy,* because if you want to get somewhere, complacency is what is in your way: satisfaction with yourself as you are. If you are not satisfied with yourself as you are, then you will do something.

Now, a lot of people know that meditation is an important part of Zen Buddhist practice, and they ask, "Why do you do meditation?" "Why do Soto Zen practitioners meditate by sitting and looking at a wall?" Well, it is one of the main ways that we have of looking inside us, of facing life and death squarely. Have you ever looked at your own mind? In meditation, you sit and look at a physical wall, and after a bit you realize that you're looking at it with "bricked-up spectacles"; because when you meditate, you're really looking at what's going on inside you, and there's a lovely big "wall" in there that you've got to tear down, that you've got to do something about. Because it is that wall, which you have created to protect yourself from life and death, that is actually the problem. It's a problem because enlightenment is one and indivisible, so when you try to protect yourself from anything (and thus you separate yourself from it), you also separate yourself from enlightenment. And it is that separation from enlightenment that both perpetuates the fear of life and death and causes you to sense that something is very wrong.

One of my students drew a cartoon, which he then put on the meditation hall wall: it showed a picture of him sitting there with a huge pair of bricked-up spectacles, and he was trying to peer around them and wondering why he couldn't. The next piece on the cartoon was smashed-up spectacles and him with two blind eyes, because there comes a time when if you sit with bricked-up spectacles for too long, the darkness is so great you just cannot break through it: there is not enough time left. So, this is the main thing that a person learns when he or she comes to meditation: how to do something about that wall inside. That wall is as far as psychology can take you. The Zen master can take you from the wall to what lies behind it, if you have the courage to go. And understand me clearly: most people haven't. They are much happier to just be able to "get by"—it's simpler, it's easier. But Zen does not accept that; there is much more to life than that. So, that which brings people to religion is fear of life when they are young and fear of death when they are older, and you need to know that both are really the same thing: both are the result of that inner wall that separates you from enlightenment.

I would like to quote from the teachings of Dogen, the patriarch on whose work we base our teachings of Soto Zen. This is from the first paragraph of the *Shushogi*, which is probably his most important teaching. It says simply this:

> The most important question for all Buddhists is how to understand birth and death completely, for then, should you be able to

find the Buddha within birth and death, they both vanish. All you have to do is realize that birth and death, as such, should not be avoided and they will cease to exist, for then, if you can understand that birth and death are Nirvana itself, there is not only no necessity to avoid them but also nothing to search for that is called Nirvana. The understanding of the above breaks the chains that bind one to birth and death; therefore this problem, which is the greatest in all Buddhism, must be completely understood.

"Should you be able to find the Buddha within birth and death"—what is "the Buddha" for which you look? It is buddha nature, which lives within each and every one of us. It is that simple, quiet "thing" that is absolutely unmovable, completely free, which each one of us longs for and very few of us find, because we are afraid to pay the price that it takes to realize It. And the price that it takes is doing something about ourselves. You come to your brick wall and you say to yourself, "All right, books have got me this far; science has got me this far; where do I go from here?" Then you realize you must do something about yourself. But what is it that causes us to ask the question, that motivates us to search for buddha nature? It is precisely buddha nature itself, the "Higher Being," which patiently calls us from within. Thus, Zen says that the mind that seeks the Way is the buddha mind and that the merit of the mind with which we first start Zen training is fathomless. I don't know what psychology calls it, but I know what I'm talking about. It's something that says, "Well, if you're satisfied, I'm not." I had this discussion going on in my skull many, many times when I was younger: "Are you satisfied with this?" "Yes, I'm happy with it." "A dog who sleeps in the sun is happy. You want to be a dog asleep in the sun?" "Of course not; no one does."

The first thing I have to teach you then, if you want to undertake serious Zen training, is don't be scared. Religion is a dangerous "game," because it is the "game" of living; it is to be able to be fully alive—alive and vibrant and worth knowing. If religion makes you quiet and sluggish, then you have got religion the wrong way up. If sitting looking at the wall makes you go around in a half-dazed dream, then you are not meditating correctly. It should make you able to be a hundred percent better than you are right now.

Now, if life and death must not be avoided, this means that you have to accept them. Therefore, all-acceptance is the key to the "gateless gate" of Zen. You know, people often come to me and talk about how beautiful it is going to be when they have this wonderful enlightenment experience, when the whole world is one. And I sit back and say to myself, "Yes, and when is it going to be that you're completely accepting the chap who is sitting beside you who's got body odor, and the one who's slurping his soup, and you're not complaining about *any* of it?" "Acceptance" means what it says: acceptance. Either you accept or you don't. Don't play games with it; don't play games with religion. This is a serious business, and you can get hurt. If once you tear down that brick wall, if once you stare at that wall within you and you really break it up, then you must go the whole distance. So don't try meditating unless you want to get "grabbed by the Cosmic Buddha."

A certain gentleman from England, who had better be nameless, came to Japan once, when I was over there, and informed the abbot that he didn't want to go to ceremonies and he didn't want to do various other things; all he wanted was the "true experience of Zen." And my master, who was the Archbishop of Tokyo, stretched, looked across at me, and then said to him, "Do you realize that anybody who meditates runs the risk of being grabbed by the Cosmic Buddha? Do you object to being grabbed?" The gentleman frowned and said, "And what is the Cosmic Buddha?" And he got into this lovely little discussion of ideologies and doctrines, and he was still talking when he suddenly realized there was a snore coming out of the old abbot. If you tear down that wall, you will get grabbed by the Cosmic Buddha, you will be face-to-face with your buddha nature: there's no way out because that is what is there. And because of that, as Dogen quite rightly says, "If you can understand that birth and death are Nirvana itself, there is not only no necessity to avoid them but also nothing to search for that is called Nirvana."

Incidentally, I warn you that atheists and agnostics are not safe from this "getting grabbed"; in fact, they're anything but safe. You see, they think that their refusal to believe will defend them, and they don't realize that when they are ripe for the plucking, the Cosmic Buddha just picks them off because they've got no ideological defenses up. Beliefs are not the issue; indeed, the man or woman who has the most problems is the one who suffers from dogmas and similar things in his or her head and is so busy running around with them that he or she can't see straight. So don't think that if you are a scientist and just simply meditate, you will be safe simply because you're a scientist: you won't be. If you sit down and look at a wall and you don't get your mind in the way and you don't theorize, then your buddha nature will pick you off like a ripe plum.

Nirvana is: here and now. The buddha mind is: right here, right here in this room, within you. All you have to do is tear down the watertight door, the brick walls, and all the other things you have carefully locked it up in, to be able to live completely. You cannot live completely until you accept life completely; you cannot live completely until you accept death completely. You cannot know nirvana until you recognize that it is here and now. You can make a mess of it or you needn't; you can get your own ideas in the way, or you needn't: it's entirely up to you. The buddhas and ancestors aren't going to turn a hair whether you are with them or you are not, because they are. They are as "iron beings." One of the things you are told when you are transmitted by your master is that to know the buddha mind is to become an iron being: absolutely immovable. And it is iron: the buddha nature within you cannot be pulled over, toppled, by anyone. This is why you can't brainwash a Zen master; it's physically impossible. She or he cannot be controlled, cannot be held. You can physically kill the master, but you cannot harm his or her mind. It is impossible because the master has touched the iron being within. If you are really willing to sit as an iron being, no matter if earthquakes or anything else hits you, you will still sit. And if you're willing to sit as an iron being, you will get rid of this wall. You won't care what happens: you'll lay your life on the line to realize enlightenment.

Then, and only then, will you know the Unborn. So if you haven't got the courage to do that, don't try it. Just stay happily with your psychology; it's a lot simpler and a lot easier. You can get by. You can go and play golf on Sunday; you can go to the country club. But if you want to live, and I mean live, then you have to do something about yourself.

Every one of you can do it, if you want to. But you're not going to do it until you get fed up enough with being the dog asleep in the sun. There is no way that you will manage it without that, because if you train thoroughly, your whole lifestyle will have to change. You cannot take anything for granted any longer. Enlightenment will not bring you happiness, but it will bring you complete peace and the ability to live utterly and be unafraid of life. But the price is that you will have to change everything you do, and in so doing you will change everybody else around you, because there is no way you can avoid it. Doing something about yourself also does something about the world, because there is no way you can do something about yourself without having an effect on everyone else around you. This is the main way you deal with the problems of the world: you don't go out to deal with the problems, you go out to deal with yourself. When you have dealt with yourself, other people (when they come up against you) say, "This one is different; I like what I see." And so, perhaps ten or twelve people reverberate off you, and they start doing something about themselves. Ten or twelve do it off each one of those: that's how you cure the world. You don't go out to cure the world, you go out to do something about yourself.

There were a lot of problems when I was first leaving Japan in that several people over in England were terrified that I was coming to the West to take over their Buddhist organizations, and then they got very worried when they discovered that I wasn't interested, because they were convinced that meant I was going to convert the whole world. They had missed the whole point of Buddhism: I went to Japan to do something about myself; I didn't go to Japan to do something about England. However much other people didn't like me, I liked myself a lot less; so I went to convert myself, I did not go to convert the world. In converting myself, I helped a lot of other people, but that was by accident. It's that simple. That is how Buddhism is spread, that is how the signs of enlightenment spread. Charity, benevolence, tenderness, and sympathy, are the four signs of enlightenment, and if a Zen master does not exhibit them, then that person is not a Zen master. But don't expect the master to exhibit them in the same way as you understand the terms, because sympathy is not saying, "Oh, I'm sorry that the cat was chased by the dog." It is understanding how the cat actually felt when the dog was behind it, which is a very different matter, and therefore, making quite sure that the door is not left open so that it happens again; responsibility comes into it too. The signs of enlightenment are not making pretty noises about religion; they are acts, actual acts.

At some level we're all at least vaguely aware that we need to do something about that brick wall inside us. But most of us don't want to do that just yet, and this is why people who undertake serious Zen training both benefit many people and also tend to lose all of their friends. Your friends will wonder what on earth is wrong with you. Now, you may take a few with you: it's just possible, though you may not. But you will pick up with the next group that is on a stage higher. That's an atrocious way of putting it: "a stage higher"; we're all marching along the same road. But you will catch up with the next lot, who will be a lot better than the previous bunch—a lot more enjoyable, a lot more interesting, because they'll be people who have done the same thing you have done. They took a look at themselves and said, "Yeah, I'm not content with 'getting by,' because I know that I can do more, much more, than just 'get by.'"

And you may not just catch up to them but may pass them, because an awful lot of people get satisfied partway along the way and then sit down and picnic on the road of life, and before they know what's hit them, it's evening. Over the meditation hall door in a Zen monastery hang the words "Time flies as an arrow from a bow: I wish to obtain the Lord's teaching. Birth and death are a grave event: time flies as an arrow from a bow." I have only now in which to live. Am I going to sit and waste it? Am I going to run away from it? Or am I going to lay my life on the line and say, "Right, I don't care what happens, I am going to do something about myself."

Thus do you start on the road of getting rid of that huge blockage that most of us have, of the watertight door that we set between the serenity of the years before we are seven and the time that comes after. It is interesting that the Buddha did not find peace of mind, did not find understanding, until he went back to doing that which he did as a child. At the age of seven, he achieved the first understanding through simple meditation. When he was older, he left his palace and went off in search of truth. He went around going through all sorts of harsh disciplines, every imaginable torment that the body could stand, and he only found that he was making life worse and he was getting hallucinations. One day he got really fed up with this and said, "I know what I am going to do. I can remember, when I was small, when all I did was just sit, I got incredible peace of mind. Why don't I try that? I know: I'll go off, I'll have a bath, I'll get a meal, and I'll try that. And I'll go on doing that until it works." And he did just that, and that was the night that he got his understanding. He had to go back, in other words, to the naive mind of a child. He had to drop all of these silly ideas of hanging himself upside down and walking around on hot coals and various other things he'd employed. He had to go back to the naive mind of a child and just sit with his mind still. There, in that stillness, he found the iron being within himself. He had pulled down all the walls he had built: walls with his ideas and his concepts, his notions of right and wrong, good and evil, how it is done, how it is not done, what is wise, and what is not wise. He had dropped all that stuff, and he just sat still, completely still, and found enlightenment.

Khandro Rinpoche

JETSÜN KHANDRO RINPOCHE was born in India in 1967 as the eldest daughter of Mindrolling Trichen, the eleventh Mindrolling throne holder. A Nyingma lineage of Tibetan Buddhism, Mindrolling features a unique line of female Buddhist masters known as the Jetsünmas, who, over the centuries, have been the daughters of various Mindrolling Trichens. Khandro Rinpoche is a continuation of this remarkable tradition of female teachers.

She is also a lineage holder in the Kagyu school because, as a small child, she was recognized by His Holiness the Sixteenth Karmapa as the reincarnation of the renowned female master Great Dakini of Tsurphu, Khandro Ugyen Tsomo.

For more than two decades, Khandro Rinpoche has been teaching extensively in North America, Europe, and Asia. In 1993 she established the Samten Tse Retreat Center in India. Then ten years later, in Stanley, Virginia, she founded Lotus Garden Retreat Center, the North American seat of Mindrolling International.

Khandro Rinpoche has taught that a human birth is as rare as a pea dropped from an airplane getting caught on the head of a pin held by someone on the ground. And this human life is precious not only because it is rare but because it is brief. In the following teaching, Khandro Rinpoche reminds us of our impermanence.

The Great Impermanence of Death

THE BUDDHA TAUGHT that death comes because of life. In the same way, sickness comes where there is health, old age comes where there is youth, destruction comes where there is construction. This logic establishes the law of existence itself—and meditators must not only understand this, they must be able to put it into practice.

The actual fact of death cannot be denied. Even individuals endowed with a precious human existence are subject to impermanence and death. No matter how far we travel in the ten directions, we won't find anyone who has not experienced this. The simplest mind can understand that nothing remains the same: there is constant generation, degeneration, transformation, and change. All of our experiences—of people, places, and other outer phenomena as well as inner thoughts and feelings—are impermanent. A mind that does not genuinely understand this provides the ground for distraction and habitual patterns.

It takes a genuine sense of urgency to use this very moment to bring our positive endowments to fruition. For this we must actually have some feeling for the *experience* of impermanence. Reflecting on the impermanence of all phenomena should truly give rise to a sense of fear—not a paralyzing fear that keeps us from generating positive tendencies or bringing our potential to fruition, but a genuine sense of urgency in the face of impermanence.

Just as change and impermanence arise in infinite ways, so too death arises. Death arising as impermanence can be caused by any number of things. There may not be any one cause that disrupts a life or causes death. There are also many different experiences of impermanence, given the various life spans of sentient beings. The Tibetan tradition talks about life spans from thousands of years long to those in the degenerate age that can be as short as ten years, a few days, or less. Contemplate the infinite numbers of beings that are going through a vast variety of experiences based on the fruition of their karma.

If the urgency of impermanence still does not arise, think of examples from your personal experience. Think of all the people you've known who are no longer with you today. How many of these relatives or friends have actually passed away? In *The Words of My Perfect Teacher,* Patrul Rinpoche talks about all of the realized teachers and great meditators who nevertheless have been subject to impermanence and are no longer alive today. When you light your shrine and hang beautiful pictures of your teachers, keep in mind that impermanence hits everyone, even those to whom you've done prostrations. Then relate this understanding to the impermanence of other circumstances in your life.

We can see that every movement is a step closer to death. Simple acts such as eating, walking, or sitting down bring us closer to the exhaustion of these experiences and closer to death. We may tell ourselves that a human life span is seventy or eighty years, but each month and year marks the passage of time. And regardless of our life span, death can strike at any moment. We could calculate the time that has passed and the time that remains, but even if we were sure we had that much time left, there is less of it with each passing moment—and it's not possible to add on any time. Given the fact of ever less time and our approaching old age—when we will truly experience impermanence—why would we still succumb to distractions and hesitations?

When we look back, at the time of death, the experience of this life will seem like a dream. And—just as with our nighttime dreams—it will seem useless to have put so much effort into it. The fear we experience in a dream is gone when we wake up; feeling afraid was just an unnecessary exertion of effort causing us to lose sleep! When we look back on our lives at death, the amount of time we spent in hesitation, aggression, ignorance, selfishness, jealousy, hatred, self-preservation, and arrogance will seem like an equally useless exertion of energy. So be able to regard all of these illusory thoughts and concepts as dreams. Within this illusory existence, what, if anything, is the logic behind any stubbornness, distraction, hesitation, or habitual emotions of aggression, desire, selfishness, and jealousy? What is the use of holding on to these useless emotions within impermanence? Impermanence is the nature of everything.

Contemplation

Begin your contemplation with the awareness that even the ground you are sitting on is subject to change. Ask yourself if you have ever seen or met any sentient being on, above, or below this earth who has not experienced death. If the answer is no, sit in meditation with the awareness that you too will experience impermanence. Even your view and understanding and all the effort you put into thinking about things—beneficial or not, distracted or awake—is impermanent. Contemplate the impermanence and death of everything inside and outside you as much as possible.

Then think of all the time wasted in distractedness, nonawareness, hesitation, and sleep—and in simply waiting for the right circumstances. Add to that the number of years that have already passed and the number of years you will spend in such states in the future. How much time do you actually have left to regard this life as a dream?

Impermanence lurks in all conceivable and inconceivable causes. An outer cause such as medicine could be life sustaining or the cause of death. Natural elements such as earth, water, fire, or wind, and other external phenomena such as mountains and trees, could cause one's death. Inner circumstances such as illness and our own doubts, hesitations, and thoughts themselves can arise as the cause of death. All such outer and inner phenomena have the full potential to cause impermanence and death.

Impermanence is the fruition of all of the impermanent causes, or karma, we've created. The Buddha himself explained that everything that originates from a cause—every perception, movement, and form—must inevitably be left behind at the moment of death. Other than our own karma, we take nothing with us at the moment of death. No matter how strong our grasping and attachment, we cannot take our material wealth, physical body, friends, relatives, teachers, retinues, or disciples. No matter how many dear ones surround us in this life, wanting never to be separated from us; no matter what our rank or power; no matter how much effort we've put into cultivating a home, a position, or knowledge or oratorical and debating skills, none of it can be brought into the experience of death.

Trying to maintain anything at the moment of death adds nothing to our time or happiness—and it does not allow for the simplicity of letting go. It does not allow us to have a sense of accomplishment at the time of death or to be the cause of happiness for anyone else.

Understanding this, why do we still grasp at material possessions and all of our other attachments? Grasping and attachment can survive only in a mind where there is still some hope: "Maybe someday it will be possible to take a little something with me—if not these samsaric things, at least a little something Buddhist: my devotions, teachers, teachings, ritual objects." Nothing, however, can be brought into death other than the simple cause and effect of our accumulated karma and the transcendence of our mind and view—to the extent that view is truly useful.

Ayya Khema

As a young Jewish girl in Nazi Germany, Ayya Khema was evacuated to Glasgow, Scotland along with two hundred other children. She was eventually reunited with her parents in Shanghai, China, but there they were put in a Japanese prisoner-of-war camp, in which her father died. After the war, Khema emigrated to the United States, married, and had two children. Yet in the early 1960s she returned to Asia and learned to meditate. In 1975 she began teaching, and three years later she established Wat Buddha Dhamma, a forest monastery in the Theravada tradition in Australia. In 1979 she was ordained in Sri Lanka, making her the first Western woman to become a nun in the Theravadin tradition.

Khema died in 1997, but she's remembered for her remarkable contribution in providing women opportunities to practice Buddhism. In addition to starting the International Buddhist Women's Centre and Parappuduwa Nuns' Island for women, she also coordinated the first international conference of Buddhist nuns—a conference that resulted in the creation of Sakyadhita, a worldwide alliance of women and men dedicated to empowering Buddhist women to work for peace and social justice and to advance their spiritual and secular lives.

Khema's teachings are direct and generally free of jargon. According to Khema, the Buddha's teachings—while profound—are simple. They can be realized within our own hearts.

Nothing Special

SPIRITUAL PRACTICE is often misunderstood and believed to be something special. It isn't. It is one's whole body and mind. Nothing special at all, just oneself. Many people think of it as meditation or ritual, devotional practice or chanting to be performed at a specific time in a certain place. Or it may be connected with a special person without whom the practice cannot occur. These are views and opinions that lead to nothing.

In the best case they may result in sporadic practice, and in the worst case they lead to fracturing ourselves, making two, three, or four people out of ourselves when we aren't even one whole yet. Namely, the ordinary person doing all the ordinary worldly chores and the other one who becomes spiritual at certain times in diverse ways. Meditation, rituals, devotional practice, chanting, certain places, certain people, can all be added to our lives, but they are not the essence of our spirituality.

Our practice consists of constant purification; there's nothing else to be done. Eventually we will arrive at a point where our thought processes and feelings are not only kind and loving but also full of wisdom, bringing benefit to ourselves and others.

That is possibly a designation of a goal. In order to get to that goal, however, we need to know exactly where we stand; otherwise how can we start on this journey? Many people go around in circles in their spiritual practice, having either exaggerated or underrated ideas of their own worth. Both are detrimental to a fundamental recognition of ourselves.

We need to inquire into any discomfort arising within. Imagine you are sitting on a pillow with one leg bent in such a way that the discomfort becomes greater and greater. Would you do something about it or would you just keep sitting like that for the rest of your life? Physical discomfort is something that all of us wish to escape from or alleviate and discard as quickly as possible. What about mental and emotional discomfort?

What can be compared in importance to that, and why do we feel uncomfortable so often? Nobody feels at ease in an untidy, messy household, or likewise when there are unwholesome aspects arising in our inner household, such as resistances, dislikes, fears, feeling threatened, worries about our past or future. How can that be comfortable?

Only when we realize that we are the manufacturers of our own discomforts is there any opening for change. If we still believe that other people or situations or the lack of appreciation, praise, love, or opportunities are at fault, we haven't started our practice yet.

We must arrive at a starting point. If one runs a race, one has to find the starting line. We have to find a point of departure for this practice, which is found within our own inner being. Only those people who are determined to grow in spirituality will find that fundamental basis within, from which inner growth can be generated.

The whole person becomes involved and not just for the few hours of meditation or scattered moments of remembrance. The whole of each of us working the whole time at it can become purified.

There must be no lip service; it has to be real. All discomfort within us, all unhappiness, fear, or worry, has been created by us. Only then is the field wide open for change. That moment of acceptance and realization changes our whole world, because now we can do something about our lives. Until then we were helpless victims. We cannot change the world or other people; we can hardly even change the behavior of a dog, but we can change ourselves. As long as we only believe this but don't do it, we haven't started to practice. We can even sit in meditation, but no results will show in our lives.

It starts with inner softness, acceptance, and pliability. We become open to people and situations around us. If we retain our own ideas and viewpoints, continually liking or disliking the same areas of life, we are not sensitive to our inner reactions. Softness, acceptance and sensitivity may result in a great deal of pain, but that's part of practice. However, because it's painful, it's often rejected. Surely that is the wrong way of dealing with ourselves. If we break a leg and don't want to have it set because that is painful, it would mean limping for the rest of our lives.

That is equivalent to looking for a lifelong anaesthetic, which dulls all awareness and keeps us in a semiawake state.

Because all of us have the six roots of greed, hate, and delusion and their opposites of generosity, love, and wisdom, we are constantly manifesting one of these. Love and hate, greed and generosity, are usually equally distributed in most people. Delusion, however, is the underlying factor of all of our mental emotional activities, and wisdom is rare. We are not actually hating anyone because the person is hateful but, rather, because our inner hate is looking for an outlet. This is one of the great absurdities of humanity, and only a very few people are aware of this simple fact that could change our whole life. When we hate, we don't do so because there's anything worth hating or disliking but only because hate wants to manifest itself.

The one who becomes unhappy in the first instance is the one who hates. This negative emotion is like a barb that we would like to use to hurt others but first pricks the one who is holding on to it. This is a law of nature and so simple that most people overlook it completely. We go through life having a distinct demarcation line: on the right everything we like and on the left everything we dislike. Certain qualities and characteristics are always either good or bad in our opinion. Sometimes it does not work out quite that way and we hate to shift our demarcation line. It's not a comfortable way of living. One is a person who cannot be happy because it's impossible to find only people and things that one likes. Since there is no perfection in existence, there's no hope for happiness in such a mode of reacting. It is amazing that most people have not woken up to this fact. Many have spoken and written about it, but it remains a matter of spiritual practice.

To recapitulate: First, we know that we are the doer. We are responsible for whatever is arising within us. Second, we can change because we realize that the dislikes, hates, fears, and worries are creating unhappiness for us.

Change necessitates substitution. Here we can appreciate the training in meditation, where we are constantly called upon to substitute being attentive to the breath for our thinking. For one who doesn't meditate, the substitution of one thought for another is an unknown factor. To exchange all unwholesome thought for a wholesome thought is an almost unbelievable idea for people who do not know anything about spiritual practice. We are prone to believe what we are thinking. That anybody else is thinking the same has never occurred to us. To be the only one with such a thought among billions of inhabitants is an absurdity rarely noticed.

The next important step in our maturing process is the recognition of our own *dukkha*. This seems so simple that one wonders why it is often difficult to follow through with it. If we have dukkha, like everybody does, we are in the first instance inclined to blame someone or something. We can start with people, continue with situations, and include our sense contacts, what we hear, see, taste, touch, and smell. The possibilities for blame are infinite. But when we indulge in them, we are refusing our first insight; namely, that we ourselves are responsible. If we hold fast to that understanding, then we begin to see dukkha in a different way. Namely, as part and parcel of being human, as a universal and not a personal truth. However, when we are disliking our painful feelings and are not willing to accept the fact that our own mind is the culprit, then we will look for a scapegoat. This is a very popular pastime, and possible scapegoats are innumerable. When we remember that we're causing our own dukkha, we are back to spiritual practice. As we dislike our own dukkha, hate arises at the same time, which results in "double dukkha."

Using insight into self-made dukkha as our next step, we have a chance of changing the discomfort within us from dislike and hate to, at least, acceptance. Eventually a feeling of being at ease with oneself arises, without which meditation cannot flourish.

These are fundamental aspects of ourselves that we need to investigate and experience. Spiritual practice involves one's whole being and the exploration of our reactions, developing sensitivity and vulnerability to others, and being able to roll with the punches. We begin to realize that there are certain necessary learning situations in our lives and if we don't make use of them, we will get the same ones over and over again. If we look back for a moment, we may be able to see identical situations having arisen many times. They'll continue to do so for many lifetimes, unless we change.

Spiritual practice is not just sitting on a pillow but more an opening of the mind to what is actually going on inside. If that opening is closed the moment we stand up, then we haven't really been meditating successfully. It is not so much how long we can attend to the breath or the sensations but rather how aware and awake we become. Then we can use that awareness in our everyday reactions and thinking processes. There is the Cartesian view: "I think, therefore I am." Actually it's the other way around: "I am, therefore I think." Unless we can get some kind of order into our thoughts and the emotional reactions that follow the thinking process, our mind will constantly play havoc with our inner household. The realization of where our dukkha comes from must be followed by the understanding that disliking it will not make it go away; only letting go of wanting makes dukkha disappear, which means unequivocal acceptance. Accepting oneself results in being able to accept others. The difficulty with other people is that they present a mirror in which we can see our own mistakes. How useful it is to have such a mirror. When we live with others, we can see ourselves as if it were a mirror image, and eventually we learn to be together like milk with water, which completely blend. It is up to each one of us to blend; if we wait for others to do it, we are not practicing. This is a difficult undertaking but also a very important one. Eventually we will create the inner comfort to expand our consciousness and awareness to universality.

The world at large is very busy, and we get caught up in extraneous matters. The world inside is also very busy, but we can do something about that. We can quieten it down to see more clearly. The way of spiritual practice is nothing special, just our whole body and mind.

Sister Chan Khong

FOR MORE THAN half a century, Sister Chan Khong has been work-ing closely with the world-renowned Zen master Thich Nhat Hanh, and she is recognized as being a major force in helping him to grow his community. But Chan Khong is an accomplished teacher in her own right, and it can even be said that her life itself is a teaching.

She was born in 1938 in a Vietnamese village on the Mekong River Delta, a land that was lush with rice fields and coconut groves yet also riddled with poverty and strife. To satisfy her parents, she studied biol-ogy, completing her degree at the University of Paris, but she always knew it was to social action that she wished to dedicate her life. At age twenty-one, she joined Nhat Hanh in establishing the School of Youth for Social Service, an organization that culminated in ten thousand young people developing medical, educational, and agricultural facili-ties in rural Vietnam and rebuilding villages decimated by war. She then went on to work tirelessly on behalf of the "boat people" who fled her homeland in the 1970s and 80s.

In "Learning True Love," Chan Khong takes readers deep into war-torn Vietnam by recounting the dangers she faced as a young woman coming to the aid of flood victims. Then, in "Deep Relaxation," she teaches a practice by that name—a highly nurturing meditation for which she has become well known in her community. Based on the idea that body and mind support each other, it involves releasing the stress in the body so as to also release the stress in the mind.

Learning True Love

IN FRANCE I had written loving letters to my mother each week, telling her how much I missed her. But when I got back to Vietnam, I spent all of my days with the poor in the pioneer villages and the slums. Sometimes Mother would tell me, "You say you love me, but then you spend all of your days working for the poor and come to see me only late at night." I gently comforted her, "Please think of me as married—not to a man but to my ideal of life. If I had married a man, I would have to spend my days and nights with him, bringing happiness only to him. But because I am married to my ideal of life, I can bring joy to many people, and I can also return home at night to be with you." My mother understood, and since that day she has always supported my work.

Among the young professionals who joined our social work in the pioneer villages, one talented and humble physician, Tran Tan Tram, fell in love with me. I enjoyed working beside him, helping the peasants in Thao Dien and Cau Kinh, but I was devoting all of my energy to these projects, and twice I declined to marry him. He waited two years and finally, under pressure from his parents, married another woman. For a Vietnamese woman, her wedding day is supposed to be the most wonderful day of her life, and on the day of Tram's wedding, I felt very sad. Looking back at my sadness, I can see that it was not because I was losing him to another woman but because I realized I would never marry. Getting married meant taking special care of one's husband and his family and one's children, and I realized that if I did that, I could not also take care of the "wild" children in the slums and remote areas who desperately needed help, nor could I devote myself to building pioneer villages as models for social change in the country. I had seen many friends who, after getting married, became caught in endless family obligations, and I knew that my life was not for the effort of bringing happiness to one person but to thousands. Because I was so active during this period, in a short time my sadness was transformed into joy in service, and I felt a great renewal of energy as I came to appreciate more and more the freedom to do the work I cared about most.

In late 1964, there were huge floods in Vietnam. More than four thousand people were reported dead, and thousands of homes were washed away. The whole nation was mobilized to help the victims, but the investigation team sent by our Van Hanh Student Committee for Flood Relief reported that victims in villages near the Ho Chi Minh Trail, where the fighting was escalating, were suffering the most. Other relief efforts concentrated on helping victims near big cities like Da Nang and Hoi An, so we decided to go to the most remote areas that no one else dared visit.

Creek bottoms there were filled with rocks, and after many days of heavy rain, these rocky gorges overflowed so quickly that it was impossible for the inhabitants to escape the floods in time. In one hour, water levels in some places increased more than twenty-five meters. (The same kind of flooding occurred again in 1992.) Thay Nhat Hanh joined us on our mission. We took seven boats filled to the brim with food supplies and went up the Thu Bon River, crossing Quang Nam Province and going high up into the mountains, through areas of intense fighting. Many times we saw soldiers shooting at each other across the river.

For five days and nights, we stayed high up in the mountains. We had no mosquito netting or drinkable water. We had to filter and boil river water before cooking or drinking, which was not easy in these conditions. But going with Thay made things easier. Everywhere we went, former students of his, including some high monks trained by him at the An Quang Pagoda in the 1950s, supported us, and on some occasions, it was thanks to the presence of these monks that we experienced some safety and respect from both warring parties. One time we were stopped and searched by nationalist soldiers and then allowed to go. Thay asked them, "What if we are stopped by the other side and given their propaganda literature? We could not refuse." "You may receive it, but when you get to the stream again, throw it into the water," the soldiers responded. Thay asked, "What if we don't have time to throw it in before we are caught again by people like you?" The soldiers did not answer.

When they saw us, old men and women who had been devastated by the floods knelt down in prayer before us, as if they were in the presence of Avalokitesvara. They could not believe that humankind still existed after what they had experienced. Many had lost sons, daughters, grandchildren, homes, livestock, and everything they owned. One old man had lost his entire family and belongings except for one water buffalo, which he floated on as the water rose. Wherever he went, the water buffalo accompanied him like a son.

We stopped at the most devastated villages, distributed gifts, and stayed the day with the people. At night we slept on our boats after a simple meal of plain rice. The smell of dead bodies was everywhere, horribly polluting the air. Although this was a remote mountain area, there was fighting between the nationalists and the guerrillas even up here. When we saw wounded soldiers from either side, we helped them without discrimination.

Seeing such immense suffering, Thay Nhat Hanh cut his finger and let a drop of blood fall into the river: "This is to pray for all who have perished in the war and in the flood."

During the war with the French, Thay had contracted malaria and dysentery, and during this trip to the remote mountain areas, both diseases recurred. Despite that, his presence was very inspiring for our whole team. Thay reminded us to be mindful of everything—the way Thay Nhu Van, a high monk who was very popular with both sides, talked to the officers of both sides; the way Thay Nhu Hue organized the local Buddhists; and the way the rowers of our boat ate in mindfulness. We observed the steep canyon of the Thu Bon River and were aware of the icy mountain wind and the homeless victims of the flood on the verge of death. The atmosphere of death permeated our whole trip—not only the death of flood victims but our own risk of dying at any moment in the ever-present cross fire.

As we were leaving the area, many young mothers followed us, pleading with us to take their babies, because they were not certain the babies could survive until our next rescue mission. We cried, but we could not take these babies with us. That image has stayed with me to this day. After that, as I went to Hue every two months to lecture on biology, I never failed to organize groups of students, monks, and nuns to help people suffering in these remote areas. We began with the daylong journey from Hue to Da Nang, where we would sleep in a temple and then travel to Quang Nam and Hoi An. In Hoi An, we rented five midsize boats to carry nearly ten tons of rice, beans, cooking utensils, used clothing, and medical supplies.

One night we stopped in Son Khuong, a remote village where the fighting was especially fierce. As we were about to go to sleep in our boat, we suddenly heard shooting, then screaming, then shooting again. The young people in our group were seized with panic, and a few young men jumped into the river to avoid the bullets. I sat quietly in the boat with two nuns and breathed consciously to calm myself. Seeing us so calm, everyone stopped panicking, and we quietly chanted the Heart Sutra, concentrating deeply on this powerful chant. For a while we didn't hear any bullets. I don't know if they actually stopped or not. The day after, I shared my strong belief with my coworkers: "When we work to help people, the bullets have to avoid us, because we can never avoid the bullets. When we have good will and great love, when our only aim is to help those in distress, I believe that there is a kind of magnetism, the energy of goodness, that protects us from being hit by the bullets. We only need to be serene. Then, even if a bullet hits us, we can accept it calmly, knowing that everyone has to die one day. If we die in service, we can die with a smile, without fear."

Two months later, while on another rescue trip, bombs had just fallen as we arrived at a very remote hamlet, about fifteen kilometers from Son Khuong village. There were dead and wounded people everywhere. We used all the bandages and medicine we had. I remember so vividly carrying a bleeding baby back to the boat in order to clean her wounds and do whatever surgery might be necessary. I cannot describe how painful and desperate it was to carry a baby covered with blood, her sobbing mother walking beside me, both of us unsure if we could save the child.

Two years later, when I went to the United States to explain the suffering of the Vietnamese people and to plead for peace in Vietnam, I saw a woman on television carrying a wounded baby covered with blood, and suddenly I understood how the American people could continue to support the fighting and bombing. The scene on the television was quite different from the reality of having a bleeding baby in my arms. My despair was intense, but the scene on television looked like a performance. I realized that there was no connection between experiencing the actual event and watching it on the TV screen while sitting at home in peace and safety. People could watch such horrible scenes on TV and still go about their daily business—eating, dancing, playing with children, having conversations. After an encounter with such suffering, desperation filled my every cell. These people were human beings like me; why did they have to suffer so? Questions like these burned inside me and, at the same time, inspired me to continue my work with serene determination. Realizing how fortunate I was compared with those living under the bombs helped dissolve any anger or suffering in me, and I was committed to keep doing my best to help them without fear.

Deep Relaxation

HAVING A SPIRITUAL practice doesn't just mean a practice for our mind. Our body and mind are two faces of one reality, and they support each other. When your mind is agitated, when you feel disturbed by a strong emotion, you have to call upon your body for help

True relaxation happens when mind and body are in harmony.

In a sutra called Mindfulness of the Body in the Body, the Buddha advised us to visit every part of our body with mindfulness so that we know what's happening inside us. He suggested we use our mindfulness like a light ray to scan and bring awareness from the top of our head to the tips of our toes.

Deep relaxation practice is based on this sutra taught by the Buddha a long time ago, but it is very relevant in our day. If we are busy with work or school and family responsibilities, we may think we can't afford to take a minute to rest. Yet it is not wise to think in that way. It's important to take even just a few minutes to rest, because if we do, we'll not only have more physical energy, but more mental clarity as well. When we rest, we're less inclined to make mistakes. Any time we feel as though we're going to burn out is the perfect moment to practice deep relaxation. I always practice it when I'm feeling overwhelmed by difficulties.

A full session of deep relaxation can last from twenty minutes to an hour. But if you only have five or ten minutes, you can still experience release. Perhaps the only opportunity you have to relax is before you go to sleep. A full session of deep relaxation at night can help you enter gently into sleep without knowing it. This can happen even when you practice deep relaxation during the day. If you happen to enter into sleep, don't resist. Let the sleep penetrate you. The sleep during deep relaxation may be very short, but it isn't agitated, so it's very rewarding. You may not even be aware that you have slept, but you will feel renewed and refreshed.

For maximum effect, a full session of deep relaxation of the body should be done at least once a day. If you live with others, consider doing deep relaxation in a group, with one person guiding the exercise, using the following cues or some variation of them. If there are young people in your family, they can also learn how to lead a session of total relaxation for the whole family.

Lie down on your back with your arms at your sides. You can lie on the floor, on a mat, or on your bed. Make yourself comfortable. Close your eyes. Allow your body to relax. Be aware of the ground beneath you and the contact of your body with whatever surface you are lying on. Allow your body to sink into the ground.

Be aware of the air as it goes in and out of your lungs. Dwell peacefully in your in breath and your out breath. Bring your attention to your abdomen, about two inches below your navel. As you breathe in gently, your abdomen rises. As you breathe out gently, your abdomen falls. If you are still distracted by thoughts, place your hand on your belly and feel it rise and fall. Be aware of your abdomen rising and falling as you breathe in and out.

Breathing in, bring your awareness to your eyes. Breathing out, allow your eyes to relax. Allow your eyes to sink back into your head. Let go of the tension in all the tiny muscles in your eyelids; send your love to the globes of your eyes. Our eyes allow us to see a paradise of forms and colors. Now allow your eyes to rest. Send love and gratitude to your eyes.

Breathing in, bring your awareness to your mouth. Breathing out, allow your mouth to relax. Release the tension around your mouth. Let a gentle smile bloom on your lips. Smiling releases the tension in the hundreds of muscles in your face. Feel the tension release on your forehead, around your eyes, in your cheeks, your jaw, and your throat.

Breathing in, bring your awareness to your brain. Let go of every thought, all thinking. Breathing in, bring your awareness to your neck. Release the tension in every tiny muscle around your neck. Let your love loosen the muscles around your neck. Breathing in, bring your awareness to your shoulders. Breathing out, allow your shoulders to relax. Let them sink into the floor. Let all the accumulated tension flow into the floor. You carry so much with your shoulders. Now let them relax. Let go of all of your heavy burdens.

Breathing in, become aware of your arms. Breathing out, relax your arms. Let your upper arms, elbows, lower arms, wrists, hands, fingers, and all the tiny muscles in your hands and fingers sink into the floor.

Move your fingers a little if you need to in order to help the muscles relax.

Breathing in, bring your awareness to your heart. Breathing out, allow your heart to relax. Continue to follow your breathing. You may have neglected your heart and brought it a lot of stress. Your heart beats for you night and day. Embrace your heart with gratitude and tenderness. Then reconcile with your heart by perhaps saying in your mind, "I will take good care of you, beloved heart. Nothing is more important to me than your well-being." Smile to your heart with gratitude.

Now embrace your liver with tenderness, silently saying, "I thank you for being there." Our liver works day and night to clean our blood, but we rarely pay attention to our liver. Smile to your liver with gratitude. We could be more mindful of what we eat and drink; we could eat less greasy food and drink more fresh water to flush out toxins. Smile to your liver with love, saying, "I will take good care of you, my beloved liver."

Now send your love to your lungs. Breathe in deeply and fill your lungs completely. People die when they struggle to breathe without success. But we can still breathe in gently, totally filling our lungs with ease. How wonderful to be able to breathe. Next send love to your kidneys. With tenderness, mentally caress your kidneys and let go of any tension held there.

Breathing in, bring your awareness to your legs. Breathing out, allow your legs to relax. Release all the tension in your legs: thighs, knees, calves, ankles, feet, toes, and all the tiny muscles in your toes. You may want to move your toes a little to help them relax. Send your love and care to your toes.

Breathing in, breathing out, your whole body feels as light as a lily pad floating on water. You have nowhere to go, nothing to do. You are as free as a cloud floating in the sky.

When you are ready, bring your awareness back to your abdomen rising and falling. Following your breathing, return your attention to your arms and legs. Move them a little and stretch. If you have the time and space, continue to lie and rest. When you are ready, open your eyes. Slowly sit up. Continue to follow your breath. When you are ready, slowly stand up. Take a moment before you begin walking to stand still, follow your breath, and feel the deep sense of relaxation and increased awareness in your whole body.

Anne Carolyn Klein

Anne Carolyn Klein is a cofounder of Dawn Mountain Tibetan Temple and Community Center and Research Institute in Houston, Texas, as well as a professor and former chair of religious studies at Rice University, where she developed a contemplative studies concentration for graduate students in the department. Her books include *Heart Essence of the Vast Expanse: A Story of Transmission; Knowledge and Liberation: Tibetan Buddhist Epistemology in Support of Transformative Religious Experience;* and *Meeting the Great Bliss Queen: Buddhists, Feminists, and the Art of the Self.*

A practicing Buddhist since 1971, Klein has studied extensively with many accomplished teachers. Two years into her practice, she became a student of Khetsun Sangpo Rinpoche and in 1995 she received teaching authorization from him. A year later, she led a women's pilgrimage to Tibet and in the process met Adzom Paylo Rinpoche—a meeting that proved significant for her. Since then, Klein has been the chief coordinator of Adzom Paylo's work in the United States, and she has translated for him and taught from his tradition.

In the following teaching, she posits that everything is either wisdom or a distortion of wisdom. Once we see this, we can relax and allow the path to dissolve the disturbed energies that give rise to our habitual reactions.

It's All Good

THE SUFI sage Rumi brings us a famous story-poem of adultery and wisdom. He describes a jealous wife who is so careful that for seven years her husband is never alone with their attractive maid. Then one day while out with her maid at the public baths, she discovers she has left her silver washbasin at home and sends the maid to fetch it. The maid eagerly runs to her task. No sooner is she gone than the wife realizes what is at stake and races home herself. Rumi sums up the narrative, saying:

> The maid ran for love
> The wife ran out of fear
> And jealousy.
> There is a great difference.
> The mystic flies from moment to moment
> The fearful ascetic drags along month to month.
> You can't understand this with your mind.
> You must burst open!

> —*The Essential Rumi,* translated by
> Coleman Barks and John Moyne

Rumi takes the occasion to contrast the burning love of the maid with the fear-based motivation of the wife. We can understand that he is describing two different qualities, or energies, of attention and intention. He is suggesting that for our spiritual work to be effective, we must plunge ahead, burning with love and longing, not burdened with fear and jealousy. Our love for the path is the only force that can counter the power of the patterns we inevitably bump up against as we practice. These are the patterns that mold our lives. But we don't generally care to look at them. We underestimate their importance. We don't love them, and we don't fully understand that they are not only the gateway to what we love but the actual fabric of it.

Not recognizing this, we sometimes feel that the thing we call "practice" is more important than the thing we call "daily life" or "our stuff." But this is just another way of expressing the dualism that is our greatest error. It is precisely this false bifurcation that keeps us from flying whole. The flight of the sage, as Buddhist paths understand this, is not a flight from the days of our lives to the nights of our realization; it is a passionately open encounter that encompasses all.

To support this possibility in ourselves, it is helpful to have an all-encompassing language, to recognize ways of expression that, like love, are inclusive, not dualistic or divisive. The language of jealousy is the language of calculation and logic; it is reason at its most impoverished, a zero-sum game. "If she has more, I have less." "If I see my afflictions, I won't see the path." Such concepts make meaning through separation and distinction. When we describe a particular object of attention, such as breath or a specific image, we also make such distinctions. But when we look at the feel of attention in the body, we see that the energy supporting attention can indeed be encompassing, acknowledging both the obstacles and the potential to remove them.

For example, in learning to focus on our breath, we can't help but notice how our attention gets deflected. Sometimes we scatter to other objects, sometimes emotion overtakes us, sometimes we go dull, sometimes we daydream. If we attend to our sensations while our mind is moving in these ways, we can experience all of these events as movements of our own energy. Asian culture in general and Buddhist traditions in particular picture the mind as riding a windhorse, a steed of wind or energy, or *lungta*. When mind moves to an object, it is our energy that takes it there. When our mind is still, the energies throughout our body are settling down. So it is important to understand that our meditation is a whole-body practice, engaging all the energies that support our mind and its habitual patterns of movement. When we train attention, we are training that windhorse to become more stable and less reactive. This is not an intellectual matter, even though an intellectual understanding of impermanence, patience, or the benefits of serenity, for example, can support our development. More fundamentally, we are training the energies on which our habitual mind rides.

The language of energy is like the language of love—inclusive and encompassing. Unlike the process of thinking, it does not make meaning through separation and distinction but through intimate connection. Recognizing how energy participates in our every interaction helps us understand how a path aimed at liberation that is based on the qualities of wisdom and compassion also encompasses the things that obstruct these qualities. This is the logos of energy, not the logic of concepts or reasoning. It is also the logos of reality itself. After all, the *dharmakaya*, the real nature of things, is everywhere. Everything participates in it, good and bad alike. In this regard its dynamic is very similar to the dynamic, or logos, of energy. Palpably sensing how this energy participates in everything we do helps us touch the endless embrace that is reality. Failing to access this dimension in a personal way means practice can't help but reinforce our obstructing dualism.

"The stink of Zen" refers to a particular type of dualism, namely, our tendency to look down with scorn at those we find less spiritual. Usually, however, these turn out to be people who are exhibiting exactly the tendencies we are trying to squelch in ourselves. When Khetsun Sangpo Rinpoche first taught the foundational practices, or *ngondro*, to American students at the University of Virginia in 1974, he told us that doing these practices intensely could "speed up our karma" and bring on unwanted states, even illness. This was a kindly and potent introduction to the dynamics of the path. He was letting us know that so long as there is anything left to stir, paths of practice will stir them. It is like taking a whirling whisk to a floor. The floor might have seemed clean enough before we started sweeping, then the air gets so thick with dust we can hardly breathe. This means our sweeping is effective. We don't say, "Oh, now the room is dusty, I should stop. I'll take the broom to another room where it's already clean."

Yet when it comes to practice, we often do just that. We find ourselves in resistance to seeing the dust, the habitual patterns we need to be scrutinizing and understanding so we can really get free of them. We may even think it's skillful not to pay attention to such things. Not understanding the inclusive nature of our own energetic sensibility, we fear that acknowledging our jealousies and attachments will somehow obstruct our goal of liberation. But that's just our deluded dualism talking. The broom must make contact with the dust, the path must make contact with our negativities. Otherwise practice is as meaningless as sweeping what is already immaculate. Luckily, the path is designed to bring this misconstrued duality to light, if we let it. This message is actually there at every level of the teachings.

The Fifth Dalai Lama advised us not to look for emptiness beyond the mountain because it is right here. Buddhist tantras teach that our afflictions are wisdom in disguise. *Dzogchen* teaches that the actual nature of everything, including our unwholesome patterns, is primordial purity. These are not abstract philosophical statements. They tell us that our wisdom and our defilements, our path and our everyday life, are not different things. Our attention need not be split. Our energy never is. The path expresses itself in part as openness, receptivity, and continuity. These energetic holdings are different from our usual ones and more conducive to unfolding optimally.

Ordinary energy will fuel our patterns if we do not recognize the energetic conversation, the interwoven dynamic, between them and our path. Such palpable recognitions gradually allow the path energies, which are not materially different from the ordinary ones, to reshape or dissolve our patterns. Water is already present in ice; we just can't drink it in that form. Our wisdom is already present in ignorant patterns; we just can't recognize it until the obscuring patterns dissolve. But their energy is always there. Everything is either wisdom or a distortion of wisdom. Once we see this, we can relax enough to let the path lead us to the disturbed energies of our habitual ways of reacting. Then we can dissolve them.

Practically speaking, it takes quite a bit of maturity and commitment to sweep where the dust is. But the path isn't functioning unless we do.

And it's helpful to recognize that the path functions in two distinct, mutually complementary and absolutely necessary ways.

On the one hand, the more access we have to wisdom, nonduality, and compassion, the more our patterns begin to dissolve. So sometimes we emphasize cultivating those enlightened qualities. Fueled by our love for these qualities, we meditate on impermanence and emptiness, we do foundational practices, we cultivate giving and taking by practicing *tonglen*. We cultivate love, equanimity, and wisdom.

On the other hand, our dualistically based patterns prevent us from experiencing these qualities right now. So we also practice to recognize, feel, and slowly thin out these patterns. (Ken McLeod's detailing of this process in *Wake Up to Your Life* is an outstanding example of how to work with this on the path.) In this way we become aware enough of our anger to dissolve it; we notice how our minds create the six realms right in this life; we feel the distasteful energies of our hungry-ghost envy or sense of inadequacy, our godlike pride, our animal dullness, and so on. Especially for those of us active in the world, those of us who don't sit in solitary retreat for months or years, it is essential that we work the path in both of these ways.

Gautama Buddha said so too. From the very first discourse on the four ennobling truths, Buddha made it clear that we practitioners must carefully and experientially identify our suffering and its causes down to their most subtle manifestation. Only then are we ready to cultivate the causes of its cessation.

The wholeness of the path is evident in traditional presentations of the four ennobling truths. The first pair, suffering and its causes, describes the process of samsara. The second pair, suffering's cessations and the path to that state, describes the process of nirvana. Nirvana comes only through seeing what goes on in samsara.

In this way we see that the path, like energetic sensibility, is a wholeness. It is not a dualistic emphasis on nirvana to the exclusion of samsara. Whether we speak of the path's emphasis on nirvana, liberation, buddha nature, or emptiness, all of these terms are ways of naming what we really are. And our love for what we really are, our most intimate possible knowing, gives us the power and confidence to, as Rumi put it, "burst open"—to acknowledge and feel all the elements, however miserable, now operating in our lives. Then the path becomes real. And we realize our all-encompassing love for it. Like sunshine on ice, love melts away self-holding and our patterns along with it. Having melted, the water flows and then evaporates. Our inner radiance remains, ready to share warmth with everyone.

Judith L. Lief

Judith L. Lief was a close student of Chögyam Trungpa Rinpoche, who trained and empowered her as a teacher. She worked with him as executive editor of Vajradhatu Publications, and now she's the editor of *The Profound Treasury of the Ocean of Dharma*, a three-volume series presenting his Hinayana, Mahayana, and Vajrayana seminary teachings.

Lief is also the author of *Making Friends with Death*, a guide both to working with the dying and exploring our relationship with our own mortality. She leads an annual retreat for women touched by cancer entitled Courageous Women, Fearless Living and is a member of the Madison-Deane Initiative, which produced the award-winning documentary *Pioneers of Hospice*. She serves on the board and is a member of the faculty of the Clinical Pastoral Education program at the Fletcher Allen hospital in Burlington, Vermont, and offers international workshops and retreats on contemplative care to pastoral counselors, hospice workers, caregivers, and medical personnel.

According to Lief, "Our life is a journey that begins with birth and ends with death, and once we begin that journey, we are on our way, nonstop. There are no breathers, no time-outs. It is a one-shot deal."

In the following teaching, she offers a Buddhist perspective on stress—where it really comes from, how it manifests, and why we need it on the spiritual path.

The Middle Way of Stress

LIFE IS STRESSFUL. Although some people claim that contemporary life is especially stressful, I am skeptical about whether that is so. Living beings have always had to struggle for food, for shelter, and for safety. They have always had the stress of finding a mate and reproducing. The world is no Garden of Eden.

You could say that the question of suffering, or stress, and what to do about it is central in Buddhism. This is the question that set the Buddha on his journey at the very beginning, and over the course of its development, the Buddhist teachings have examined the topic at many levels and from many different perspectives. Like medical researchers, Buddhist scholars and practitioners have catalogued the details of this syndrome in order both to treat its symptoms and to find the ultimate cure.

So what is stress and what do the Buddhist teachings have to say about it? What is our proper relationship to stress? Should it always be avoided, or can it be productive? To what extent is it inherent in life or our own creation? What are its symptoms and what is its cure?

The Experience of Stress

The experience of stress could be looked at as a family of unpleasant sensations. We may experience stress as pressure, anxiety, or claustrophobia. Sometimes there are so many challenges facing us that it is as though we were drowning. We feel overwhelmed, capsized by it all like a sinking ship. Stress may make us feel cornered and that we have no way out. We may simply freeze up, or we may stir up so much anxiety that it feels as if we were choking to death. With stress there is no air. No space. No looseness or freshness. Under the influence of stress, what once may have seemed easy becomes completely impossible, and no matter where we turn, there seems to be no escape. With stress we become distressed, as though we were being pulled apart and were about to break.

When we are stressed, our body gets tighter, as if it were shrinking into itself. Mentally, our thinking gets tight and does not flow freely. Emotionally, we are edgy and fearful. The slightest irritation may set us off, and we may lash out in anger. Or we might withdraw into ourselves, close off, and shut down. We forget to breathe; it is as if the core of our body were one big ache of pain.

Once you start thinking of all the things to be stressed out about, the list goes on and on. It could start with the close-at-hand problems such as the need to pay the rent or find a job. But merely by reading the newspaper, it can quickly expand to include global problems such as famine, war, overpopulation, and environmental destruction. We may even use the fact that we are stressed out about such global issues as a credential, as though our stress and worry were a virtue or a proof of our insight, empathy, and sensitivity.

When we experience stress, we struggle to find someone or something to blame. We assume that there must be some external reason we are feeling this bad and that if we just remove that situation, we will be okay. If there is an obvious external cause, we should simply remove it. We could stop seeing the person who drives us crazy or stop agreeing to put ourselves in situations we know to be upsetting. However, there are many situations we may not be able to do much about, no matter how stressful they may be.

Four Styles of Hope and Fear

There are many different maps or geographies of stress in the Buddhist teachings. Because it is considered to be important to make a commitment to do what we can to improve the conditions of life for all beings, it is necessary to understand how we needlessly tangle ourselves in layers and layers of stress and how we can begin to unravel some of that entanglement.

To begin with, we need to look at the underpinnings of emotional stress, which are described in terms of entrenched patterns of thought. Because of such mental preoccupations, we take stressful situations and actually make them worse. Through our confusion, we change neither the situation nor our attitude but just add fuel to the fire.

Classically this is described in terms of an endless cycle of hope and fear that dominates our lives from day to day and moment to moment, from beginning to end. The Indian Buddhist philosopher Nagarjuna describes hope and fear in terms of what are called the eight worldly preoccupations: hope for happiness and fear of suffering; hope for fame and fear of insignificance; hope for praise and fear of blame; and hope for gain and fear of loss. Basically we spend our lives trying to hold on to some things and get rid of others in an endless and stressful struggle.

You could ask, What's wrong with preferring happiness to sadness or praise to blame? Isn't the pursuit of happiness what it's all about? Isn't it obvious that gain is better than loss? But it is one thing to recognize what we would like to attract and what we would prefer to get rid of and quite another to be obsessed with getting our way and terrified of things going wrong. The problem is that hope is joined at the hip with its partner, fear. We can't have one without the other. When we are caught in this hope-fear cycle, our attitude is always tense, and even our most satisfying experiences are bounded by paranoia.

Happiness versus Suffering In the first style of hope and fear, we look at things in terms of happiness versus suffering, pleasure versus pain. We hope for happiness, but once we have it, fear arises, for we are afraid to lose it. Out of that fear we cling to pleasure so hard that the pleasure itself becomes a form of pain. And when suffering arises, no amount of wishful thinking makes it go away. The more we hope for it to be otherwise, the more pain we feel.

Fame versus Insignificance In the second style of hope and fear, we are obsessed with fame and afraid of our own insignificance. We scramble our way to the top, hungry for confirmation, and when it is not forthcoming, we get pissed off and huffy. And when it dawns on us how hard we need to work to be seen as someone special, our fear of insignificance is magnified. Behind our facade of fame we suffer from a kind of inner desolation and hollowness.

Praise versus Blame With the third style we are obsessed with praise and fearful of blame. We need to be pumped up constantly or we begin to have doubts about our worth. When we are not searching for praise, we are busy trying to cover up our mistakes so we don't get caught. But there is never enough praise to satisfy us, and we are never free from the threat of being found wanting. Only if we are perfect can we count on continual praise, but although we struggle for perfection, we can never attain it. The slightest little mistake is all it takes to retrigger our fear.

Gain versus Loss Finally, with the fourth style we are obsessed with gain and loss. We invest situations with high hopes, and we expect that if things have been improving, they will continue to do so. That quality of hope is so seductive that we forget how easily situations can turn on us. But just as we are about to congratulate ourselves on our success, the bottom falls out, and fear once again holds sway. Our hope falls apart, and we are afraid that things will keep going downhill forever. Over and over, things are hopeful one moment, and the next they are not, and in either case we are anxious.

These cycles of hope and fear occupy our minds and capture our energy. No matter what is happening to us, we think it could be better or at least different. No matter who we are, we think we could be better or at least different. Nothing is ever good enough, and we can never relax.

Six Patterns of Stress

Another way of looking at stress is through the teachings of the six realms of being. These six realms are the god realm, jealous-god realm, human realm, animal realm, hungry-ghost realm, and hell realm. They represent the experiential worlds we create out of ignorance and inhabit out of fear. They describe worlds in which struggle is the underpinning, and no matter how hard we try, we never truly get what we want. It is said that we cycle through these realms constantly and it is hard to get out.

Each of the six realms has its own dominant preoccupation, its own pattern of hope and fear, and its own form of stress. But even when we are caught in one of these realms, there are ways to break free from the fixations that entrap us and perpetuate our stress and suffering.

The God Realm and the Stress of Perfectionism   The god realm refers to a world of refinement. It is one of spiritual bliss, material pleasure, or psychological satisfaction. The god realm is fueled by pride joined with ignorance, which allows you to dwell in a self-absorbed haze. Finding yourself in such a realm is like a dream come true. But when you finally have everything you ever wanted, you worry that it might all be lost. You might create hideouts, whether in the form of spiritual retreat centers, gated communities, or mental la-la lands. But to maintain such islands of perfection, you need to close your eyes to suffering. You need to close off your heart. Since you don't want your bubble to burst or to experience unpleasantness of any sort, you have to ignore anything that threatens it.

It may seem that this realm has very little stress. But under the surface of spiritual pride and tranquillity there runs a river of fear. You have to hold yourself very tight to prolong your special experiences and to protect them from decaying. You hope that your transcendent experiences will go on forever, but you are afraid that you will not actually be able to hold on to them.

The problem is that as soon as you create a protected area and surround it with a wall, whether it is a literal wall or a psychological wall, there will be not only constant struggle but also the stress of realizing that your experience is a manufactured one, not real. However, there are moments when you let go of that striving and something fresh arises. The more you pay attention to such gaps in your scheming, the more expansive is your perspective. With your roomier mind, that mentality of striving begins to dissolve into insignificance.

The Jealous-God Realm and the Stress of the Rat Race The jealous-god realm is marked by envy, speediness, and competitiveness. In this realm, you are never satisfied with what you have as long as someone else has more. You are striving all the time, afraid to ever stop, afraid you might get passed by. You have no sense of yourself except in comparison with those who are ahead of you and those who are coming up from behind.

Once you step onto this kind of treadmill, you cannot get back off. You are always competing and see everything in terms of winning and losing. Fueled by envy, you are ground up in the maws of competitiveness, trapped in a rat race that never slows down.

If you continue to be obsessed with success and failure, with winning and losing, your actions will be constricted and stressful. But there are times when the actions speak for themselves, and whatever you do becomes more simple and effective. This gives you a glimpse of the possibility of another way of doing things, a way to act more skillfully and with less effort.

The Human Realm and the Stress of Insecurity The human realm is the realm of passion and longing for relationship. You feel incomplete and look for ways to fill that empty feeling. When you are lonely, you try to connect, but once you make a connection, you feel claustrophobic and disappointed. When you choose one person to connect with, you wonder whether you could have found someone better. Whatever you do, you think there might be something better that you have missed out on.

In the human realm, you are fueled by neediness and desire. You worry about how you are perceived by others and obsessed with your popularity. Although you create shifting coalitions of relationships, none of them is all that stable. You are always insecure, and your mind hops all over the place. On top of it all, you think too much, which complicates everything. In the human realm, you long to feel more substantial and are afraid of your own vulnerability.

If you are always looking outside yourself for some kind of confirmation, you will be stressed out all the time. But from time to time moments of spontaneous insight arise from within you. This clarity needs no external confirmation. You find that you do not need to second-guess yourself. You can appreciate what you are experiencing whether or not there may be something better going on somewhere else.

The Animal Realm and the Stress of Habit In the animal realm you establish habits of stability that are boring and repetitive, but you lack the imagination to do anything else and are afraid to change. You are set in your ways and find new ideas are threatening. You might have glimmers of inspiration to change, but laziness and inertia drag you down. You would like not to be stuck, but you keep doing the same things over and over again nonetheless. You are fueled by ignorance and are afraid to rock the boat or to venture out from what is familiar, even if it is unsatisfactory. You create bureaucracies with incomprehensibly mindless regulations and procedures.

A person in this realm may seem to be calm and stable, but this is not true stability. It is more like a pillowy buffer protecting the person from facing the energy and intensity of life. The stuck quality of the animal realm is a refuge of sorts. However, it begins to feel very heavy and depressing, and you are afraid that this will never change.

The stress of this realm is not sharp but dull. Your habits of body and mind seem completely solid and invincible. There is a frozen, mind-numbing energy. Murky as this is, there are occasional openings when something sharp comes through. You begin to recognize how painful it is, which is driven home by the negativity and fallout your ignorance has created around you.

The Hungry-Ghost Realm and the Stress of Never Having Enough In the hungry-ghost realm, you want more and more and never get enough. No matter how many riches you accumulate, you still feel poor. There is always more money, more power, more gravitas you could acquire. If you can't play with the big boys, you no longer know who you are. You are fueled by greed and are always hungry. Without all of your things around you, you begin to feel naked, so you pile on more and more. There is a kind of delight in having the most and the best, but there is no stopping point and no real contentment, no matter how much you have.

In the hungry-ghost realm there is a painful contrast between inner poverty and outer richness. The need to satisfy that inner hunger can come to dominate your life, but it is possible to break that pattern and bring the inner world and outer world into greater balance so that your appreciation of outer wealth is matched by the recognition of your inner richness.

The Hell Realm and the Stress of Eternal Warfare In the hell realm you are always enraged. You find enemies everywhere, and you are always fighting. You are always on edge, ready to defend yourself or to lash out. You are afraid that if you relax, you will be threatened or destroyed, so you strike first if you can. You are either red-hot or ice-cold. Fueled by hatred, you create wars and conflicts both large and small. You are fearful and in pain, like a cornered rat, and all you can do is attack.

This mix of resentment, pain, and anger makes it hard even to breathe. Seeing the world in terms of us and them, for us and against us, keeps fueling this anger and warfare. But there are moments when you are not caught in those polarities. Rather than living on a battlefield, you begin to open to the textures and nuances of your experience.

The Three Culprits Underlying all of these styles of stress—the engine that keeps them going—is a gang of three culprits. They are ego fixation, emotional grasping, and habitual actions. If you look into your anger, poverty mentality, competitiveness, or greed, you will find them there. If you examine how you continually cycle between hope and fear, you will find they are the cause.

This threesome is like an internal Mafia to which we pay protection money daily. Once we lose our sense of the whole and identify with this one little part, which we label "me," "myself," or "I," there will be conflict and struggle. In order to prop up and defend that "I," we need to apply our arsenal of negativity: our grasping, ignoring, hating, and all the rest. And once those energies are unleashed, we start doing stupid and harmful actions. For those actions we reap consequences, and once again the cycle is set up as we react to those consequences in the same harmful manner.

Fundamentally, until we penetrate these deeper supports for the stresses we experience on the surface of life, we will continue to be tossed about by hope and fear and cycle through the six realms. Our stress level may fluctuate, and we may have good times and bad times, but there will continue to be an undercurrent of stress in whatever we do.

Stress and Growth

Relating to stress is not as simple as just trying to reduce our stress or to relax. A certain amount of stress is necessary for growth, and at times we need to purposefully put ourselves into stressful situations. It is easy to confuse the virtue of contentment or peacefulness with the pseudo-peacefulness born of inertia and the fear of change. It is an oversimplification of the Buddhist ideal of ease to think that it means the avoidance of stress. Great teachers like Nagarjuna and Sakya Pandita have pointed out that to learn we need to exert ourselves, and that to progress along the path, we have to give up our attachment to ease. According to Nagarjuna: "If you desire ease, forsake learning. If you desire learning, forsake ease." And Sakya Pandita wrote that "the wise, when studying, suffer pains; without exertion, it is impossible to become wise." In fact, there is no such thing as a stress-free life. Life is movement, and movement is stressful. Without stress there would be no path, no wisdom, and no attainment. Ironically, without stress, we could not be at ease.

Chögyam Trungpa Rinpoche encouraged students to "lean into the sharp points" of experience. What all of this points to is that although stress can be an obstacle, it can also be a catalyst for growth. Trungpa Rinpoche routinely placed students in positions beyond their comfort zone and encouraged them to do the same to themselves. He was particularly pointed in his critique of the approach of always looking for comfort, whether it was loose, comfortable clothing; air-conditioned housing; or comfortably unchallenging belief systems. He taught that a bit of discomfort was not just an annoyance but a reminder of the need for ongoing discipline.

Not only do we have to lean into our own stress at times, but we also have to be willing to allow others to learn in that same way. It is hard to watch someone struggle without feeling anxious and wanting to help out—and often that is what you should do. But it is not always so simple. For instance, I was told that if you see a butterfly struggling to break out of its cocoon and you try to ease its struggle by prying open the cocoon for it, that butterfly will emerge in a weakened state and may even die. The butterfly needs the stress of working its way out of the cocoon to build up strength and to dry its wings. Likewise, a master gardener told me that when you plant a sapling, it is better not to stake it if possible. She said that if the sapling has to secure itself in the wind and weather, it will put down stronger roots and be healthier for it. In this example, once again there is acknowledgement that growing inevitably involves a degree of pain or stress. The hothouse flower or the overprotected child simply does not acquire the tools needed to survive.

The Middle Way of Stress

Clearly, a certain amount of stress is a part of life, but how much stress and what kind of stress? How can we navigate a course that is challenging but not overwhelming?

The Buddhist tradition acknowledges the reality of stress and discomfort. It is realistic, uncomfortably so, in describing the stress, pain, and suffering that accompanies our individual and collective lives from beginning to end. The simple teaching of the first noble truth, the truth of suffering, may be the most difficult to understand and accept. We keep thinking that if we just fix this or fix that, tweak here or there, we can avoid it. We think that if we were smarter, prettier, wealthier, more powerful, living somewhere else, younger, older, male, female, with different parents—you name it—things would be different. But things are not different; they are as bad as they seem! Since it is unrealistic to hope for a stress-free life, which would not be all that good in any case, it makes more sense to learn how to deal with the stresses that inevitably arise.

In dealing with stress we need to look at both the conditions we face and how we are dealing with them. It is sometimes possible to remove the causes and conditions that are stressing us out, but other times it is not. So it is important to distinguish between the two. If we can change our situation for the better, we should do so. There is no point complaining about it— it is better to fix it. However, we may be stuck with a stressful situation we cannot change. In that case, we still have the option of changing our attitude.

We need to be realistic and honest with ourselves so that, on one hand, we do not hold back when we could act, and on the other hand, we do not act just to do something, when there is no benefit in doing so. In looking at your external situation, there is no need to cover up problems or look at the world through rose-colored glasses. But you also do not need to stew and fret over all the world problems you are bombarded with daily in the news or let yourself be mentally glued to the endless vicissitudes of ordinary living.

When the great Cambodian teacher Mahagosananda was asked how he maintained his cheerfulness and equanimity in light of the violence and horrors of the Khmer Rouge he had gone through, he smiled and said, "Life is full of ups and downs." There is great teaching in that statement. If we take that kind of attitude, we can release some of our heavy-handed expectations about how life is supposed to go for us, which frees us to deal more simply with whatever we encounter. If our experiences are just what they are, nothing more and nothing less, we can see that they are not out to get us, nor are they a confirmation. They are simply the impersonal play of causes and conditions.

This attitude is different from passivity or detachment in the negative sense of disengagement, defeatism, or fatalism. It instead points to a form of engagement with the world that is intelligent and not merely reactive, that is realistic rather than dreamy. To paraphrase the great Mahayana teacher Shantideva: When you can do something about a problem, then just do it. Why worry about it? And when you do not have the ability or the circumstances to do anything about a problem, why worry? Worrying and stressing about it is not going to help anyone.

Training the Mind and Heart

What I like about Buddhism is that it is so practical and hopeful. You may be the type of person who gets stressed out at the slightest little thing, or you may be more thick-skinned, even oblivious. But either way, you are not doomed to be under the control of the stresses you encounter because you were just "born that way." No matter where on the spectrum you start out, you can begin to change your relationship to stress for the better. This is not accomplished by wishful thinking or pretending to be other than you are but by training your mind and opening your heart.

A primary mind-training tool is mindfulness practice, through which you learn to settle your mind and to tame its wildness. As you repeatedly bring your attention back to the breath, you are becoming more familiar with your own mind and it is getting stronger. It is as though your mind had more weight, so it is not easily blown about by every little breeze. It is reassuring to discover that, amid all the mental commotion and ups and downs, there is something steady and reliable about your mind at the core. When things get tough and you feel stress beginning to take you over, you can draw on that inner strength.

Along with mindfulness comes the tool of training the heart to be more open and compassionate. Compassion practices draw you out of yourself and remind you to think of others. When you feel the force of stress narrowing you down and drawing you into yourself, you can resist the tendency to close down. You can look around you and through compassion get a larger perspective.

Stress is exaggerated when your mind is flighty and unbalanced, and it is also heightened when you are weighed down with self-concerns and preoccupied with yourself. The practices of mindfulness and compassion give you a way to work with both of these problems. It is unrealistic to expect your life to be free of stress, but there is a real possibility that you could transform the way you deal with it. Stress brings to light harmful habits of mind and heart. So instead of viewing it as an enemy, you could regard stress as a teacher and be grateful for it.

Joanna Macy

JOANNA MACY was introduced to Buddhism in 1965 while working with Tibetan refugees in northern India. One day as she was walking down a narrow Indian road, she mulled over what someone had recently told her: "So countless are all sentient beings and so many their births through time that each at some point was your mother."

Macy felt this idea was quaint, though not relevant for her, since she didn't believe in reincarnation. Nonetheless, she paused on the path as a man approached, struggling under his unwieldy burden—the trunk of a cedar. Macy was used to seeing such laborers in the area and was equally used to the discomfort they sparked in her. Usually, she looked away from their gaunt, bent forms while mentally casting judgments about the social and economic system that oppressed its own people.

On this particular afternoon, however, Macy did not avert her eyes. She simply stood and gazed at the man's bowed legs, his rag turban, and his gnarled hands, and her heart trembled. For the first time she wasn't seeing before her an oppressed social class but, rather, a precious being—her mother, her child. Desperately she wanted to share the man's terrible load, yet out of respect or shyness she made no offer, nor did she do anything else to better his life or reveal her discovery of their relationship. Nonetheless, as Macy put it in her memoir, *Widening Circles*, their meeting rearranged the furniture of her mind. It didn't matter that she didn't believe in reincarnation.

After living in India, Macy went on to become an internationally renowned activist and scholar of Buddhism, general systems theory, and deep ecology. She's also authored and coauthored numerous books, including *Active Hope: How to Face the Mess We're in without Going Crazy* and *Pass It On: Five Stories That Can Change the World*. Macy currently resides in Berkeley, California, near her children and grandchildren.

Gratitude: Where Healing
the Earth Begins

WE HAVE RECEIVED an inestimable gift. To be alive in this beautiful, self-organizing universe—to participate in the dance of life with senses to perceive it, lungs that breathe it, organs that draw nourishment from it—is a wonder beyond words. It is an extraordinary privilege to be accorded a human life, with self-reflexive consciousness that brings awareness of our own actions and the ability to make choices. It lets us choose to take part in the healing of our world.

Gratitude for the gift of life is the primary wellspring of all religions, the hallmark of the mystic, the source of all true art. Yet we so easily take this gift for granted. That is why so many spiritual traditions begin with thanksgiving, to remind us that for all of our woes and worries, our existence itself is an unearned benefaction that we could never of ourselves create.

In the Tibetan Buddhist path, we are asked to pause before any period of meditative practice and precede it with reflection on the preciousness of a human life. This is not because we as humans are superior to other beings but because we can "change the karma." In other words, graced with self-reflexive consciousness, we are endowed with the capacity for choice—to take stock of what we are doing and change direction. We may have endured for aeons of lifetimes as other life-forms, under the heavy hand of fate and the blind play of instinct, but now at last we are granted the ability to consider and judge and make decisions. Weaving our ever-more-complex neural circuits into the miracle of self-awareness, life yearned through us for the ability to know and act and speak on behalf of the larger whole. Now the time has come when by our own choice we can consciously enter the dance.

In Buddhist practice, that first reflection is followed by a second, on the brevity of this precious human life: "Death is certain; the time of death is uncertain." That reflection awakens in us the precious gift of the present moment—to seize this chance to be alive right now on planet Earth.

Even in the Dark

That our world is in crisis—to the point where survival of conscious life on Earth is in question—in no way diminishes the value of this gift; on the contrary. To us is granted the privilege of being on hand: to take part, if we choose, in the Great Turning to a just and sustainable society. We can let life work through us, enlisting all of our strength, wisdom, and courage, so that life itself can continue.

There is so much to be done, and the time is so short. We can proceed, of course, out of grim and angry desperation. But the tasks proceed more easily and productively with a measure of thankfulness for life; it links us to our deeper powers and lets us rest in them. Many of us are braced, psychically and physically, against the signals of distress that continually barrage us in the news, on our streets, in our environment. As if to reduce their impact on us, we contract like a turtle into its shell. But we can choose to turn to the breath, the body, the senses—for they help us to relax and open to wider currents of knowing and feeling.

The great open secret of gratitude is that it is not dependent on external circumstance. It's like a setting or channel that we can switch to at any moment, no matter what's going on around us. It helps us connect to our basic right to be here, like the breath does. It's a stance of the soul. In systems theory, each part contains the whole. Gratitude is the kernel that can flower into everything we need to know.

Thankfulness loosens the grip of the industrial growth society by contradicting its predominant message: that we are insufficient and inadequate. The forces of late capitalism continually tell us that we need more—more stuff, more money, more approval, more comfort, more entertainment. The dissatisfaction it breeds is profound. It infects people with a compulsion to acquire that delivers them into the cruel, humiliating bondage of debt. So gratitude is liberating. It is subversive.

It helps us realize that we are sufficient, and that realization frees us. Elders of indigenous cultures have retained this knowledge, and we can learn from their practices.

Learning from the Onondaga

Elders of the six-nation confederacy of the Haudenosaunee, also known as the Iroquois, have passed down through the ages the teachings of the Great Peacemaker. A thousand years ago, they had been warring tribes, caught in brutal cycles of attack, revenge, and retaliation, when he came across Lake Ontario in a stone canoe. Gradually his words and actions won them over, and they accepted the Great Law of Peace. They buried their weapons under the Peace Tree by Onondaga Lake and formed councils for making wise choices together and for self-governance. In the Haudenosaunee, historians recognize the oldest known participatory democracy and point to the inspiration it provided to Benjamin Franklin, James Madison, and others in crafting the Constitution of the United States. That did not impede American settlers and soldiers from taking by force most of the Haudenosaunee's land and decimating their populations.

Eventually accorded "sovereign" status, the Haudenosaunee nations—all except for the Onondaga—proceeded in recent decades to sue state and federal governments for their ancestral lands, winning settlements in cash and licenses for casinos. All waited and wondered what legal action would be brought by the Onondaga Nation, whose name means "keepers of the central fire" and whose ancestral land, vastly larger than the bit they now control, extends in a wide swath from Pennsylvania to Canada. But the Onondaga elders and clan mothers continued to deliberate year after year, seeking consensus on this issue that would shape the fate of their people for generations to come. Finally, in the spring of 2005, they made their legal move. In their land-rights claim, unlike that of any other indigenous group in America, they did not demand the return of any ancestral land or monetary compensation for it. They asked for one thing only: that it be cleaned up and restored to health for the sake of all who presently live on it and for the sake of their children and children's children.

To state and federal power holders, this was asking a lot. The land is heavily contaminated by industrial development, including big chemical processing plants and a number of neglected toxic waste sites. Onondaga Lake, on whose shores stood the sacred Peace Tree, is considered to be more polluted with heavy metals than any other in the country. Within a year, at the urging of the governor of New York, the court dismissed the Onondaga claim as invalid and too late.

On a bleak November afternoon, when the suit was still in process, I visited the Onondaga Nation—a big name for this scrap of land that looks like a postage stamp on maps of Central New York. I had come because I was moved by the integrity and vision of their land-rights claim, and now I saw how few material resources they possess to pursue it. In the community center, native counselors described outreach programs for mental health and self-esteem, bringing young people together from all the Haudenosaunee. To help with the expenses, other tribes had chipped in, but few contributions had been received from the richer ones.

They were eager for me to see the recently built school where young Onondagans who choose not to go off the nation to U.S.-run schools can receive an education. A teacher named Frieda, who was serving for a while as a clan mother, had waited after hours to show me around. The central atrium she led me into was hung about with shields of a dozen clans—turtle clan, bear clan, frog—and on the floor, illumined by a skylight, was a large green turtle, beautifully wrought of inlaid wood. "Here is where we gather the students for our daily morning assembly," Frieda explained. "We begin, of course, with the thanksgiving. Not the real, traditional form of it, because that takes days. We do it very short, just twenty minutes or so." Turning to gaze at her face, I sank down on a bench. She heard my silent request and sat down too. Raising her right hand in a circling gesture that spiraled downward as the fingers closed, she began: "Let us gather our minds as one mind and give thanks to grandfather Sun, who rises each day to bring light so we can see each others' faces and warmth for the seeds to grow." On and on she continued, greeting and thanking the life-giving presences that bless and nourish us all. With each one—moon, waters, trees—that lovely gesture was repeated. "We gather our minds as one mind."

My eyes stayed riveted on her. What I was receiving through her words and gesture felt like an intravenous injection, right into my bloodstream. This, I knew, can teach us how to survive when all possessions and comforts have been lost. When our honored place in the world is taken from us, this practice can hold us together in dignity and clear mind.

What Frieda gave me is a staple of Haudenosaunee culture. The Mohawks have written down similar words, in an equally short form, so the rest of us can have it too. Known as the Mohawk Thanksgiving Prayer, it begins:

The People

Today we have gathered and we see that the cycles of life continue. We have been given the duty to live in balance and harmony with each other and all living things. So now, we give greetings and thanks to each other as people.

Now our minds are one.

The Earth Mother

We are all thankful to our mother, the Earth, for she gives us all that we need for life. She supports our feet as we walk about upon her. It gives us joy that she continues to care for us as she has from the beginning of time. To our mother, we send greetings and thanks.

Now our minds are one.

And it concludes:

The Enlightened Teachers

We gather our minds to greet and thank the enlightened teachers who have come to help throughout the ages. When we forget how to live in harmony, they remind us of the way we were instructed to live as people. We send greetings and thanks to these caring teachers.

Now our minds are one.

The Creator

Now we turn our thoughts to the creator, or great spirit, and send greetings and thanks for all the gifts of creation. Everything we need to live a good life is here on this Mother Earth. For all the love that is still around us, we gather our minds together as one and send our choicest words of greetings and thanks to the creator.

Now our minds are one.

Closing Words

We have now arrived at the place where we end our words. Of all the things we have named, it was not our intention to leave anything out. If something was forgotten, we leave it to each individual to send such greetings and thanks in their own way.

Now our minds are one.

The Spiral

There are hard things to face in our world today if we want to be of use. Gratitude, when it's real, offers no blinders. On the contrary, in the face of devastation and tragedy, it can ground us, especially when we're scared. It can hold us steady for the work to be done.

The activist's inner journey appears to me like a spiral, interconnecting four successive stages or movements that feed into each other. These four are (1) opening to gratitude, (2) owning our pain for the world, (3) seeing with new eyes, and (4) going forth. The sequence repeats itself as the spiral circles around, but ever in new ways. The spiral is fractal in nature: it can characterize a lifetime or a project, and it can also happen in a day or several times a day. The spiral begins with gratitude, because that quiets the frantic mind and brings us back to source. It reconnects us with basic goodness and our personal power. It helps us to be more fully present to our world. That grounded presence provides the psychic space for acknowledging the pain we carry for our world.

In owning this pain, and daring to experience it, we learn that our capacity to "suffer with" is the true meaning of compassion. We begin to know the immensity of our heart-mind and how it helps us to move beyond fear. What had isolated us in private anguish now opens outward and delivers us into wider reaches of our world as lover, world as self.

The truth of our interexistence, made real to us by our pain for the world, helps us see with new eyes. It brings fresh understanding of who we are and how we are related to each other and the universe. We begin to comprehend our own power to change and heal. We strengthen by growing living connections with past and future generations and our brother and sister species.

Then, ever again, we go forth into the action that calls us. With others whenever and wherever possible, we set a target, lay a plan, step out. We don't wait for a blueprint or fail-proof scheme, for each step will be our teacher, bringing new perspectives and opportunities. Even when we don't succeed in a given venture, we can be grateful for the chance we took and the lessons we learned. And the spiral begins again.

Karen Maezen Miller

KAREN MAEZEN MILLER likes to share with people what she has learned from reading about the history of horticulture: These days the word *paradise* might have fantastical connotations, but it originated in Persia, where it simply meant a walled outdoor area, natural or planted, used for sport or pleasure. In other words, true paradise is as real and ordinary as your backyard. Indeed, says Miller, paradise is never anywhere else.

The author of *Momma Zen* and *Hand Wash Cold,* Miller is gifted in revealing the spiritual dimension in everyday life—in marriage and motherhood and even in the daily grind of cleaning the mildew creeping up the shower curtain. For two good examples of how she highlights the extraordinary in the ordinary, see the following teachings. In "Waking Up Alone" she addresses breakups—what to do after the love story ends. Then in "Sanitize Option: What Children Do Not Require" she unpacks the unrealistic (and stressful) expectations we so often have for ourselves and our children.

Miller began studying Zen with Taizan Maezumi Roshi. Later, following his death in 1995, she continued her studies with his successor Nyogen Yeo Roshi. Miller is now a Zen priest and teacher at the Hazy Moon Zen Center in Los Angeles.

Waking Up Alone

IT WAS THE toothbrush that told me. Alone and overlooked in the emptied medicine chest, it was one of the few things my departed lover had left behind. When I found it, I knew with certainty something I'd been denying for some time.

It was over.

In truth, our relationship had been over for longer than I'd wanted to believe, but in beginnings and endings, one party can lag behind the other on the uptake. If the toothbrush was my messenger, what was his? Perhaps the time I kicked his suitcase to the curb? For years after the breakup, I would forget that part in the telling of the story. Everyone, after all, tells stories his or her own way, from his or her own perspective.

Whether by choice or circumstance, by the fleet seasons of romance or the final curtain of death, love ends. At least the love that is a *story* ends. And when that happens, what are we left with? A passage we might otherwise never have dared to take—a passage through denial, disbelief, and despair, through rage and madness. A portal, beyond delusive fairy tales and melodrama, into a state of wakeful grace that is true love.

True love is what is left behind when the story of love ends. But it only looks like the end. Make it through one ending and you might change your mind about all endings. That is the miracle cure, the ultimate healing, that is left behind on an empty shelf.

When Form Empties

Form is exactly emptiness. Emptiness exactly form.

—*Heart Sutra*

Practicing Buddhists may regularly read these crucial lines from the Heart Sutra, said to be the most concise and complete statement of the true nature of reality. As we study the words, we may think we understand them. Leaving aside any spiritual insight and reasoning solely on the basis of scientific fact, we can easily see the truth of impermanence. Everything changes. Nothing lasts, not even feelings. It's obvious, and yet in matters of the heart, it can be a hard thing to wake up to.

I must have been about thirteen years old when my mother hung up the phone one evening, turned, and told me that my uncle had come home from work at lunch that day, walked into the kitchen, and told my aunt that he didn't love her, had never loved her, and was leaving right that minute. Since then I've heard of many parting scenes with a similar script and even uttered a variation of it myself. But at such a young age, hearing the words that shattered a family and dissolved its story made the ground give way.

Whether we notice it or not, the ground is always giving way, disappearing into the vast chasm of impermanence and inconceivability, where our understanding of a line or two of ancient text doesn't begin to reach. To suffer a loss or heartbreak is to live the irrevocable truth through which one's own wisdom awakens. It's the hard way to wisdom, but it's the only way, and the path is well-worn. When the love story ends, take the path that lies before you, and it will always lead you out of suffering.

Not What You Think

The thought of enlightenment is the mind
that sees into impermanence.

—*Dogen Zenji*

A broken heart can seem like an undignified or even trivial way to start a spiritual transformation, but it's a powerful one, as the life of the great Dogen Zenji attests. His mother died when he was but a boy of seven, and some scholars trace his prodigiousness as the revitalizer of thirteenth-century Zen to that early event, when his mind was seized by unanswerable questions.

We experience a subtle spiritual awakening the moment we see that life goes on, even after our life has been ripped apart by loss. However unimaginable, life goes on even when we don't recognize it as *our life*. It's absent of the familiar people, places, or things we previously used to navigate it, and it's without the tenuous threads we used to bind it together. When a relationship so central to our life proves unreliable, we might wonder what is real.

If we look deeper into our discursive mind, we see how we create memory, sentiment, and meaning. Suddenly nothing means what we once thought it did. Ordinary things take on the weight of our rage and the freight of our pain, and a toothbrush is no longer just a toothbrush. Indeed, your home may be your new hell; your bed, a torture chamber; a sleepless night, an eternity.

Perhaps nothing is what we conceive or perceive it to be. When this thought occurs to you, take heart. Doubt is the dawn of faith, and faith will see you through darkness.

The Stride of No Stride

This is the greatest illusion of all.

—Marpa, weeping over the death of his child

It would be nice if we could keep from falling apart when our lives collapse around us. It would be handy if by our spiritual learning alone we could pull ourselves together, keep up appearances, and maintain our stride. We might be saved embarrassment and shame. We might look like we're coping. We might even stay positive. But that is not the way reality works. We can't outsmart it. Impermanence always knocks us off our stride. It is a pothole, a land mine, and a head-on collision. We tumble and fall, and that can be useful. Falling is the fastest way to drop our arrogance, cynicism, pretense, and indifference. Pain brings us fully to life.

Such is the lesson in the story of Marpa, the eleventh-century Tibetan teacher who wept copiously over the dead body of his young son. Finding him in the throes of inconsolable grief, Marpa's disciples were taken aback. Hadn't the master taught them repeatedly that life was an illusion? Why was he carrying on like this? Was he a liar or a fake? Marpa responded, "Yes, everything is an illusion, but the death of a child is the greatest illusion of all."

Your pain is the most piercing illusion of all. Facing it, feeling it, you will awaken your sympathy and kindness. You will feel compassion for yourself, and soon, for all. You will find your footing by losing it.

Your Angry Child

You are the mother for your anger, your baby.

—*Thich Nhat Hahn*

Face it, you're angry.

Anger is so unpleasant, so altogether ugly, that we usually attribute it to someone else. Someone else made you angry, that certain someone who tore out your heart and ruined your life. It's easy to blame others for our injuries, but if we persist in seeing our own anger as the unavoidable outcome of someone else's actions, we are going to be angry for a very long time. Anger is power, and blame is powerlessness. When we take responsibility for our anger, we take back our power to change. That power has never belonged to anyone else.

This is what Thich Nhat Hahn teaches when he suggests we view our anger as a howling baby. No one wants to be around it, but it cannot be ignored. *Someone needs to do something about that baby!* The baby is yours, and the only one who can do anything is you. However disagreeable the infant is, you pick the baby up and place it in your lap. Then you rock and comfort her, and wait. You attend to yourself without judgment or blame. In this way, anger wears itself out. The baby goes to sleep.

In the wake of anger, you may find the strength and determination to live differently. If you don't, you haven't yet seen fully to the needs of your own screaming child. You are rejecting it still.

There's time. You'll have many opportunities to quiet the rage. You'll have many chances to apply the alchemy of your own gentle attention to whatever is disturbing you. Screaming babies go to sleep eventually, and every wise parent learns to let a sleeping baby be.

Be Completely Sad

When you're sad, be sad.

—*Maezumi Roshi*

Anger, we despise, but sadness, we might cherish. At least I did. Sorrow can seem such a rich and complex place to dwell; we might forget that it too is impermanent.

One time I went to see Maezumi Roshi after a meditation session in which the tears streamed in rivulets down my cheeks. "I'm sitting in a field of sadness," I said to him. I was a tiny bit pleased by my poetic expression. I thought we might talk about it, rooting out the cause, and apply a treatment.

"When you're sad, be sad," he said. And that was all he said. I confess I found it abrupt, considering my experience with other counselors. He didn't criticize or correct me, he just didn't dwell. I was unaccustomed to making so little of what felt like so much.

We usually have an impulse to *do something* with what we judge to be a "negative" emotion. Perhaps we should explore, explain, or fix it. Surely it's not "right" or "normal." Is it possible to be sad and then be done with it?

Sadness is a good guide and even a good sign. Sadness may initiate your spiritual practice. Because most of us suffer when we are sad, it can lead us to seek solace and resolution. You might notice, for instance, that when you begin a meditation or yoga practice, you cry for no good reason at all. This can indicate that you are releasing long-held emotions and fears.

To be sure, grief is its own teacher and takes its own time. It feels good to cry. And it feels good to stop. By itself, crying always ends.

Sadness changes to something else because all things, even thoughts and emotions, change when we let them.

Soon enough you'll see that a heartbreak doesn't break anything for long. Take care that you do not turn back and take up permanent residence in the ruin, or you will condemn your life to the shadows of the past. Keep going straight on.

Sit Down for a While

Through the process of sitting still and following your breath,
you are connecting with your heart.

—Chögyam Trungpa

I copied this quotation in a personal journal I kept during my breakup eighteen years ago. Now I can see how clearly the dharma always leads us back to ourselves.

The surest way to keep going through any difficulty is to sit down and stay put—specifically by practicing meditation. It's what all the teachers tell us, and you can prove it to yourself.

Meditating while you are angry, sad, disappointed, or afraid is the most direct way to resolve the difficulty. Why? Because you're facing it. Meditation is the practice of facing yourself completely, cultivating intimacy with your breath and awareness. It is an intimacy that goes far beyond the companionship and gratification we seek from another. Keeping company with yourself can change the expectations you place on a relationship. Through a mindfulness practice, you see firsthand what it means to take responsibility for your own happiness and fulfillment, and you experience love of a different kind—unconditional love, which arises spontaneously as your true nature.

When you practice formally with a group, you'll have the opportunity to sit in silence for a day or more alongside someone you've never met. Eventually, your mind will grow quiet and your concentration will deepen. You will share proximity without the judgments and expectations we usually impose on those around us, and be in relationships that are not conditioned by what another person is doing for you or how that person is serving you. This is what happens in a silent meditation retreat. At the end of the time together, you might be inclined to do what I do: turn to the stranger sitting nearby, smile, and spontaneously say, "I love you." The thing is, I really mean it. Is it possible to love in this way? Yes, from the very bottom of your heart and mind, when everything else drops away, it is possible and it is effortless.

Now, can you live that way with people you actually know?

The Romance of No Romance

Where there is no romance is the most romantic.

—*Hongzhi*

As surely as trees bud in spring and leaves fall in autumn, couples in a long relationship encounter all the same stages as those who don't make it. Yet their union endures. They survive anger and resentments, disappointments and reversals. They watch their interests diverge and their devotions ebb. Their responsibilities grow; their families expand; their houses fill and then empty again. What is it that favors one partnership over another? Some say it is magic, the machinations of fate, the movement of stars, the right choice, or sheer luck. I think it is something we have the power to realize and actualize for ourselves.

Love that lasts allows the *love story* to end. It isn't laden with romantic fantasies or regret; it's not defined or limited, not stingy or selfish. Without form or name, this love allows all things to be as they are. It sees all of life in every season as a process of perpetual change, growth, maturation, and renewal. This love is our inherent treasure, and when we practice, it shines. It is true love because it is truth.

Several years after my lover left me peering into the emptied medicine chest, I got married to another man, and he and I have been together now for a long time. I make no claims for our future, nor do I sentimentalize the past. Our toothbrushes sit in silence side by side on the bathroom counter. They stand sentry over a life shared through mutual courage, acceptance, forgiveness, and very small kindnesses.

Every morning I reach for my toothbrush in a transcendent act that will spread boundless love wherever I go. I brush my teeth, brighten my smile, and begin again.

———————

Sanitize Option: What Children Do Not Require

STOOPING to my knees, I reach into the cabinet. This is my nightly genuflection to receive my daily absolution. Under the eerie overcast of a fluorescent kitchen light, teetering on thin timbers of fatigue, after the last feeding and before the midnight cries, I put a tall pot of water on the stove and light a high flame to boil it. I squeeze a dozen six-ounce plastic bottles one by one between stainless steel tongs and submerge them in the churn. Then the nipples and the lids, five minutes at least, but I'm not counting the time, because time no longer counts. I want to do what is best no matter what it takes.

My baby is three months old.

I boil another batch of water. This is for mixing the formula, two scoops of powder into each bottle, topped by cooled water to the mark. Powder because it is cheaper than liquid, bottles because I have already settled for what everyone knows is much, much less than the best. I have settled on the substandard because my baby, born early, is too little and weak to nurse to her satisfaction, and by that I mean to my satisfaction. It is too hard, breast-feeding. It takes too long. It hurts too much. It produces too little. We have been roundly defeated and unsuccessful from the start.

When the bottles are assembled and shaken, I line them up in pairs in the refrigerator, an honor guard at the ready for another difficult day. Every day is difficult, although I have a pretty good hunch I'm making the days harder than they need to be.

The municipal water supply is safe; the label said the bottles need only a soapy wash and dry. I could fill from the tap and skip all the sterilizing, even catch some sleep. Still, I take measured comfort in the extra inconvenience: slavish compensation from my undue care. Nothing less will pass. It is my penance for imperfection, you see. Doing the most is the least I can do to win back the superlative ground I've already lost.

And then one night I see it: a button on the control panel of my dishwasher. An elevated half-inch, up to now unnoticed.

Sanitize Option, it reads. Perfect. Bottles, lids, and nipples go in a basket on the top rack. Scientific, secure, certain. With one touch I believe I've found what a parent spends long days and nights searching for: the right way.

There are many things said by many people about parenthood; written and read about parenthood; counseled, debated, researched, and preached about parenthood—and too much of it has been by me. None of it is necessary. Not even this. So why do I write it? Because it can take a very long time to realize what is not required. I'm still hard at work on what doesn't need any work. Parenthood.

No other experience brings you so instantly into complete and inexpressible union with the divine. Nothing else is as genuine or encompassing. Nothing is more alive. No love is fuller; no intimacy, greater. Sex is close, but it's not even close.

Nothing compares to being a parent. And yet, all we do is compare. Most of us think, for instance, that we should be much better parents than we are. We infer that there is such a thing as a *good* parent, and by our own critical thinking we ensure that we are not. For when we judge ourselves as inadequate parents, we judge our children as the inadequate result. Judgment conquers our divine wholeness and separates our inexpressible union into a dueling dichotomy of incomplete parts.

The oppositional labels we assign to our life—and to the loves of our life—cause separation and alienation. Yes, just by a word or by the fleeting phantom of a word. Perfect, imperfect, best, worst, more, less, good, no good, right, wrong, early, late, not enough, enough!

Yes, well, we're only human, we tend to say in consolation, the point entirely. By merely forgiving ourselves for perceived limitations and inadequacies, we still judge the job of parenting to be beyond us, indeed, to be humanly impossible. We must go further and completely forget ourselves to see that there is no need to perfect the life that appears before us. It is already perfect *as it is*.

Once I gave what I judged to be a good talk at my Zen center about the extraordinary challenges of parenting. The parents in the room nodded in solidarity. Why, oh, why was it so hard to do it well, to do it right? Ours was the most difficult job in the world! The discussion wound on and on, going nowhere, until my teacher gave a *harrumph*.

"Even monkeys can raise their young!" he said.

"Raise them *badly*," I thought at the time, taking his comment to be little more than the rude evidence of his unique insensitivity. "He might have been a father," I reassured myself, "but was never a mother!" Mothers, I knew firsthand, could be the unrivaled experts at doing difficult things.

Parenthood is without question one of the hardest jobs in the world, and there is no one harder on you than yourself. To be fair, we're nudged along in fear and self-doubt by an unending stream of experts who don't mind telling us that the way we feed, hold, handle, speak to, and sleep with our kids is downright dangerous, particularly to their future test scores. No wonder we wake with a groan each morning as if we'd spent all night being kicked in the ribs by a little monster.

"Stop the presses!" exhorts one reviewer of a recent parenting book. "Everything you thought you knew about parenting is wrong!"

Really? By whose standards? By what measure? I can answer that myself, and every parent can, because whether we admit it or not, we're all aiming for the same bull's-eye: a perfect outcome. I can tell you what's wrong too. What's wrong is to stand over the hissing steam in a late-night kitchen as though you're going to get a better child to come out of a boiled bottle.

It's not just the experts who dole out the body blows. We do it to each other. Venture into a park or playgroup and you're surrounded by advocates for various parenting styles. Advocating what? Their way, of course. We hurt ourselves too every time we fix on one way as the right way. One bend, one blind curve, and the right way turns into the wrong way in a hurry. Perhaps we feel so inadequate as parents not because of what we don't know but because parenthood shows us the limits of what can be known.

As parents we think our job is to create an ideal future—a happier child, a smarter child, a more successful child. It's a silly notion, isn't it? That we are supposed to shape something presidential out of what looks like seven pounds of putty in our palm. The pressure alone makes us feel as though we're doomed to fail. But this focus on the future outcome blinds us to the marvel that already appears before us. It's not putty. Babies aren't blobs. Do we ever notice, and trust, the wonder of life happening continually and miraculously by itself? Do we ever see how effortless life is?

In my second, midlife marriage, I had a hard time getting pregnant. And then one day I was. Suffice it to say, I didn't use my noggin.

Stricken with pregnancy complications, I found it hard to keep going until the day my baby was born. And then one day she was. All I did was get out of the way.

It was difficult coping with a preterm infant. And then one day wasn't. I can't take credit.

It was hard with a baby who never slept. And then one day she did. Frankly, I slept through it.

One day—it seems like only yesterday—she rolled over. Crawled. Walked. Spoke. Ate with a spoon. A fork. Rode a trike. A bike. A two-wheeler. Sat up. Read. Wrote. Skipped. Made up a song. Climbed a tree. Boarded a bus. Turned a cartwheel. Played the piano. Delivered a monologue on a live-theater stage. None of it was hard for me, to tell you the truth. Monkeys raise their young; my teacher's point was true.

But they don't do it with the degree of difficulty we impose on the process by our ego-driven judgments and expectations.

We expect it to be the way we want it to be; and the way we want it to be is the way we call "right." In other words, *my way*. My way is what you have before you have children. There is no right way to parent; there is only a right-now way.

Like it or not, this is the offering that children give us, over and over: right now. We reflexively swat it from their hands—*I can't deal with that right now!*—since we are, after all, busy strategizing their brilliant futures. They return with the gift again, in fresh packaging. Children always show us the present moment unfolding. Our full attention is the only thing of value we can give them in return. Good thing too, because it is the only thing that makes a lasting difference.

When you step outside your judging mind, the mind that picks and chooses what it sees as good and what it sees as bad, what it fears most and desires least, you see that raising children is not impossible at all. It is only impossible to judge.

That's the day that you look up and see what all has happened while you had your head stuck in a cabinet. Your baby grew up all by herself.

This is bound to be an unpopular view. The popular view is that parenthood is difficult because we are inadequately schooled and supervised. I'll grant that's part of it. But I was adequately schooled and supervised in Spanish, and I still can't speak the language. I can't speak it because I don't practice it. As a parent, I make the job more difficult because I don't practice doing it the easy way. The *let's just see how it goes* way.

Those nights standing over the stove, I might have thought it would all get easier when my baby was out of bottles, then out of diapers, then out of a high chair, then out from underfoot, then out of my hair, and then finally out of the house. It was always going to be easier some other day. But I never had to wait that long. It gets easier as soon as you get out of your judging mind— the mind that picks and chooses your way as best and regards all other ways as less.

And what a happy day that is! When we liberate ourselves from the idea of parenting success, we liberate our children from failure, all without accomplishing a single thing. Freedom is instantaneous the moment we accept the way things are. Our own cruel judgment is what keeps us trapped over the stove long past the time when we should give ourselves a rest. And when we give ourselves a rest, we give everyone a rest.

I often speak to parenting groups with the aim of reassuring folks that they have everything they need to raise their children. It's a hard sell when you're not selling anything: not a lecture series, not an online class, not a packaged set of DVDs for $299. One of these talks was at a conference for parents of preschoolers where the workshops covered the usual rugged turf: handling sibling rivalry, effective discipline, non-violent communication, how to raise girls today, how to raise boys today, resolving conflicts, teaching diversity, managing transitions, and a host of terrors that have us trembling in the sanctuary of our own homes. Leaving the hotel afterward, I saw a woman from my workshop sitting in the hallway crying, and I wondered if I'd done harm.

"You were the only speaker all day who didn't convince me I was doing everything wrong!" she told me. I urge parents not to be so hard on themselves, knowing that when they are hard on themselves, they are hard on their children too.

But wait a minute, you might argue. Aren't we supposed to teach our children something? Instruct, direct, correct, persuade, dissuade and convince them to think and act the way we want them to? There are plenty of opportunities to try all of that, with spotty success. I rather like to think our children are here to teach us something: to give up and thereby gain the kingdom of heaven.

When my daughter was a year old—yes, a year!—I commenced a study of preschools. I gathered the brochures and made site visits. I compared the teacher-to-child ratios, the amount of shade in the play yards, the quality of the sand, the incidence of wooden versus plastic toys, and the pedagogy, and I ended up utterly confused. What I needed was a few hours a week to myself, and what I'd come up with was our first academic crisis.

My mother was visiting me at the time, and I laid out the prospects for her to deliberate on. Should I side with Montessori or Piaget? Waldorf or emergent curriculum? University laboratory or co-op? She spoke with the weariness born of thirty-seven years as a classroom teacher and the clarity of a sage. "Karen, all that matters is love."

That's what children require. Not what we call "the best," not what we think is right, not a push or a shove, but true love, love without judgment or condition, love for them as they are right now and for whatever they become. And equal love for our fumbling, tumbling tutelage. Within this wide-open field of possibility, anything can happen, and all of it is called *play*, not work and not the most difficult job in the world.

How do you love a willful toddler? A bossy kindergartener? An obnoxious teenager? Love is not the same as like. We love our children whether we like them or not, and let's face it, a lot of the time we don't like them at all. Unconditional love does not pick and choose. This love comes without judgment but not without action. Animated by love, not fear, and not paralyzed by preoccupation with a future measure of success, we act to correct and direct our children right here and now.

The best teaching is usually our own behavior. Taking stock of ourselves, we often find that the annoying, stubborn, and disruptive behaviors of our children are attempts to coax attention from us. Our attention lags, and they learn how to revive it.

When we focus on what is in front of us, what is truly facing us in a situation, we know what to do and not do. I'm never confused when I see my daughter reach up to touch the open flame on the stovetop; I'm confused only when I try to deduce some future impact on her performance. Since in the thinking about what to do we become terribly confused, I tell parents to stop thinking about all the worrisome what-ifs and just stay present to what is. Then, if we overreact, we can always say we're sorry. There is no right way to parent, but saying we're sorry is something we can all get good at.

"Mommy, I feel sorry for God," my daughter said not long ago, "because he has to create a million billion fingerprints!" And I am complaining about making another bowl of macaroni and cheese. As far as I'm concerned, she can call the source of creation whatever she likes;

I'm just glad she's taken the responsibility for fabricating the human race out of my hands. I can make a mess out of the simplest things.

After I located the sanitize button, I became accustomed to running the dishwasher twice daily, nearly empty, for the sole purpose of washing bottles on superhigh heat. I must have overdone it. One afternoon I detected an acrid undernote to the dense vapor that rose from its door. It was a fire, an electrical fire inside the dishwasher controls. My perfectly good idea had gone up in flames, and once the fire was doused, the dishwasher was kaput.

We didn't do without a dishwasher for long. But there *is* something I never let back into my kitchen: the jury. It's still out on my parenting. Now we can all grow up to be ourselves.

Pat Enkyo O'Hara

CARING, SOCIAL SERVICE, and creative response form the backbone of Roshi Pat Enkyo O'Hara's teachings. The very heart of Zen practice is becoming intimate with yourself, she says. "Once you really know yourself, then, automatically, you are available to serve the world."

A Soto Zen priest, O'Hara is the abbot of the Village Zendo, which she founded in 1986 with her partner—now spouse—Sensei Barbara Joshin O'Hara. She is also the guiding spiritual teacher for the New York Center for Contemplative Care and a founding teacher of the Zen Peacemaker Order, a spiritual, study, and social-action association. O'Hara is well known for her activism on behalf of HIV and AIDS patients and for her twenty-year career as a professor of interactive media at New York University's Tisch School of the Arts.

In the teaching that follows, O'Hara recounts a street retreat during which she spent four days and nights in lower Manhattan eating in soup kitchens and sleeping outdoors or in abandoned housing. Plunged into this shadow world of her very own city, O'Hara came face-to-face with fear, disgust, anger, and uncertainty. Yet she also ran headlong into the true nature of compassion.

Include Everything

I WANT TO speak to you about the koan "Seizei, a Poor Monk."

> Seizei, a monk, once said to Master Sozan, "I am poor and destitute. I beg you, oh Master, please help me and make me rich."
> Sozan said, "Venerable Seizei?"
> "Yes, teacher," replied Seizei.
> Sozan said, "Having tasted three cups of the best wine of Seigen, do you still say your lips are not yet moistened?"

How did the monk taste that best wine of Seigen? What is it to be poor and destitute? Koans reveal themselves in different ways. Though one can see this koan from the perspective of spiritual poverty, I want to highlight the material poverty that arises when we don't recognize our own value.

In October a group of twelve of us, led by my old friend Genro Gauntt Sensei and me, lived on the streets in lower Manhattan for four days, practicing meditation and experiencing how it is to survive without money or cell phones. It was a renunciation and a pilgrimage, a way to give up all of our habitual comforts and resources and to open up to reality, to the conditions of the world of which we are a part. What's it like to live in the city without anything? What's it like to find that you need to use a phone when you don't have a quarter?

The week before the retreat, I attended a Soto Zen conference in San Francisco. While there, I met with my beloved dharma sister Egyoku Roshi, and she told me something that struck me powerfully. Roshi's community, Los Angeles Zen Center, was spending a year studying "What is 'vow'?" One of Roshi's students had decided that for the whole year, her practice would be to investigate the vow "Include everything."

Just imagine what it would be like if you were to include everything that arises. Usually, all of us include only a certain amount. We include what we like, what we are willing to see about ourselves and others. We don't include the things we don't like about ourselves or our situations. In denial, we push them away.

So, I took this idea of "include everything" onto the street retreat. To deny nothing, not even my disgust. While trying to sleep, I thought, "Something is touching me—a rat? A bedbug?" (The worst fear of a New Yorker.) Then at the soup kitchen, I thought, "Is this man going to throw up on me?"

One of the points of Street Retreat is that things are right in your face, so there is no way to exclude anything. Every one of us on the retreat had issues come up: "Begging shows me what it's like to be rejected or given something." Or "Living on the street shows me I need to be seen" or "I have my anger."

Fear was a huge thing. Living on the street is scary. But the minute you include the fear, it's much less scary, because then the fear is there. You can touch it, you can feel it, and it's not this black cloud that's following you around.

The first night, we slept in an alley by the World Trade Center. We were very fortunate because, though it started raining in the middle of the night, we were under an overhang. There was also much joy and celebration when we realized there was a MacDonald's around the corner with a bathroom open all night. One of the great challenges when you live on the street is to find a bathroom.

In case you're ever homeless, I want to tell you about cardboard. Cardboard is the best thing to sleep on. It insulates nicely and it softens the concrete, but even so the ground was still hard, especially for some of us older ones, and it got cold. We used ponchos or plastic garbage bags and newspapers, which make good insulation. Every day, we spent time in Washington Square doing *zazen* and reflecting on the precepts.

During those four days, one thing that happened, which challenged me to "include everything," concerned the places where we went to receive food. Many people are doing hands-on work with the poor in Manhattan, offering various kinds of support and aid, including food and shelter. By chance, all the places we visited were Christian.

Every day we had breakfast at the Bowery Mission, which is right next to the New Museum and is quite a shocking contrast to it. But the mission is an amazing place. Founded in 1879, it serves three meals a day, has a shower program for men, and offers medical attention, clothing, and emergency shelter—all free. However, if you want to eat, there is a price you have to pay: chapel! Be in the chapel for service one hour before a meal is served . . . or no meal. The chapel experience was very daunting for our group, as most of us have a lot of opinions about what is appropriate and what is not.

Because the Bowery is a gospel mission, the chapel program would always begin with gospel music, though each day's program was different. Our first night, there were young people singing, accompanied by an electric guitar and piano. Everyone was invited to sing along, but most of the audience was asleep, heads on pews, or else they were looking around. The last day, a Latino man sang gospel hymns a cappella. It was very sweet.

After the music, a sermon was given using forceful language—a Manichaean conception of good and evil, of blame and shame, fire and brimstone. Looking at the people there—nodding off, impatient—it was not hard to feel they were being abused by this unremitting barrage of sermonizing: "There is only one right way. Come to Jesus. Be saved or you will be lost."

After the sermon, people were dispatched in groups to go to the cafeteria; and, inside, the food was plentiful. There were all kinds of donations from Whole Foods—food that was just going out of date, such as croissants and Greek yogurt, as well as vats of oatmeal and chili. But staff monitors paced around, hurrying us: "All right, women and disabled, let's go, let's go, keep moving." People were sleepy, tired, drunk, detoxing, and there was a lot of noise and pushing. It was very brusque. There was not a lot of dignity, none of what we would call compassion. So the overwhelming impression for us was one of brainwashing, indoctrination, and a sense of demeaning these poor victims.

On the other hand, at the Catholic Worker soup kitchen, nothing was asked of recipients. We came in and sat down at a beautiful wooden table holding a great big bowl of homemade soup and bread, and kind-looking people walked around serving coffee and tea. I asked one server, "Do you work here?" It turned out she was a volunteer who lived in the neighborhood and came once a week to help out. The Catholic Worker is a left-wing group inspired by Peter Maurin and founded by Dorothy Day, whose idea of Christian mercy was simply to serve food. Just that. It's a very small organization; they serve at 11 A.M. only. But we thought they had the best food—all organic, all donated.

A lot of the people whom we saw eating there had been so abused and mistreated over the course of their lives that they were not particularly nice to the servers. They weren't gracious; they just put their faces into their bowls. Yet the servers were there with a sense of generous dignity that I think is very important. When we want to give someone something, we need to check ourselves to be sure that we're not putting them in an up-to-down situation, that we're not victimizing. At the Catholic Worker, there was something about the tenor and tone that was simple acceptance.

At another soup kitchen—this one Methodist—the people who served tended to be "church lady" types who had a little time to come in for a day and help make food. I commented on the collards, and a woman said enthusiastically, "Yes, I made the collards. I always make the collards." She told me a whole story about how she had learned to make collards from her mother and now she still makes them the same way. I loved her—a woman in her late seventies. Much of the time we think we're special, compassionate Buddhists, so I just wanted to share that this compassionate work is being done by people of other religions all the time, all around us.

The McAuley Mission was founded in 1872 by Jerry McAuley, an Irish immigrant who actually grew up on the streets of New York, did time in Sing-Sing, and even after several spiritual experiences, struggled for years with alcoholism. At that time in New York, there was a phrase that breaks my heart: "the unworthy poor." There were wonderful charities for "the worthy poor," that is, women and children, but nothing was being done for "the unworthy poor," that is, men who weren't working. McAuley decided that his life mission was to care for these men. He convinced another ex-hoodlum who had done well to give him a property, and he and his wife (said to have been a prostitute) set up the McAuley Mission, which is still on White Street.

When we visited, we found a raw, rather dilapidated place, and once again a disciplinary style: silent, crowded, dense. Monitors shouted at people in the lines, not unlike in a prison. But this whole time I was trying to include everything, trying not to make a judgment, trying to learn to "not know," as we say, to not judge the style of operation because it was not in alignment with "my" style of operation.

Then on our last morning, I heard two young men testify at the Bowery Mission. They were called students, like we call ourselves Zen students, and I perked up and thought, "Oh, they're here to learn something, to learn how to shift their lives onto a kind of spiritual axis, a kind of acknowledgment of their own worth." After all, you can call it the Absolute or you can call it Jesus, but ultimately it's recognizing our own worth. When I listened to those men at the Bowery Mission, I saw how skillful what I had thought of as brainwashing and indoctrination could be.

What were they doing there at that mission? I saw my mind shift from all the opinions I'd had about the program as a kind of fundamentalist brainwashing to seeing it as a style of training. What is religion anyway? Many American Buddhist converts have opinions about religion; we don't care very much for it. We think of religion in terms of abuse of power, in terms of fundamentalist views of right and wrong, good and bad.

I began to think about the origin of the word *religion*. Cicero said the word came from *re*, "to once again," and *leger*, to read. He thought it meant "to read again" or "to study deeply." But there were other people in the classical era who said it came from *relegare*, which is to bind fast, to hold fast, to bring together the spiritual and the human. Still another group said, no, no, no, it comes from *relegere*, which means careful, the opposite of *nelegere*, negligence. I love the idea of this binding fast, this reading over and study, this carefulness. And I think we tend to disdain these useful aspects of what we call religion. They show the healing power of religion, the transforming power. Religion, great compassion—this is what motivates the volunteers of the spiritual groups who are out there serving food.

The very last night, we went to a Sufi mosque and visited with some Sufi friends. We chanted the Songs of the Beloved, which are so beautiful, so full of devotional love, and in accord with Buddhist meditation practice. Chanting seemed to make our hearts open. The love of Muhammad, the love of Jesus, and the teachings of Zen—all center on trusting and recognizing the unity, the humanness, the absolute in each of us.

It is that recognition of our absolute value as humans, as individuals, that Seizei, the poor monk, couldn't quite see in the koan we looked at earlier. He said to Sozan, "I am poor and destitute. I beg you, oh Master, please help me and make me rich."

When anyone asks us for help, what is the greatest gift we can give the person at that moment? The key is right in this exchange: "Sozan said, 'Having tasted three cups of the best wine of Seigen, do you still say your lips are not yet moistened?'"

Isn't the greatest gift to goad someone to realize his or her own incomparable value and uniqueness? Isn't that what we do, when we offer the gift of our attention and love, when we include everything?

Toni Packer

Toni Packer (1927–2013) was born in Germany but spent most of her life in western New York. In 1967 she began her Zen training with Roshi Philip Kapleau, author of *The Three Pillars of Zen*, and she made such quick progress in koan study that he eventually chose her to succeed him at the Rochester Zen Center.

Packer, however, had grown up in a secular household, and she became increasingly uncomfortable with certain doctrines taught at Rochester, including rebirth and karma. She also felt disconnected from some of the practices, such as praying to bodhisattvas, bowing, and wearing robes. After a great deal of difficult self-questioning, Packer cut her ties with conventional Zen and began focusing on what she saw as the essence of meditative practice—attending to what is happening within and without, moment by moment. Today in the West practitioners widely and openly contemplate what should constitute Western Zen, and Packer is considered a seminal figure in bringing this question to light.

In the early 1980s she founded Springwater Center, located in the bucolic Finger Lakes region of upstate New York. At the center there are no rituals, required beliefs, or assigned practices, and the aim is to be nonhierarchical. As Packer once said, "We are human beings, not 'students' and 'teacher,' coming together and questioning, looking together, not having made up our minds about what we're looking at, but starting afresh."

What Is the Me?

A SOMBER DAY, isn't it? Dark, cloudy, cool, moist, and windy. Amazing, this whole affair of the weather!

We call it weather, but what is it really? Wind. Rain. Clouds slowly parting. Not the words spoken about it but just this darkening, blowing, pounding, wetting, and then lightening up, blue sky appearing amid darkness, and sunshine sparkling on wet grasses and leaves. In a little while there'll be frost, snow, and ice covers. And then warming again, melting, oozing water everywhere. On an early spring day the dirt road sparkles with streams of wet silver. So—what is weather other than this incessant change of earthly conditions and all the human thoughts, feelings, and undertakings influenced by it? Like and dislike. Depression and elation. Creation and destruction. An ongoing, ever-changing stream of happenings abiding nowhere. No real entity *weather* exists anywhere except in thinking and talking about it.

Now, is there such an entity as *me* or *I*? Or is it just like the weather—an ongoing, ever-changing stream of ideas, images, memories, projections, likes and dislikes, creation and destruction that thought keeps calling *I, me, Toni,* and thereby solidifying what is evanescent? What am I really, truly, and what do I merely think and believe I am?

Are we interested in exploring this amazing affair of *myself* from moment to moment? Is this, maybe, the essence of this work? Exploring ourselves attentively beyond the peace and quiet that we are seeking and maybe finding occasionally? Coming upon an amazing insight into this deep sense of separation that we call *me* and *other people, me* and *the world,* without any need to condemn or overcome?

Most human beings take it for granted that I am *me,* and that *me* is this body, this mind, this knowledge and sense of myself that feels so obviously distinct and separate from other people and from the nature around us. The language in which we talk to ourselves and to each other inevitably implies separate *mes* and *yous* all the time. All of us talk *I-and-you* talk. We think it, write it, read it, and dream it with rarely any pause.

There is incessant reinforcement of the sense of *me,* separate from others. Isolated, insulated *me.* Not understood by others. How are we to come upon the truth if separateness is taken so much for granted, feels so commonsense?

The difficulty is not insurmountable. Wholeness, our true being, is here all the time, like the sun behind the clouds. Light is here in spite of cloud cover.

What makes up the clouds?

Can we begin to realize that we live in conceptual, abstract ideas about ourselves? That we are rarely in touch directly with what is actually going on? Can we realize that thoughts about myself—I'm good or bad, I'm liked or disliked—are nothing but thoughts and that thoughts do not tell us the truth about what we really are? A thought is a thought, and it triggers instant physical reactions, pleasures and pains throughout the body-mind. Physical reactions generate further thoughts and feelings about myself—"I'm suffering," "I'm happy," "I'm not as bright, as good looking as the others." That feedback implies that all of this is *me,* that I have gotten hurt or feel good about myself, or that I need to defend myself or get more approval and love from others. When we're protecting ourselves in our daily interrelationships, we're not protecting ourselves from flying stones or bomb attacks. It's from words we're taking cover, from gestures, from coloration of voice and innuendo.

"We're protecting ourselves, we're taking cover." In using our common language, the implication is constantly created that there is someone real who is protecting and someone real who needs protection.

Is there someone real to be protected from words and gestures, or are we merely living in ideas and stories about me and you, *all* of it happening in the ongoing audio-video drama of ourselves?

The utmost care and attention is needed to see the internal drama fairly accurately, dispassionately, in order to express it as it is seen. What we mean by "being made to feel good" or "getting hurt" is the internal enhancing of our ongoing *me* story, or the puncturing and deflating of it. Enhancement or disturbance of the *me* story is accompanied by pleasurable energies or painful feelings and emotions throughout the organism. Either warmth or chill can be felt at the drop of a word that evokes memories, feelings, passions. Conscious or unconscious emotional recollections of what happened yesterday or long ago surge through the body-mind, causing feelings of happiness or sadness, affection or humiliation.

Right now words are being spoken, and they can be followed literally. If they are fairly clear and logical, they can make sense intellectually. Perhaps at first it's necessary to understand intellectually what is going on in us. But that's not completely understanding the whole thing. These words point to something that may be *directly* seen and felt, inwardly, as the words are heard or read.

As we wake up from moment to moment, can we experience freshly, directly, when hurt or flattery is taking place?

What is happening? What is being hurt? And what keeps the hurt going?

Can there be some awareness of defenses arising, fear and anger forming, or withdrawal taking place, all accompanied by some kind of story line? Can the whole drama become increasingly transparent? And in becoming increasingly transparent, can it be thoroughly questioned? What is it that is being protected? What is it that gets hurt or flattered? *Me?* What is *me?* Is it images, ideas, memories?

It is amazing. A spark of awareness witnessing how one spoken word arouses pleasure or pain throughout the body-mind. Can the instant connection between thought and sensations become palpable? The immediacy of it. No *I* entity directing it, even though we say and believe I am doing all of that. It's just happening automatically, with no one intending to "do" it. Those are all afterthoughts!

We say, "I didn't want to do that," as though we could have done otherwise. Words and reaction proceed along well-oiled pathways and interconnections. A thought about the loss of a loved one comes up, and immediately the solar plexus tightens in pain. Fantasy of lovemaking occurs, and an ocean of pleasure ensues. Who does all of that? Thought says, "I do. I'm doing that to myself."

To whom is it happening? Thought says, "To me, of course!"

But where and what is this *I*, this *me*, aside from all the thoughts and feelings, the palpitating heart, the painful and pleasurable energies circulating throughout the organism? Who could possibly be doing it all with such amazing speed and precision? Thinking about ourselves and the triggering of physiological reactions takes time, but present awareness brings the whole drama to light instantly. Everything is happening on its own. No one is directing the show!

Right at this moment wind is storming, windows are rattling, tree branches are creaking, and leaves are quivering. It's all here in the listening—but whose listening is it? Mine? Yours? We say "I'm listening" or "I cannot listen as well as you do," and these words befuddle the mind with feelings and emotions learned long ago. You may be protesting, "My hearing isn't yours. Your body isn't mine." We have thought like that for aeons and behave accordingly; but at this moment can there be just the sound of swaying trees and rustling leaves and fresh air from the open window cooling the skin? It's not happening to anyone. It's simply present for *all* of us, isn't it?

Do I sound as though I'm trying to convince you of something? The passion arising in trying to communicate simply, clearly, may be misunderstood for a desire to influence people. That's not the case. There is just the description of what is happening here for all of us. Nothing needs to be sold or bought. Can we simply listen and investigate what is being offered for exploration from moment to moment?

What is the *me* that gets hurt or flattered, time and time again, the world over? In psychological terms we say that we are identified with ourselves. In spiritual language we say that we are attached to ourselves. What is this *ourselves*? Is it the feeling of myself existing, knowing what I am, having lots of recollections about myself—all the ideas and pictures and feelings about myself strung together in a coherent story? And knowing this story very well—multitudes of memories, some added, some dropped, all interconnected—what I am, how I look, what my abilities and disabilities are, my education, my family, my name, my likes and dislikes, opinions, beliefs, and so on. The identification with all of that, which says, "This is what I am." And the attachment to it, which says, "I can't let go of it."

Let's go beyond concepts and look directly into what we mean by them. If one says, "I'm identified with my family name," what does that mean? Let me give an example. As a growing child I was very much identified with my last name because it was my father's and he was famous—so I was told. I liked to tell others about my father's scientific achievements to garner respect and pleasurable feelings for myself by impressing friends. I felt admiration through other people's eyes. It may not even have been there. It may have been projected. Perhaps some people even felt, "What a bore she is!" On the entrance door to our apartment there was a little polished brass plate with my father's name engraved on it and his titles: "Professor Doctor Phil." The "Phil" impressed me particularly, because I thought it meant that my father was a philosopher, which he was not. I must have had the idea that a philosopher was a particularly imposing personage. So I told some of my friends about it and brought them to look at the little brass sign at the door.

This is one meaning of identification—enhancing one's sense of self by incorporating ideas about other individuals or groups or one's possessions, achievements, transgressions—anything—and feeling that all of this is *me*. Feeling important about oneself generates amazingly addictive energies.

To give another example from the past: I became very identified with my half-Jewish descent. Not openly in Germany, where I mostly tried to hide it rather than display it, but later on after the war ended, telling people of our family's fate and finding welcome attention, instant sympathy, and nourishing interest in the story. One can become quite addicted to making the story of one's life impressive to others and to oneself and feed on the energies aroused by that. And when that sense of identification and attachment is disturbed by someone's not buying into it, contesting it, or questioning it altogether, there is sudden insecurity, physical discomfort, anger, fear, and hurt.

Becoming a member of a Zen center and engaging in spiritual practice, I realized one day that I had not been talking about my background in a long while. And now, when somebody brings it up—sometimes an interviewer will ask me to talk about it—it feels like so much bother and effort. Why delve into old memory stuff? I want to talk about listening, the wind, and the birds.

Are we listening right now? Or are we more interested in identities and stories?

We all love stories, don't we? Telling them and hearing them is wonderfully entertaining.

At times people wonder why I don't call myself a teacher when I'm so obviously engaged in teaching. Somebody actually brought it up this morning—the projections and the associations aroused in waiting outside the meeting room and then entering nervously with a pounding heart. Do images of teacher and student offer themselves automatically like clothes to put on and roles to play in these clothes? In giving talks and meeting with people, the student-teacher imagery does not have to be there—it belongs to a different level of existence. If images do come up, they're in the way, like clouds hiding the sun. Relating without images is the freshest, freest thing in the universe.

So, what am I and what are you—what are we without images clothing and hiding our true being? It's un-image-inable, isn't it? And yet there's the sound of wind blowing, trees shaking, crows cawing, woodwork creaking, breath flowing without need for any thoughts. Thoughts are grafted on top of what's actually going on right now, and in that grafted world we happen to spend most of our lives.

Yet every once in a while, whether one does meditation or not, the real world shines wondrously through everything. How is it when words fall silent? When there is no knowing? When there is no listener and yet there is listening, awaring in utter silence?

The listening to, the awaring of the *me* story, is not part of the *me*. Awareness is not part of that network. The network cannot witness itself. It can think about itself and even change itself, establish new behavior patterns, but it cannot see itself or free itself. There is a whole psychological science called behavior modification that, through reward and punishment, tries to drop undesirable habits and adopt better, more sociable ones. This is not what we're talking about. The seeing, the awaring of the *me* movement is not part of the *me* movement.

A moment during a visit with my parents in Switzerland comes to mind. I had always had a difficult relationship with my mother. I had been afraid of her. She was a very passionate woman with lots of anger but also love. Once during that visit I saw her standing in the dining room facing me. She was just standing there, and for no known reason I suddenly saw her without the past. There was no image of her and also no idea of what she saw in me. All of that was gone. There was nothing left except pure love for this woman. Such beauty shone out of her. And our relationship changed; there was a new closeness. No one changed it. It just happened.

Truly seeing is freeing beyond imagination.

Images in Relationship

IN MANY HUMAN beings there is a deep fear of relationship, of being rejected, hurt, or misunderstood. We may avoid relationship yet long for it, because human beings are born into relationship, for better or worse. And we are born out of relationship. We wouldn't be here if there hadn't been a relationship between our parents. There is a great yearning in human beings for companionship, for being together, for sharing.

Little children gravitate toward each other, play together, or often just watch each other. When they are being pushed in shopping carts in a supermarket, they will find each other with their eyes and watch each other with consuming interest.

A man who had been coming to the Springwater Center for many years spent a vacation in a remote place in the Canadian Rockies to hike alone over mountain ranges, glaciers, and streams. He had arranged to be dropped off by plane and to be met again after six weeks of solitary wandering. He wanted to find out what it is like to be really alone. Alone in the wilderness, on his way back to the plane's pickup place, he saw a tiny figure in the distance, which he knew must be a human being. Immediately he noticed his drained energies picking up. He began walking more briskly, then running, and upon meeting this stranger, he embraced him. He didn't know who the man was; he had never seen him before. It wasn't that he wanted anything of that person, he just hugged him because he was there.

There is a great yearning in us for love and companionship. Yet our relationships cause immense conflicts, violence, and heartaches. Why? Why does the joy of just being together on a walk, sharing a meal, playing together, or having sex so quickly turn into something else? Can we examine this? We first have to understand where our yearning for companionship comes from.

Is the fear of being lonely, of being unloved, the driving force for seeking companionship? Are we seeking someone to fill the aching inner emptiness?

What about insecurity? Not being sure of myself, feeling negative about myself, I want somebody to tell me that I'm attractive and lovable. When someone says those things to me, the chemicals get going. I feel alive. I long to be with this person so that I'll continue to feel good about myself. The one who makes me feel this way appears in glowing images in my mind. When I'm with him or her, I don't see the actual person. I see him or her through the image of the ideal companion who makes me feel alive. Not only do I love the verbal flattery, but I also love the way he or she approaches, looking at me with adoring or longing eyes. I adore myself through this person.

I remember experiencing this in my teens in World War II Germany. It was after I developed my first real crush on a young soldier who was home on leave. There weren't many young men around then because they were in the war. Just a few came home on leave occasionally, maybe for a week or two. So mostly they weren't around. And I felt a tremendous yearning to be with a young man.

Finally I met one, but he was already on his last day of furlough, and then he'd be off to the front again. He wrote letters. How I read and reread those letters to bathe in the magic words about me: that I was beautiful, that he loved me, and how much he missed me. I was much more concerned with myself than I was with this young man, but that wasn't clear to me at the time. If you had asked me then, I would have said that I was in love with *him*. But I was in love with *myself*. I was looking for *me* in his letters.

And there never seemed to be enough of them either. There was always the need for more, because chemicals come and go; eventually they get flushed out. One needs new stimulation, a new rush from more affirmation, more words, more touch.

We human beings do this to each other at the time of courting. We're at our best then, saying to the other what we sense he or she wants to hear. We're like a bird displaying his brightest feathers or a bullfrog croaking his finest song. But for the animals, when the mating season is over, the courting rituals end. Animals go back to "normal." Not so with human beings. For us the season goes on.

Being on our best behavior, though, is hard to keep up. We are projecting our own image onto the other person, and then we are relating to the image we have created of the other person. Then if two people start living together, in the nitty-gritty of daily life, things change somehow. For one thing, we find out more about each other's habits and rigidities. We also discover that flirting and courting behavior isn't the basis for a continuing relationship. And getting used to each other, we may find the present relationship boring and start flirting with someone else.

When the courtship wears off and we're with each other day in and day out, the partner may increasingly trigger the memory, the image of someone else—the father or the mother, the stereotyped male or female, the dominant one who always gets his or her own way. Projections arise from our memories of past relationships, and what happens in the present relationship is interpreted according to our earlier experiences. Whatever we have done to each other has been recorded in the brain and becomes a distorting filter through which we behold each other now. So we're not together freshly and spontaneously; we're reacting to each other through the filters of our past experiences.

In childhood our parents were able to punish us by withholding what we needed for survival: affection and life sustenance. To avoid this threat, most of us have put up with a lot from our parents. Now all of a sudden, in relationship with a partner who reminds us of one of our parents, we come upon a lot of stored-up fear, anger, and vindictiveness. It may be active or passive. We may say things that we couldn't say to our elders, who were all-powerful. We may rage at our companion for trying to dominate us or tell us what to do, or we may sulk with a vengeance. None of this is clear, because we're not clear about what's memory, what's image, what's the past, and what's right now.

Parents, children, you, and I—we all react in conditioned patterns most of the time. We *think* we are responding to each other consciously, spontaneously, out of the present situation, but we're not. Instead, stored-up images and programs, with their connected feelings and emotions, are constantly being triggered and projected. *They* are doing the "relating"—the reacting and the clashing.

We all have physical and psychological needs: to be touched, held, to be taken care of, to be comforted, to be loved, and so on. Do these needs dovetail in two people? Or does each person want to have his or her needs fulfilled with little regard to the needs of the other? The end result of that disregard is friction, disappointment, turning away, and maybe looking for another relationship.

Can we become aware of this whole process as it is happening, not in order to change it, but to clarify what is unclear, to bring into light what is confused and hidden?

Our usual reaction is to try to change the other person so that we can live with him or her to our own satisfaction. That is what was once done to us: "Behave, and Mom (or Dad) will love you." We were always told what to do for the sake of the peace of the parents or the family. Our parents never asked what *they* could do, at least not in our presence. They may have asked that of a therapist, but in my time parents didn't go to therapists. They knew everything! At least we thought they knew everything. They were always right, and we were always wrong.

Thus ideas and images of what we are and what others are—right or wrong, good or bad, lovable or unworthy—were programmed into our brains and bodies from the beginning. And these programs are actively functioning now in what we call our "relationship." Can we wake up to this as it is taking place? Not so that we can find fault or blame ourselves or each other; that doesn't clarify anything. Blaming only perpetuates old images.

Attention brings images to light. It clarifies without judging. With attention there can be a lightening, an opening up to each other, free of the past. Then it is no longer images that are relating to each other but real people who have an astonishing capacity for kindness.

Tenzin Palmo

BORN DIANE PERRY in the east end of London, Ani Tenzin Palmo came across her first Buddhist book at the age of eighteen. Halfway through, she said to her mother, "I'm a Buddhist." And her mother said, "That's nice, dear. Finish reading the book and then you can tell me all about it." Six months later, her mother also became a Buddhist.

But besides her mom, Tenzin Palmo didn't know anyone else on the same path. She only had books to guide her in the practice, and all the books seemed to advocate eliminating desire. As a result, Tenzin Palmo broke up with her boyfriend, stopped using makeup, and began wearing what she believed was appropriate Buddhist attire: black stockings and a yellow garment resembling a Greek tunic.

This extremism went on for months, and all the while Tenzin Palmo's mother refrained from complaining. Then one day Tenzin Palmo found the Buddhist Society in the telephone directory, decided to connect with them, and in this way discovered that English Buddhists did not sport Greek tunics but rather ordinary garb, even high heels. "What a pity I gave all my clothes away," Tenzin Palmo lamented to her mother. And with that, her mom revealed that she'd secretly saved them, just in case.

At this time, Tenzin Palmo was Theravadin, but after about a year of exploring Buddhism, she read a book that listed the four main Buddhist traditions in Tibet: the Nyingmapa, the Sakyapa, the Kagyupa, and the Gelugpa—all forms of Vajrayana, or Tantric, Buddhism. Immediately, according to Tenzin Palmo, a voice inside her said, "You're a Kagyupa."

"What's a Kagyupa?" her thinking mind shot back.

"It doesn't matter," answered the voice. "You're a Kagyupa."

It became clear to Tenzin Palmo that she needed a teacher, and so at the age of twenty she traveled to India, where she met her root guru, Khamtrul Rinpoche, a high Drukpa Kagyu lama. She then went on to become one of the first Western women to be ordained as a Tibetan Buddhist nun and to spend twelve years living in a remote cave in the Himalayas, three of those years in strict meditation retreat. Of her time in the cave, Tenzin Palmo has said, "Solitude was very rewarding because I had to learn to deal with whatever happened, be it internal or external, on my own. When you live in such isolation, you can't get on the phone and call a technician or have a chat with your best friend. You can't turn on the television to divert yourself. In the winter, you can't even go for a walk. Whatever happens, you have to sit there and deal with it! This period helped me develop inner resourcefulness and confidence."

In 2008 Tenzin Palmo was given the rare title *Jetsunma* (Venerable Master) in recognition of her spiritual achievements as a nun and her efforts in promoting the status of female practitioners in Tibetan Buddhism.

Vajrayana

ACCORDING TO THE Hinayana school of Buddhism, we are trapped in this realm of endless birth, death, rebirth, and redeath because we desire things and hold on to them so tightly. Even though this wheel of life brings us so much suffering again and again, we cling to it. The Hinayana school places emphasis on eradicating even the finest roots of our desire. According to the Mahayana, it is because of our ignorance that we are trapped on this wheel. We accept as real that which is not real, and we think unreal that which is the only true reality. Everything we think reflects a misapprehension of how things really are. Therefore, our task is to develop what is called "transcendental wisdom," which will eradicate the very roots of our ignorance.

According to Vajrayana, we are trapped in this realm of endless birth and death because of our impure perceptions. We believe that what we see is solid, ordinary, and defiled. We see ourselves as impure beings. The antidote to this is to develop pure perception, or pure vision. If we understand this, the whole Vajrayana path makes sense. The way to go beyond samsara is to realize that it has always been nirvana. It is our basic ignorance that causes impure perceptions to manifest so that everything appears as ordinary, suffering and defiled. We have to "clean the lenses" in order to see that what looks so ordinary is actually a pure realm of utter transcendence. This is a basic fundamental of the Vajrayana view and can be realized only by an awakened mind. One of the Mahayana sutras tells about a time when Ananda, the Buddha's attendant, asked the Buddha, "How is it that all of these other Buddhas like Amitabha, Akshobhya, and Ratnasambhava have beautiful pure lands full of realized beings, whereas your mandala, your pure land, is full of defiled beings and foul places? How is it that you are a buddha, yet your pure land is so impure?" The Buddha replied, "There is nothing wrong with my pure land. When I look around, I see that it is immaculate. The problem is with your impure perception, which sees it as defiled."

Once His Holiness the Sixteenth Karmapa, head of the Karma

Kagyu tradition, was very ill in Delhi. At that time, I went to see His Holiness Sakya Trizin, who was also there. His Holiness Sakya Trizin is the head of the Sakya order, one of the four traditions of Tibetan Buddhism. I said to him, "It's awful that Karmapa is so sick!" He replied, "Karmapa isn't sick. Karmapa is beyond birth and death. It's just your impure perception that sees Karmapa as sick." And I said, "Well, yes, but Tai Situ Rinpoche, a very high-level bodhisattva who presumably has pure perception, is nonetheless worried and concerned because Karmapa is sick." His Holiness replied, "Situ Rinpoche is not worried or concerned. It's your impure perception that sees Situ Rinpoche as worried and concerned." You get the idea! We have to purify our perception. Then we will see that this has been nirvana all the time. It is only because of our perverted view that there was ever any problem.

Vajrayana shares its philosophy with Mahayana. The Vajrayana is not a philosophy. It is a practice technique and a view, or vision. It takes its philosophical stance from the Mahayana. The Tibetans say it takes it from the Prasangika-Madhyamaka school. Actually it seems to be a combination of Yogachara and Madhyamaka viewpoints. In the Mahayana, the practice path is this: we are here, and we have the inherent potential for Buddhahood, called our buddha nature, which is like a seed. The path is the means to water and nurture that seed until it grows and grows and finally ripens into full Buddhahood.

We ordinary, defiled sentient beings have the potential for enlightenment. We all have embryonic buddha nature, and we cultivate it through aeons of time. It takes a long time to become a buddha in the Mahayana school. We have to nurture this seed for endless ages until it grows and puts out leaves and branches and finally manifests as a full-grown Tree of Enlightenment. This could be considered as a wonderful vision, but it might also be considered totally discouraging. You might think, "Well, if it takes aeons and aeons, what's the point?" In reaction to such concerns, the Vajrayana takes a very radical step: it turns the whole thing around.

The Sutrayana division of the Mahayana school is referred to as the "path of the cause." This is because we start with the cause, which is our embryonic buddha nature, and nurture it until we produce the fruit. The Vajrayana is called the path of the fruit. This is because it maintains that from beginningless time, we have already been buddhas. Our problem is that we don't recognize this. Therefore, why not use our inherent buddha nature as the path itself? So we start from the fruit and use that as the path. In other words, we start from the opposite direction. Therefore, Vajrayana places great emphasis on visualizing ourselves as a buddha or as a particular tantric deity that symbolizes some aspect of a fully flowered buddha nature.

Most Buddhist meditation focuses on the breath, on the mind itself, or sometimes on very simple geometrical designs. Vajrayana meditation depends on a faculty called "creative imagination," or visualization. This is what makes it different from other forms of Buddhist practice. Although nobody knows when the Vajrayana first entered the Buddhist stream, it was certainly in existence by the early centuries of the common era. It might have been there from the beginning. Tibetans believe that it was always there and was taught by the Buddha himself. In any event, by the fourth or fifth century it was extremely prolific, although still a very secret form of practice.

At that time there were huge monasteries in India that were also universities, including Nalanda, Vikramashila, and Takshila. They contained thousands and thousands of monastic scholars who were studying all the schools of Buddhist philosophy. Within that complex, there were many masters who were also practicing these Vajrayana teachings. But they did it quietly. It is said that although outwardly these masters looked like monks, inwardly they were yogis. They didn't talk about it, and it did not become widespread and open, with public initiations and so forth, until it became the state religion of Tibet. I don't think the Vajrayana was ever intended to be a state religion. It was intended to be quiet and secret, just between the master and a few disciples. Before you can practice the Vajrayana, you need to receive an initiation. If you look at the early records in India, they show that a disciple was usually initiated only after years and years of testing by the guru, and then it was a one-on-one, mind-to-mind transmission.

Nowadays, His Holiness the Dalai Lama gives the Kalachakra initiation to a hundred thousand people at a time.

As I mentioned earlier, the practice of Vajrayana relies heavily on the use of creative imagination. I will give an example for those who have never done anything like this before. Suppose we take the example of Guru Padmasambhava, whom the Tibetans call Guru Rinpoche. Guru Padmasambhava is very appropriate to this topic, because he was the master who came from India and established tantric Buddhism in Tibet during the eighth century. He has become a focus for popular devotion. Suppose we were to do a practice centering on Padmasambhava. Whatever we do, it is extraordinarily important to proceed with the correct motivation, which is the wish to break through to the unconditioned reality and, having gained access to our innate wisdom and compassion, benefit others. No other motivation is valid. First we would take refuge in the Buddha, his doctrine, and the community of realized practitioners. Next we raise the aspiration to attain enlightenment for the benefit of others. At this point, we begin the meditation.

If we were doing the Padmasambhava meditation, we would visualize ourselves sitting. Then our body would dissolve into space. In the space, at the heart center, a syllable would appear. In this case it would be a PAM, standing for Padma. This is called a seed syllable. That PAM would then emanate light in all directions, purifying the entire universe. Then the whole universe and everything in it would become a realm of absolute immaculate purity, and all the beings there would be purified of their defilements and become like gods and goddesses. Then the lights would come back into the PAM, and in an instant one would appear as Padmasambhava. One must then see oneself as Padmasambhava, who embodies the wisdom and compassion of all the buddhas.

When we are doing these meditations, it is very important for us to believe them. None of this is made up—everything is exact and precise. One of the problems Westerners face is that we are simply not accustomed to such detailed imagery. Many of us find it very difficult, at least in the beginning, although people who are visually oriented may find it easier. But even more important than the very detailed visualization is the belief that this is real. It doesn't work if you don't believe in it. Normally when people do these meditations, they are really thinking, "Here am I, Pat, pretending to be Padmasambhava. The reality is that I'm Pat. The fantasy is that I am now supposed to be Padmasambhava." But the truth is that we are Padmasambhava, who represents our primordial wisdom and compassionate mind. We are Padmasambhava pretending to be Pat. You see, these forms, which might seem quite alien to you, are actually emanations of our wisdom mind. They are emanations of our inherent buddha nature, as they have appeared to realized masters throughout the ages. They arose in minds that had access to their wisdom nature. Therefore, they are an extremely skillful conduit back to very profound realms of our psyche that we cannot access by means of logical, linear thinking.

There are very subtle levels of our psychological makeup that we can access only through enlightened imagery. These meditations, if we really become one with them, open up profound levels of the mind very quickly. They have quite an extraordinary effect. The amount of effort we expend is tiny compared with the enormous benefits to be attained. People are often startled because there is a part of us that doesn't really believe it, that thinks that we are just playing games. To gain the benefits, we must become absorbed in the practice and cease this duality of "I" doing the practice. Just become the practice. As soon as we get rid of that subject-object dichotomy and become the meditation, the results come quickly. This is why Tibetan Buddhism has remained so popular, despite that fact that it initially seems so alien to many Westerners.

Now we are seeing ourselves as Padmasambhava, and we have the certainty of being Padmasambhava. At this point, if our original wisdom nature could take form, it would take form as Padmasambhava. This is the glow of our buddha nature. It is like a rainbow. This visualization is not solid; Padmasambhava does not possess a liver, guts, and a heart. He is made up of rainbow light. Every feature has a meaning. The two arms are wisdom and compassion. He is a conglomeration of the elements of the Buddhist path distilled into a single form. That is who we really are. This is the important thing to know. This is what I really am, not the transient identity I usually think of as "me." Then we sit and see ourselves as Guru Rinpoche (Padmasambhava), trying very hard to visualize as clearly as possible all the details, going through the visualization part by part, getting a flash of the whole thing together. Padmasambhava is sitting there, radiating light. At the heart center is a lotus, and upon that, a moon disk. On the moon disk is the syllable PAM, and around that, the letters of the mantra, standing upright. Light radiates from Padmasamhhava's mantra. These radiating lights go out and purify the entire cosmos. All the beings within it will naturally be purified because now we are Buddha.

This is what I was describing before as "taking the fruit as the path." Now we are Buddha, and the Buddha has the capacity to purify beings. In our minds we are doing this activity that a buddha would do, that is, radiating light in all directions, completely purifying everything and all beings everywhere within it. By "beings," we are not referring simply to human beings. "Beings" includes animals, insects, fish, spirits, those in the heavens and hells and everywhere. All beings throughout the incredibly vast universe are liberated. They become conscious of their wisdom and compassionate nature, and they turn into Padmasambhava. The whole world has become an immaculate pure land. Then the lights come back and again go out and make offerings to all the buddhas and bodhisattvas in the universe and also to all the sentient beings who are now themselves buddhas. The entire universe is now an immaculate pure land full of buddhas. While we visualize this, we say the mantra. Then, at the end, this vast universe, now completely filled with buddhas and bodhisattvas, melts into light. That light melts into us. We melt down into the center. The lotus and the moon melt into the mantra. The mantra melts into the seed syllable PAM. The seed syllable melts upward into the tiny circle called the *nada*, which then also melts. We watch this very precisely as it melts, stage by stage, until there is nothing left. Then the mind remains in its natural, immaculate state. It rests in this state that is beyond thought and beyond concept for as long as possible. When thinking starts, we again instantly appear as Padmasambhava and dedicate the merit attained by doing this practice.

Subsequently, as we are going about our business during the day, we see ourselves as Padmasambhava. We see all beings we meet as emanations of Padmasambhava. Immediately upon meeting someone, we recognize the person's inherent buddha nature. All sounds we hear are the sounds of the mantra. Nice sounds, harsh sounds, all are just the mantra. All thoughts—good thoughts, bad thoughts, intelligent thoughts, and stupid thoughts—are just the play of Guru Padmasambhava's wisdom mind. We try to maintain the awareness throughout the day that all the beings we encounter are just pretending to be ordinary but are really Guru Rinpoche in disguise. All sounds that we hear are the wonderful echo of Om Ah Hum Vajra Guru Padma Siddhi Hum (Padmasambhava's mantra). All the thoughts we have are just the essential nature of the empty play of wisdom. Nothing to worry about. If we can maintain that throughout the day, we will learn what it is to develop pure perception.

This is the way the Vajrayana works. I have given a very simplified illustration, but it is basically the way it works. Sometimes when people come to the Vajrayana, they are intimidated by its seemingly endless complexity. There are so many deities, so many levels, so many different practices and approaches, where does one begin? It can become quite mind-boggling. But the essential focus of the practice is actually very simple. The problem is that, as with any other practice, we have to do it. It's not enough to just do it for ten minutes a day. We need to incorporate our practice into our daily life. We have to transform our minds. It's not about playing with nice ideas. It is about transforming the very core of our being. It doesn't work unless we really take the practice and eat it, digest it, and use it to nourish ourselves, not just nibble at it from time to time. Some people do these practices a little bit every day, and then they forget them. Then they wonder why nothing is happening. But the texts are very clear that this is not just something you do when you are sitting on your mat. You have to take the visualization with you into your everyday life. This is what the early masters did. They transformed their vision into pure perception because they were using it all the time, in all of their encounters.

There is another aspect of the Vajrayana that builds on this. It involves manipulating the inner energies. This is done once our visualization has become stable and we have performed the requisite number of mantras. The mantra is considered to be the essence of the nature of the deity. Every buddha and bodhisattva has his or her own special mantra that is the way to connect with and experience that deity. When we say the mantra with perfect concentration and visualization, we actualize the qualities the deity represents. They are locked inside the mantra, which is like a code. We decode it and access that energy through our meditation and visualization and by saying the mantra. If we say it with perfect concentration, really focusing on the visualization and becoming one-pointed in the practice, the results come very quickly. If we harbor doubt in our minds, nothing will happen even after aeons of practice. The texts are very specific in pointing this out.

There is so much one can say, but I hesitate to say too much, because many of you may never have taken Vajrayana initiations. However, I will touch on something that often confuses people. Non-Vajrayana people are often puzzled when they enter a Vajrayana temple and find themselves surrounded by all the representations of these beings on the walls. They often ask, "What's this got to do with Buddhism?" Many of the images are naked. Many of them appear to be wrathful and look like demons. Some are even shown copulating. But this iconography is not as bizarre or as complex as it first appears. The images of the deities represent one or another of three basic levels of mood. The first mood is peaceful, represented by figures such as Avalokiteshvara, the Bodhisattva of Compassion; Manjushri, the Bodhisattva of Wisdom; and Tara, the Savioress. They are shown as quiet, peaceful, and gently smiling. People don't usually have any problems with them, although they sometimes have problems with the fact that Tara is green or somebody else is blue. But basically there is no problem, because they look nice and friendly, as if they were on our side.

Then you get the second level, which is called *shi ma tro* in Tibetan. This means "neither peaceful nor angry." These are the heroic deities, known as the *heruka* and *dakini* forms. They represent the thrust of energy toward enlightenment. Their particular quality is passion. Now, in the earlier forms of Buddhism, desire was seen as the major obstacle to liberation. But in the Mahayana, and especially in the Vajrayana, it was understood that emotions such as passion and anger, when traced to their source, consist of vast amounts of energy. At some stage this energy has become perverted into a negative force. But nevertheless, this energy is in itself very clear and wise. In other words, the flip side of what looks to us like negative energy is an innate wisdom. This was a tremendous volte-face in the attitude toward negative emotions. Instead of having to uproot emotions such as anger, pride, jealousy, and passion, we could take that energy and use it as the fuel for attaining enlightenment. These emotions were no longer enemies to be vanquished. They had become our main helpers on the path. This is an underlying motif throughout Vajrayana. When we understand this, we will understand the iconography of Vajrayana.

The Tibetan texts tell us that the greater the negative emotion, the greater the wisdom. The corollary to this is that without negative emotions, there is no wisdom. Does this mean that we are encouraged to run rampant, giving full rein to our greed, passion, hatred, and desire in the name of spiritual practice? Some people think it does, but this is a misconception. These negative qualities, if left in their uncontrolled and unmitigated state, are indeed the cause of samsara. But if we control and transform them, we can use them as the fuel to propel us beyond samsara. The example that always comes to my mind is that of a rocket. You need enormous amounts of fuel to launch the rocket beyond the earth's gravitational pull, but once it's out in space, you no longer need much power. It becomes virtually self-propelling. So also with the spiritual path. The gravitational pull of our ordinary nature, of our ordinary, ignorant, ego-based mind, is extremely strong. It is incredibly difficult to make that first thrust into the unconditioned, because our conditioned mind is so powerful. Even if we are doing ordinary calming and insight meditations, it is difficult to make that thrust through. We need everything we can possibly muster for the initial push.

Vajrayana takes everything we have, even the garbage, and uses the whole lot as fuel to power the breakthrough to the unconditioned nature of the mind. That's why it can seem so threatening, and that's why it can be very dangerous and why we need the guidance of a teacher. The need for a perfect teacher is continually emphasized in the Vajrayana texts. Otherwise, it can be a very dangerous path. It is said that we won't get into much trouble driving an oxcart along the road, but when we get behind the wheel of a sports car, we have to be very careful. You really need a good teacher before you take the wheel. This is because the Vajrayana uses the energies, especially the sexual energy, which in earlier Buddhism was sublimated or transformed in much more genteel ways. In the Vajrayana, that energy is transformed into a means to open up all the inner wisdom centers.

It is a misconception to imagine that Vajrayana gives you a license for uninhibited sexuality, to be as angry as you want, to get drunk, or to abuse the senses in any way whatsoever. On the contrary, it is the most disciplined and the most controlled practice there is. There are many, many Vajrayana vows that deal with the mind. It is not at all a path of license. But it is a path that takes everything we have. It requires great dedication and very clear guidance.

The third level of deity, which comes after the heroic level, is the *tro wa*, which means "fierce." You can tell the difference between the heroic and the fierce representations by looking at the flames around them. The peaceful forms have auras surrounding them. In the heroic forms, they have a very neat frame of flames. In the fierce form they are surrounded by wild flames. The heroic deities are based on lust. The fierce deities are based on anger. They deal with all of these emotions we have inside us, from mild irritation to total fury. Although they look very angry, at their heart there is total love, wisdom, and compassion. They are not really angry at all. They just manifest in that form. It is the transformed anger that has such tremendous energy. I don't know any lamas who are angry, but many of them manifest very wrathful deities in their meditation. The deities in union with their consorts represent a number of things. We are within these opposites, but these opposites are always joined in a higher unity. They represent the unity of wisdom and compassion, of bliss and emptiness, and so on. But the idea is always that we are taking two qualities of mind that become united into one. This is shown in a very graphic way through the unity of the male and female. It doesn't mean they have wild orgies in tantric monasteries.

Tibetan Buddhism places a lot of emphasis on the guru. The guru is a very difficult subject to deal with because, as I said earlier on, in the early days in both India and Tibet, the relationship between the guru and the disciple was a very personal one. The teacher had just a small circle of intimate disciples. He knew them all very well, and they knew him. There was mutual trust. The practices were very individual. When I was with my teacher in India, apart from his monastery and the Tibetan laypeople, he had a very small number of Western disciples. Usually when Westerners came to him, he would send them away to other lamas. But occasionally he would select a few whom he would allow to stay. And although we all started doing the same things, within a very short time we were doing widely divergent practices. I never received teachings together with anyone else. There was also an American nun, a Dutch nun, and a Swiss nun, who came some years after I had become a nun. We were dharma sisters. Sometimes one of us would ask for an initiation, and my lama would say, "Let's wait until the three or four of you are together, and I will give it to all of you." So we would get the initiation and the oral transmission together, but we didn't get the teachings together.

For instance, Khamtrul Rinpoche would ask me to do a particular practice, and I would think, "Fantastic, that is just the practice I would want to do." And I would tell my dharma sisters, and they would say, "Oh, I hope he doesn't tell us to do that." And I would say, "If that's your reaction, he wouldn't." And he didn't. I knew that my lama knew me better than I knew myself. He would tell me to do things that had never occurred to me but that were so completely right. That kind of confidence is very important, and you get it when you know you have a teacher who completely understands you. How could you not have trust and confidence in someone like that?

A problem has arisen now because Vajrayana has become so popular in the West and in the East, and many lamas are constantly jet-setting around the world. Say they come here. They are here for a few days, maybe they give an initiation and some teachings, and then they are off. Maybe they won't come again for another five years. First of all, how are you going to make contact with that teacher, and second, if you do make contact, how are you going to meet him or her again? And how is the teacher going to remember who you are? It's a big problem. In the Vajrayana texts, it says that you must examine your teacher, or rather your potential teacher, for up to twelve years before accepting him or her.

A genuine guru is not just for this lifetime. He or she is for all of our lifetimes. We must trust that the guru can take us to enlightenment, because the guru him- or herself has that level of realization and can bestow it on us. Also, the genuine guru is the one who shows you the original and inherent wisdom, awareness, and clarity of your mind. This is the unconditioned state, beyond thought, beyond concepts. The guru who shows you this mind so that you see it for an instant is the true guru. It's difficult to make that connection, but it's not impossible. In the meantime, however, we can manage quite well for quite a long time without having such an intense relationship. We can manage by receiving occasional teachings and instructions from the hands of visiting lamas who are qualified and who inspire confidence. It is not necessary for this lama to be our lama for our lifetime. We have devotion toward the lama, and that will suffice in the meantime. It is necessary to have devotion toward a lama because when we do Vajrayana practice, there is always a lama at the center. We can't pretend to have devotion. Either we have devotion or we don't.

Personally, I don't think Vajrayana is for everybody. I also think that if you are going to follow the Vajrayana path, unless you are prepared to give up everything and go off to do extensive retreats, it is important to keep the practice simple. Several lamas have remarked to me how difficult it is for them. As lineage holders they have to study many different practices, but they never really get the time to observe and digest any one practice fully. They all agree that the real way to success is to concentrate on and keep at one simple practice that is meaningful to you.

One of the advantages of Tibetan Buddhism is that it's like a big spiritual supermarket. If we go into Zen meditation, we are told, "This is the way we meditate." If you don't go along with that, you have to go somewhere else. If you go to a vipassana center, you will be told, "This is how we do vipassana meditation." If you don't like it, it's your bad luck. But in Vajrayana, there are so many practices. There is vipassana, there is Zen-like meditation, there is study, there is the whole panoply of Technicolor Vajrayana visualizations with buddhas and bodhisattvas in every possible color combination. There is something for everybody—peaceful, angry, sort of peaceful, and sort of angry. Male, female, green, red, blue, white, lots of arms and legs, two arms and legs, one head, standing up, sitting down, lying down; any way you want. There is a lot of variety, and everybody can find something to practice. When you find something you like and really identify with, then you can stay with that.

Every lama who comes to town will tell you that his or her particular practice is the most special, the most secret, ultimate, highest, unrevealed treasury that's ever been heard of. And you'll think, "Oh, I've got to have that." Then next week somebody else will come along with another one, and you'll finish up completely confused, completely frustrated, and worst of all, completely unrealized! The important thing is not to be too ambitious. We must go back to the foundations. First of all, the motivation. Why are we doing this anyway, what is it all for? Cultivate a compassionate heart, bodhichitta, the aspiration for enlightenment for the sake of other beings. Really get your ethical life together. Deal with nonharming, not lying, refraining from sexual misconduct. We must be realistic. If we are serious about following a spiritual path, we have to get our life together on a very fundamental basis. We must be responsible for our actions and understand what is virtuous and what is nonvirtuous.

First we have to get our fundamental dharma life together. Then we should do a practice that is simple and accessible to us and that we can incorporate into our daily life. Then it can work, and it can be very ful-filling. Then we can really feel things transforming. But we must avoid the pitfall of becoming too ambitious. I know people who go all around the world, taking very high initiations, then end up with all of these commitments. When you take higher initiations, you often have com-mitments. This means that you have to do this practice every day. It might take one or two hours. If you have many such practice commit-ments, you end up with a meditation program of maybe three or four hours. On top of that you have your work, your family, your social life, and this terror that if you don't honor your practice commitments you'll go to hell. What is intended to be a transformation of your life into real meaningfulness and joy then becomes just a heavy burden. I know one lama who told me he had a daily commitment of three hours. If he got up early enough and did it first thing in the morning, he felt great relief. If he didn't, then for the rest of the day he felt he had this heavy burden on him because he knew that at night, when he was exhausted, he would have to do these three hours of practice. Now that is not very helpful, especially for laypeople. My lama always said to me, "Don't undertake big commitments. Keep your practice very small and simple, but do it." This is very good advice. I have always been very clear with lamas when it comes to initiations. Sorry, I am not keeping this commitment. I say this before taking the initiation, then the lama can decide whether or not it's okay for me to take it. Usually, the lama says it's okay.

It is easy to get sucked into undertaking all of these commitments. It's another kind of dharma greed. You don't want to miss anything. The point is that in Vajrayana it is important to know your teacher and your path. We should keep it as simple as possible but do it. It should be enough to challenge us but not so much that it overwhelms us. We must be able to continue it and integrate it more and more into our lives, our relationships, and our work, until there is no separation between prac-tice time and everyday life.

Sharon Salzberg

CｈÖＧＹＡＭ Tｒｕｎｇｐａ Rｉｎｐｏｃｈｅ was the first practicing Buddhist with whom Sharon Salzberg ever had personal contact. In 1970 she attended a talk he gave in Buffalo, New York, and afterward he invited people to submit written questions. By chance, Salzberg's was the first that he selected from the stack, and he read it aloud with his British accent: "In a few days I am leaving for India to study Buddhism. Do you have any recommendations as to where I should go?" For a moment the rinpoche was silent. "In this matter," he finally said, "you had perhaps best follow the pretense of accident."

For months, however, it seemed that accident would only lead Salzberg to frustration. Nonetheless, she persevered and eventually made her way to Bodhgaya, where—almost as soon as she arrived—she met an old man wearing burgundy robes. He was by the Bodhi Tree, and he offered Salzberg one of its seeds, indicating with gestures that she should eat it. So she did—without hesitating or thinking about the symbolism. Only later did she learn that this ragged, unassuming man was Khunu Rinpoche, an accomplished scholar and practitioner who counted the Dalai Lama as one of his students. Khunu Rinpoche invited Salzberg to sit down with him, and in his presence she saw the possibility of defining herself by something more than the sorrow she'd faced in her young life. Then this feeling bore fruit in the meditation retreat that Salzberg had come to Bodhgaya to attend.

S. N. Goenka was the teacher, and Salzberg had a profound connection with him. While he was teaching, she felt he was speaking directly to her—his words going straight to her heart. Yet, as she describes it, her faith wasn't blind. It was, rather, a "bright faith." Healing and commonsensical, it allowed her to surrender cynicism and apathy and to sit through days of discomfort during meditation practice. Her back ached, her knees throbbed, and even worse her mind swirled with long-buried grief and anger. Then a significant shift occurred. At times the pain lifted and she felt a lightness and clarity, which showed her something entirely new about herself.

Salzberg went on to spend the next several years engaged in intensive study with highly respected Buddhist teachers before returning to the United States, where she herself began teaching vipassana (insight) meditation. In 1976 Salzberg, along with Joseph Goldstein and Jack Kornfield, established the Insight Meditation Society (IMS) in Barre, Massachusetts. Then in 1989 she and Joseph Goldstein expanded their vision by founding the Barre Center for Buddhist Studies. Today Salzberg is celebrated as the best-selling author of various books, including *Lovingkindness: The Revolutionary Art of Happiness* and *A Heart as Wide as the World: Stories on the Path of Lovingkindness.*

The Journey of Faith

EACH OF US tells ourself some kind of story about who we are and what our life is about. Our theme might be the pursuit of money, sex, or prestige; it might center on love or spirituality. Some of us figure as a hero in the story, some as an antihero. Our story might be picaresque, romantic, or tragic. We might frame ourselves as optimists or pessimists, winners or losers. How we interpret our own experiences gives rise to the narratives to which we dedicate our lives. Some stories weave the fragments of our experience into a greater whole in a way that reveals relationship and connection. Other stories lock us into the fragments, leaving us nowhere to turn.

As is the case for many, the story I told myself for years was that I didn't deserve to be happy. Throughout my childhood, I believed that something must be intrinsically wrong with me because things never seemed to change for the better. My father, whom I adored, disappeared when I was four, and my mother and I moved in with my aunt and uncle. One night when I was nine years old, my mother and I were home alone. She had recently undergone surgery and seemed to be recovering well. In celebration of her return, I was wearing my ballerina Halloween costume. We were sitting close together on the couch, watching her favorite singer, Nat King Cole, on television, when suddenly she began bleeding violently. I ran out into the hallway to get someone to help us but couldn't find anyone. My mother managed to tell me to call an ambulance immediately and then to call my grandmother, whom I hardly knew, to come get me. Shaking uncontrollably, I complied. After that evening, I never saw her again. About two weeks later she died in the hospital. After that I lived with my father's parents and rarely heard mention of my mother again.

My childhood continued to unfold through terrifying, uprooting turns and incomprehensible losses. When I was eleven my grandfather died, and one day my father returned. The handsome prince I'd secretly imagined had been replaced by a disheveled, hard-bitten, troubled stranger. A few days after he arrived, my entire body broke out in hives. When I got back from the doctor's office, my father told me, "You have to be tough to be able to survive life." Six weeks later he took an overdose of sleeping pills. I stood outside in the cold, holding my grandmother's hand among a crowd of gawking neighbors as he was carried out on a stretcher. I watched as the flashing red lights receded and the sirens faded. Now both of my parents had been spun away from me in the back of an ambulance. That night my father entered the mental health system. He was never able to function outside of it again.

One of the hardest parts of all the loss and dislocation was that it was surrounded by an ambient, opaque silence about what was happening. Because no one spoke openly or even acknowledged all the changes as loss, my immense grief, anger, and confusion remained held inside. Whenever the cover slipped, I scrambled to hide the feelings, or distort them, so no one would really know, especially not me. When John Kennedy was assassinated, I couldn't stop crying. My grandmother asked me why, and I replied, simply, "Because his children have lost their father."

The story I was telling myself was that what I felt didn't matter anyway. It seems as if I spent most of my childhood, and even my teenage years, curled up in bed, lost in a separate shadowed existence built of sadness. I repeatedly invented scenarios of having parents just like anybody else. The dream of answering, just like anybody else, the schoolteacher's question, "What does your father do for a living?" was the kindling that fed the fire of many of my secret fantasies. I'd summon images of my mother coming back, as though from a long trip, like anyone else's mother might. But I wasn't at all like anybody else seemed to be. Of course, none of them were like they seemed either, but I didn't know that then. Feeling so different, I liked playing it safe more than anything, seeing life from a distance, never really engaging, preferring to lose myself in the seductive play of listlessness.

While silent dreams and desires played out within me, in most situations I'd insist with bravado, "I didn't want that anyway." When I lived with my grandparents, color television was just becoming the rage. I longed for one, but they couldn't afford it. To compensate, my grand-mother, who cared a lot about me, bought a special plastic sheet to place over the black-and-white screen to create a faint illusion of color. This rainbow aura bore no relationship to the figures and settings of the stories depicted in the programs. I wanted to rip off that bizarre front and plead for the real thing; instead I silently tolerated the charade, not betraying my desire. I didn't care about anything, or so I hoped it seemed. I came to know very well the protection of distance, of a nar-rowed, compressed world. Though it was my own act of pulling back, I felt forsaken. I told myself a story that there was no way out of the world that turned me in upon myself.

Years later, as an adult, I would find the phrase that perfectly described my dilemma. Some friends and I had rented a house near the ocean where we could practice meditation on our own for a few days. In my designated bedroom I found a *Peanuts* comic strip on the desk, which went something like this: Lucy is sitting in a little booth, a DOCTOR IS IN sign prominently displayed. She tells Charlie Brown, "You know what your problem is, Charlie Brown? The problem with you is that you're you." Crushed, Charlie Brown asks, "Well, what in the world can I do about that?" Lucy responds in the final frame, "I don't pretend to be able to give advice. I merely point out the problem."

"The problem with you is that you're you" was a very familiar phrase—the "me that was me" was someone I had often considered a problem. Many of us seem to have an internalized Lucy who tells us that our problem is who we are and that there is no way out, little reason to have faith in ourselves or in the possibility of turning our lives around.

In fact, until I was eighteen, Lucy ruled. My resistance to participat-ing more fully in life came to feel like the most alive, vibrant thing about me. I often found myself, in many endeavors, not really trying because I was secretly sure that I'd fail. I'd learned well to hold life in abeyance. For years I hardly spoke. I barely allowed myself a full-blown emo-tion—no anger, no joy. My whole life was an effort to balance on the edge of what felt like an eroding cliff where I was stranded. I was waiting, suspended. Though it mimics death, waiting isn't necessarily death's prelude but might rather be the life force conserving itself. When I was a child, my favorite animal was a caterpillar, never a dog or a cat, and somehow never a butterfly. Like the body being cooled down before surgery to slow its vital functions, my very life depended on stepping out of time and expectation, depended on waiting for . . . *something*.

At sixteen I entered the State University of New York at Buffalo, feeling as lost and afraid as ever. By this time the smooth, monochromatic shelter of abeyance, which had once saved me, was now engulfing me. I was slowly being forced to wake up out of my slumber. Having to choose an academic major confronted me with defining what I wanted out of life. Just that one choice provoked the uncertainty and risk of discovering what it might mean to be alive. Sometimes I thought of majoring in history, sometimes in philosophy. I heard that the Asian Studies Department offered a philosophy class on Buddhism, and I enrolled.

One of the Buddha's basic teachings is that because we are born, we experience suffering—not only suffering as grave pain but also suffering as the instability, the sorrow, the hollowness of life. Sometimes the distress is simply dissatisfaction that things don't go the way we wish they would. Sometimes the discomfort is minor; sometimes the pain is unspeakable. When I heard this first noble truth, I knew it to be true. The circumstances of my own life proclaimed it.

The second noble truth talks about the causes of suffering as ignorance and attachment. I wasn't too sure what attachment meant but figured I might understand by the end of the semester. The teaching about ignorance of who we are was intriguing. The second noble truth says that we look at our personal histories, our bodies, our thoughts and feelings, and we conclude, "That's who I am." But when we look to these things to know who we actually are, we become consumed and exhausted. Within ten minutes we might see sadness, amusement, anger, kindness; we might feel physical pleasure, then discomfort, then relief, then apprehension as the discomfort emerges again. We might see ourselves as powerful one moment, powerless the next. As our thoughts and feelings and sensations shift and change, any superficial idea of who we are unravels. We may strive mightily to hold it together, because we fear being nothing, being nowhere. As long as we are ignorant of what lies below our surface identifications, the teachings say we will be unhappy.

Is there a way out? The third noble truth affirms that without reservation. This truth is described in different ways: as wisdom that understands fully the nature of life; as liberation from distorted concepts of who we think we are by seeing clearly who we actually are; as boundless, unimpeded love for ourselves and all others without exception; as experience of that which lies beyond our conditioning, that which frees us from suffering.

The meditation techniques developed by the sages of old, embedded in the fourth noble truth, were said to be the way to achieve this liberation. All of this suggested a radically different way to tell a life story—the way the Buddha told it. In commenting on the power of a story to give our lives cohesion, writer Hannah Arendt says, "The story reveals the meaning of what otherwise would remain an unbearable sequence of sheer happenings." To perceive the events of our lives as "sheer happenings" is indeed unbearable. I was about to explore a story that would take the scattered shards of my life and fit them all together in a new and different way.

The Buddha's story is about freedom from suffering. It is a way out of Charlie Brown's problem. A way to trust our immense potential instead of that belittling Lucy voice. I was captivated by the possibility of turning my life around, of lifting it out of the resignation and sorrow that had been the background notes of my own personal story. Some inner knowing of what I had been waiting for was stirred.

The pivotal point of the Buddha's story is his enlightenment. Siddhartha Gautama, born an Indian prince, was a bodhisattva: he aspired to become a buddha, an awakened one, so that he could help relieve all beings of suffering. After years of trying various methods to purify his mind and attain understanding, he sat down under a tree one night, determined not to move until he was free of all confusion, all ignorance, and all limitation. While he sat deep in meditation, he was attacked by the legendary figure Mara—killer of virtue, killer of life. With enticing and lustful visions, with ferocious rain and hailstorms, with vile images, Mara attempted to dissuade him from his course. But through it all, Siddhartha sat tranquilly.

It is significant that Mara's ultimate attack was on the bodhisattva's faith in his own potential. In essence Mara said, "Who do you think you are to be sitting there with that immense aspiration? What makes you think you can actually be enlightened?" This was Lucy in the voice of Mara. In response to that challenge, the bodhisattva reached his hand down and touched the earth, asking it to bear witness to all the lifetimes in which he had practiced generosity and morality, loving-kindness and wisdom. He asked the earth to bear witness to his right to be sitting there, his right to aspire to full understanding and infinite compassion. As the legend goes, when the bodhisattva touched the ground, the earth shook, testifying to his right to be free. With that, Mara was vanquished and fled. The bodhisattva sat through the rest of the night in deep meditation, and with the rising of the first morning star was enlightened.

In this story is the Buddha's promise that freeing the mind from habits of anguish and fear is a real and attainable goal, not just for him, not just for a few others, but for everyone who makes the effort. That all beings want to be happy, and in fact deserve to be happy, is emblazoned throughout.

Our ingrained habit of viewing life as though standing with our noses pressed against the bakery window, believing that none of the goodies inside could possibly be for us, runs right up against this boundless, breathtaking inclusivity. The voice of the inner Lucy puts us outside that bakery window, saying, "Life, freedom, happiness, love are for others, not for you." The Buddha holds out his hand, offering to bring us directly inside. Here was a promise that I could finally live unencumbered by the pain of my past. This view of what life could be drew me like a magnet.

In my second year of college, although my life was slowly opening up, the only time I really came alive was for an hour and a half on Tuesdays and Thursdays, in my Asian philosophy class. I found myself beginning to wonder if I might one day be truly happy, even though my family didn't look at all like anything I'd dreamed it should be. Maybe I didn't have to be lonely and afraid forever. Maybe I didn't have to be so pressed down by my circumstances forever. While the repeated disintegration of my family had kept me frightened, this glimmer of possibility kept me alive.

Like a subliminal message being played under the predominant music, a sense of possibility, no matter how faint, drives a wedge between the suffering we may wake up with each day and the hopelessness that can try to move in with us on a permanent basis. It inspires us to envision a better life for ourselves. It is this glimmer of possibility that is the beginning of faith.

When I learned about the school's junior-year-abroad program, I felt strongly attracted. Despite the fact that the only time in my life I had even left New York State was for a short trip to Florida, I felt ready to leave everything I had known and travel to a place about which I knew nothing. I could no longer simply endure, could no longer be half-alive and willing merely to get by. I yearned for embodiment, for a sense of belonging; I yearned to transform the waiting into finally coming alive. I wanted to take up my place in the world.

When I tell people I decided to go to India when I was only eighteen, they often think I knew what I was doing. Once someone remarked, "You must have been such a clear thinker," and I had to reply, in all honesty, "No, in fact, I had only one clear thought," which was that I could solve the "problem" that was me if I learned how to meditate. That one clear thought was enough. It would set me on a journey that would remake my life.

In Pali, the language of the original Buddhist texts, the word usually translated as "faith," "confidence," or "trust" is *saddha*. *Saddha* literally means "to place the heart upon." To have faith is to offer one's heart or give over one's heart. The "unbearable sequence of sheer happenings" that had been my life began to come together in the teachings of the Buddha, and I was ready to place my heart upon those teachings. Perhaps I already had. The promise of happiness had touched a place within me so deep and unknown that what it had awakened there was wild, inchoate, primal. I recognize that now as the stirring of faith.

In Pali, faith is a verb, an action, as it is also in Latin and Hebrew. Faith is not a singular state that we either have or don't have but is something that we do. We "faithe." Saddha is the willingness to take the next step, to see the unknown as an adventure, to launch a journey. Writer and philosopher John O'Donohue holds up the story of Aeneas, hero of Virgil's epic poem about the founding of Rome, as an archetypal journey of faith. When Aeneas flees the battle of Troy, he has no idea of where he is going or what lies before him. On his way to do one thing, he finds himself, blown by storm and fortune, doing another. His ships and crew are battered, plundered, attacked, but guided by a faint yet compelling sense of mission, Aeneas again and again faces the unknown. Only when he has the courage to step into the darkness, as O'Donohue depicts it, does the light to guide him to the next step reveal itself.

Often it is the journey itself, not the destination, that is the real point of setting forth. For me, the journey from the isolation of my early life to the doorway of freedom has been the unfolding of my faith, because I had to be willing, like Aeneas, to keep moving forward, even when I felt I was walking in the dark. With faith we move into the unknown, openly meeting whatever the next moment brings. Faith is what gets us out of bed, gets us on an airplane to an unknown land, opens us to the possibility that our lives can be different. Though we may repeatedly stumble, afraid to move forward in the dark, we have the strength to take that magnitude of risk because of faith.

The first step on the journey of faith is to recognize that everything is moving onward to something else, inside us and outside. Seeing this truth is the foundation of faith. Life is transition, movement, and growth. However solid things may appear on the surface, everything in life is changing, without exception. Even Mount Everest—the perfect symbol of indomitable, unyielding, massively solid reality—is "growing" a quarter of an inch a year, as the landmass of India pushes under Asia. People come and go in our lives; possessions break or change; governments and whole systems of government are established or disintegrate. Eager anticipation precedes a meal, which soon ends. A relationship is difficult and disappointing, then transforms into a bond we trust. We might feel frightened in the morning, reassured in the afternoon, and uneasy at night. We know that at the end of our lives we die. There is change, breath, oscillation, and rhythm everywhere.

With faith we can draw near to the truth of the present moment, which is dissolving into the unknown even as we meet it. We open up to what is happening right now in all of its mutability and evanescence. A pain in our body, a heartache, an unjust treatment may seem inert, impermeable, unchanging. It may appear to be all that is, all that ever will be. But when we look closely, instead of solidity, we see porousness, fluidity, motion. We begin to see gaps between the moments of suffering. We see the small changes that are happening all the time in the texture, the intensity, the contours of our pain.

No matter what is happening, whenever we see the inevitability of change, the ordinary, or even oppressive, facts of our lives can become alive with prospect. We see that a self-image we've been holding doesn't need to define us forever; the next step is not the last step; what life was is not what it is now and certainly not what it might yet be.

Some years ago, when I was teaching meditation at a federal women's prison in California, one of the inmates observed, "When you're in prison, it's especially important to try to live in the present moment. It's easy to get lost in the past, which you can't change anyway, or to get lost hoping for the future, which is not yet here. If you do that, it's like you're not really alive." Then she paused and looked at me, her eyes shining, and said, "I choose life."

Such faith is not superficial or sentimental. It doesn't say everything will turn out all right. As we all know, as I knew profoundly by the time I was eighteen, a lot of times things don't turn out "all right," according to our wishes, according to our demands or ideas of how they should. Life is not likely to deliver only pleasant events. Faith entails the understanding that we don't know how things will unfold. Even so, faith allows us to claim the possibility that we ourselves might change in ways that will allow us to recognize and trust the helping hands stretched toward us. It enables us to aspire to a better life than the one we have inherited.

Without faith in change we would be compelled to repeat patterns of suffering—like an abused child who grows up to find an abusive partner, at least reassured by being able to predict mortification and pain. Without a sense of possibility, we would be stuck—isolated, hopeless, and unspeakably sad.

Faith is the animation of the heart that says, "I choose life, I align myself with the potential inherent in life, I give myself over to that potential." This spark of faith is ignited the moment we think, *I'm going to go for it. I'm going to try.*

I once asked a psychiatrist friend what he considered the single most compelling force for healing in the psychotherapeutic relationship. "Love," he replied. I agreed with him about the transforming power of love but wondered if there wasn't something else even more fundamental. "For all we know," I suggested, "what is most important to healing in therapy is that people show up for their appointments." The therapist's love can nurture healing, but it is our own faith in that possibility that impels us to show up and take each new step into the darkness.

To seize such possibility for myself, I first had to reach within the lassitude coiled tightly around my heart and begin transforming how I felt about my heart and about myself. I had to give up my protective distance, alter my habit of withdrawal, and learn to participate, engage, link up. I had to acknowledge that underneath my facade of indifference, I cared, and in fact cared a lot. I cared about what happened to me and what happened to others. I cared about life.

I stepped onto the spiritual path moved by an inner sense that I might find greatness of heart, that I might find profound belonging, that I might find a hidden source of love and compassion. Like a homing instinct for freedom, my intuitive sense that this was possible was the faint, flickering, yet undeniable expression of faith.

———————

Living Our Love

With an eye made quiet by the power
Of harmony, and the deep power of joy,
We see into the life of things.

—*William Wordsworth*

WE ONCE BROUGHT one of our teachers to the United States from India. After he had been here for some time, we asked him for his perspective on our Buddhist practice in America. While he was mostly very positive about what he saw, one critical thing stood out. Our teacher said that those practicing here in the West sometimes reminded him of people in a rowboat. They row and row and row with great earnestness and effort, but they neglect to untie the boat from the dock. He said he noticed people striving diligently for powerful meditative experiences—wonderful transcendence, going beyond space, time, body, and mind—but not seeming to care so much about how they relate to others in a day-to-day way. How much compassion do they express toward the plumber who is late or the child who makes a mess? How much kindness? How much presence? The path may lead to many powerful and sublime experiences, but the path begins here with our daily interactions with each other.

All living beings, all of us, want to be happy, yet so few have any idea about how to realize this desire. This fact is said to be the inspiration behind the Buddha's decision to teach the dharma. When he looked around the world, he saw beings with this desire for happiness doing over and over again, in their ignorance, the very things that were bringing them suffering.

Once the Buddha did decide to offer the teachings, he began by teaching people to be generous and to be very careful about what they say and do. If we want to enjoy happiness, taking the care to be ethical is a cardinal means for that aspiration. The Buddha taught that if the heart is full of love and compassion, which is the inner state, the outer manifestation is care and connectedness, which is morality; they are both aspects of the same radiance.

Ethical conduct—*sila* in Pali—is, along with generosity, the necessary foundation for liberation. It is the beginning of the path and is also one of the path's great fruits and culminations. The Buddha taught moral conduct as the source of true beauty, more fundamental than any relative, conventional, or transitory sense of beauty.

Moral conduct is the reflection of our deepest love, concern, and care. The Buddha once said that if we truly loved ourselves, we would never harm another, because we are all interconnected. To protect another is to protect oneself. To protect oneself is to protect another. Sila works on all levels of our relationships: our relationship to ourselves, to other people, and to the environment around us.

Everything is interwoven. The things we do, the things we think about, the things we care about, all make a difference in the totality we are part of. If we want to quiet our minds, to bring our lives into spiritual truth, to see into the life of things, we need to live in harmony.

There is no way to disregard our behavior and then sit down in a formal posture on a meditation cushion and experience freedom, because each part of our life is thoroughly intermeshed with every other part. That is why we consider what the Buddha called "right livelihood" an intrinsic aspect of the liberating path. We cannot engage for eight hours a day in work that involves lying, for example, or harming in some other way, and also feel whole within, unfragmented, when we undertake spiritual practice. Thus we need to look to all of life, to our relationship to all beings, in our aspiration to be free.

The Buddha was an example of a fully integrated being. Compassion, honesty, and wisdom were true for him whether he was alone or among others, wandering or staying still. We have the possibility for just such wholeness and integrity in ourselves as well. We attain it through the practice of sila.

Sila, ethical conduct, rests on aspiring to fulfill certain commitments. Traditionally, laypeople in our Buddhist tradition undertake the practice of honoring five basic precepts of conduct:

1. to refrain from killing or physical violence;

2. to refrain from stealing, or taking that which is not given;

3. to refrain from sexual misconduct, or using our sexual energy in a way that causes harm;

4. to refrain from lying, from harsh speech, from idle speech, and from slander;

5. to refrain from taking intoxicants that cloud the mind and cause heedlessness.

Many of us consider ourselves good-hearted people. In fact, I am sure that many of us are indeed good-hearted. So when we hear or read a teaching about morality and reflect on these five basic precepts, many of us feel that as a matter of course we might not kill, steal, rape, slander, or hang out in crack houses. However, I have found in my own life that it is possible to continually refine my understanding of and commitment to these precepts. Honoring them is actually a profound and subtle practice. As we practice them, we discover more and more deeply the levels of strength and protection the precepts can give us.

For example, most of us feel very deeply the gravity of killing other humans because we feel a sense of connection to what it is to be human; we know the value of human life because we value our own lives. But it is not so easy for us to know and feel our oneness with other forms of life.

We tend to hold the view that the value of life increases according to the size of the being. So we encounter something like a fly and find it easy to kill. When we do not recognize some sense of connection to a fly, it is very easy to do. But is life as it appears in a fly so very different from life as it appears in a human? Does our feeling of separateness from other life-forms actually bring us joy and a sense of wholeness?

If we look carefully and deeply, we can see quite clearly the oneness of all living beings. The Buddha taught that all beings want to be happy. Every single creature of every type and form of life wants to experience happiness. As we come to understand deeply this profound commonality, our relationship to killing of any kind quite naturally changes, and our understanding of the first precept becomes more refined.

To refrain from stealing also has greater implications. It not only means to accept only that which has been offered but also implies being careful with our resources. If we are so lost in grasping that we are ready to steal, then we are viewing other people, other demands, or other responsibilities simply as obstacles to our fulfillment. We would just as soon push them away in order to get what we want. There is an echo of this feeling of competition and separation even when we are only taking a little of someone's toothpaste or shampoo without asking. Look at what is happening in your mind if you find yourself in that situation— you actually feel quite disconnected from others. A yet more refined understanding of this precept melts barriers of division and exclusivity, reminding us that this entire planet is interdependent and that we have to share its resources.

There is a collection of stories in the Pali literature known as Jataka tales, which are Indian folk stories that depict the previous lives of the Buddha as the Bodhisattva, before his enlightenment. One is about a king who one day offered half of his kingdom and the hand of his daughter in marriage to any man who could steal something without anyone at all finding out about it. This announcement was proclaimed throughout the land, and many young men started showing up with various items. Somebody would come up and say, "I have this ruby necklace that I stole, and nobody knows about it." The king would say, "No, forget it." Somebody else would come up and say, "I have this splendid chariot and I stole it and nobody knows about it." The king would again say, "Sorry, forget it." Everybody got quite confused, until one day a young man showed up with nothing. He said, "I don't have anything at all." The king said, "Well, why not?" The man said, "It is not really possible to steal something with absolutely *nobody* knowing about it, because I myself would always know about it." This was the right answer. The king had been looking for an heir with wisdom.

We always do know, even if at the time we are acting we do not fully register the fact that we have caused harm; we have planted a seed of pain for ourselves or for others. Somehow we have diminished ourselves and our deepest happiness of connection.

We see the same principle in the precept concerning sexual misconduct. One of my favorite sayings of Sayadaw U Pandita is "Lust cracks the brain." All too often, people will sacrifice love, family life, career, or friendship to satisfy sexual craving. Abiding happiness is given up for temporary pleasure, and a great deal of suffering ensues when we are willing to cause pain to satisfy our desires. Stories abound of adultery, abuse, exploitation, and obsession. These stories illustrate how often our sexual energy is used in harmful ways.

A friend was once at a community meeting at which a member was being rather self-righteously denounced for sexual misconduct. My friend's comment was, "Who in this room has never made a fool of themselves over sex?" In fact, no one raised a hand. Sexuality is a very powerful force. A mature spirituality demands that we, without self-righteousness, commit to not harming ourselves or others through our sexual energy.

We try not to harm others physically, which means not killing, harming through sexuality, or being abusive or exploitive. We also try not to harm others verbally, seeing that our speech has tremendous power. Words do not just leave our mouths and disappear; they have great effects in this world. We particularly attempt not to lie, because of the delusion that gets generated.

I had an experience some years ago that I think perfectly illustrates the delusion that arises from not telling the truth. At the time, I was living in a house with some friends, and another friend of ours who lived nearby decided to go to India to practice meditation. Because she knew that her mother would worry, she did not want her to know that she was going alone. So she lied by telling her mother that her husband was going to India too, when in fact he was not. She also gave her mother the number at our house to call if any emergency should come up.

About twenty-four hours before my friend was due home from India, her mother called us to ask, "Have you heard from my daughter or her husband?" The person who answered the phone did not remember the lie in that moment, so he blurted out, "Oh yes, her husband was just here for dinner." When he realized what he had done, he tried to set things right by telling another lie. He said, "You know, he went to India with her, but he had a business meeting and came back early for it."

Right away our friend's mother knew that something was wrong, that she was not being told the truth. She panicked. "What aren't you telling me? She's sick, she's very sick, she's beyond sick! What's going on?" My housemate said, "No, no, she's fine. She'll be home in another day."

A few minutes after that phone call, another friend called and said, "Do you know who just called me? Our friend's mother." This woman was so ill at ease about what she had been told that she started calling around the community to see if someone would tell her the truth about her daughter. Now we thought that we had better call everybody before she did so that we could instruct them as to what lie to tell.

At one point someone none of us knew called. It turned out that the mother had enlisted a neighbor, thinking that if we would not tell her the truth, we might tell someone else the truth. Then we had to call everybody again to alert them about another person who might call and which lies to tell.

Right in the middle of this whole episode, we began receiving anonymous obscene phone calls. Normally with such calls we would have just stopped answering the phone. But we had to answer because someone might call about the situation with our friend's mother, and we had to be ready to tell the person the right lie!

Finally one of our friends just gave up. She could not bear it anymore. The next time she talked to our friend's mother, she said, "You're right, we haven't been telling you the truth. This is the truth: the husband never went to India. Your daughter went alone. She's fine. She'll be home in a day."

Two interesting things happened at that point. First, the mother had been lied to so much that she did not believe the truth when she heard it. The other thing was that *I* saw in my own mind that I had told so many lies by then that I did not know what was true anymore. Confusion reigned. "Did he go to India? What's going on?" I began to see, once again, the power of truth and what it means for another or for oneself to deny that power. In the light of seeing the effects of untruthfulness, we can make a commitment to truthfulness.

One of the points of the precepts is to minimize delusion in all of its forms. The last precept is about not taking substances that cloud our mind or cause heedlessness. This concept has been the source of a lot of debate for Westerners. What does it mean to "cloud the mind and cause heedlessness"? What about one little drink if I do not get drunk? I can generally understand such questions. We are each exploring what such commitments would mean, trying to find the balance, the Middle Way that is uniquely right for us at each particular moment in our unfolding.

When I began working with Sayadaw U Pandita, someone asked him about the precept regarding intoxicants: "Is there ever a time when it is all right to have a drink?" I think the question was asked with either the expectation or the hope that U Pandita's answer would be "Well, it's fine in moderation" or "You can do it in a social occasion when it would hurt someone's feelings if you did not accept a drink, or when you're visiting your grandmother and she offers you a glass of wine." The actual answer was "If someone ties you down and pours it down your throat, and you don't enjoy it, then it's all right to have a drink."

I heard that answer and thought, "That's a little extreme!" However, on the strength of U Pandita's words, I later thought, "Who am I just to dismiss what he said? Why not consider it with some humility and take it to heart?" So I decided that, as an experiment, for a period of time I was not going to take a drink. For several years after that decision, I did not drink any alcohol.

It is quite interesting to me that I clearly felt something different as a result of this experiment, which became a part of my practice. I felt as if I had laid something to rest. There was some new clarity and strength, however subtle. I did not feel self-righteous about it and did not go around telling people, "Put down that glass of wine!" or anything like that. It was something inside, a kind of delight I felt within. I felt simpler, stronger, clearer, more confident; I felt more self-respect.

It is very simple but significant in working with these precepts to take the risk of trying such experiments. We find that we can continually refine our understanding of them and can enjoy a deepening sense of radiance and happiness through our attention to them.

Don't I Know You?

A FRIEND ONCE told me about repeated fights he had with his wife early on in their marriage. Much of their conflict centered on how to have dinner. He liked to eat hurriedly, standing up in the kitchen, getting it over with as quickly as possible. She liked to set the table elegantly, sit down and eat leisurely, together. Many nights they fought instead of eating. Finally they sought the help of a marriage counselor.

As they examined the layers of meaning hidden in the simple and familiar word *dinner,* they each discovered how many associations, and how many people, they were actually bringing to that table. He talked about his father, a brutal man who was often at home only at dinnertime, which became a nightmarish experience to be escaped from as quickly as possible. She spoke of her fractured family and her mentally ill brother who consumed her mother with worry. It was mainly at dinner that her family made an effort to talk to *her*, to find out about her day—where she felt she indeed belonged to a family.

For both of them dinner was rarely just dinner, and their partner was often not the person standing in front of them but an "other" made of an amalgam of past hurts and long-held dreams and tentative new yearnings.

Can we ever actually see another person? If we create an "other" out of our projections and associations and ready interpretations, we have made an object of a person; we have taken away his or her humanity. We have stripped from our consciousness the person's own sensitivity to pain, the person's likely wish to feel at home in his or her body and mind, the person's complexity and intricacy and mutability.

If we have lost any recognition of the truth of change in someone and have fixed the person in our mind as "good" or "bad" or "indifferent," we've lost touch with the living essence of that person. We are dwelling in a world of stylized prototypes and distant caricatures, reified images, and, often, very great loneliness.

Meditation practice is like a skills training in stepping back, in getting a broader perspective and a deeper understanding of what's happening. Mindfulness, one of the tools at the core of meditation, helps us not to be lost in habitual biases that distort how we interpret our feelings. Without mindfulness, our perception is easily shaped by barely conscious thoughts, such as, "I'm shaking and my stomach is roiling with what seems to be fear, but I can never allow myself to admit that. I'll pretend it never came up." If we do that, it is a great struggle to be kind. There is no ready access to kindness without awareness.

Mindfulness also helps us to see through our prejudices about another person. For example, a person might think, "All older women are fuzzy thinkers, so she can't possibly be as sharp as she is pretending to be." Mindfulness helps us to see by showing us that a conclusion such as that one is simply a thought in our own mind. Mindfulness enables us to cultivate a different quality of attention, one where we relate to what we see before us not just as an echo of the past or a foreshadowing of the future but more as it is right now. Here too we find the power of kindness because we can connect to things as they are.

Making the effort to truly see someone doesn't mean we never respond or react. We can and do attempt to restore a failing marriage or protest at loud cell phones in public places or try with everything in us to rectify injustice. But we can do it from a place that allows people to be as textured as they are, that admits our feelings to be as varied and flowing as they are, that is open to surprises—a place that listens, that lets the world come alive.

One essential step in learning to see each other more genuinely is to bother to look. If someone yells at us or annoys us or dazzles us with a gift, we do pay attention to the person. Our challenge then is to see this person as he or she is, not as we project or assume the person to be. But if this person doesn't make much of an impression on us, we have a different challenge: it is all too easy to look right through him or her.

In particular, the meditation exercise of offering loving-kindness (*metta*) to a neutral person confronts our tendency to look through people we do not know. We choose a person whom we don't strongly like or dislike; we feel, indeed, rather neutral or indifferent toward the person. Very often it helps to select a near stranger or someone who plays a certain role or function in our lives—the checkout person in the grocery store, for example, or the UPS delivery person. We may not know much about the person, not even his or her name.

When we send a neutral person loving-kindness, we are consciously changing a pattern of overlooking the person, or talking around him or her, to one of paying attention to the person. The experiment in attention we are making through these benevolent wishes asks of us whether we can practice loving "thy neighbor as thyself" when we don't know the facts about someone's dependent, elderly parent or at-risk teenager, and so our heartstrings have not been tugged.

When we think of our neutral person, we haven't learned the story of his or her suspicious mole or empty evenings. We have no knowledge of the person's inspiring triumphs or admirable philanthropy, and so we are not in awe of him or her. We aren't seeing the person's tension after a disappointing job interview or sadness after his or her lover leaves. We practice wishing the person well anyway, not knowing any of this, but simply because the person exists and because we do know the beauty, the sorrow, the poignancy, and the sheer, unalterable insecurity of existence that we all share.

On trains and on the streets, and in our homes and in our communities, we practice paying attention—through developing mindfulness, through developing loving-kindness, through letting go of projections—because a more complete attention proffers many special gifts. These gifts can penetrate through the exigencies of social roles, through the seeming hollowness of chance encounters, and even through terrible hurt.

Paying attention in this way provides the gift of noticing, the gift of connecting. We find the gift of seeing a little bit of ourselves in others, of realizing that we're not so awfully alone. We can let go of the burden of so much of what we habitually carry with us and receive the gift of the present moment.

Through paying attention, we learn that even when we don't especially know or like someone, we are nonetheless in relationship with the person. We come to realize that this relatedness is in itself like a vibrant, changing, living entity. We discover the gift of caring, of tending to this force of life that exists between us, and we are immeasurably enriched by that.

Maurine Stuart

NOT ONLY WAS she one of the first female Zen masters in the United States, Maurine Stuart was also the mother of three, an accomplished concert pianist, and a piano teacher.

"Maurine had a full, balanced life," says her student Trudy Goodman, who is now the guiding teacher of InsightLA. "She modeled that it's possible to do intensive spiritual practice while living as a laywoman and still do your hair and joke about new lipstick. I did very deep practice with her."

Stuart delighted in nature, literature, dance, food, film, and driving. According to her student and editor Roko Sherry Chayat, "She drove fast, with a single-minded intensity that brooked no interference no matter what the elements, what the traffic." Chayat has written, "Despite her respect for the traditional forms of Zen, a respect natural to one whose entire life was engaged in the demanding discipline of music, Maurine's teaching, like her life, was never circumscribed by ritual or convention."

"Maurine was not someone who needed to impress or dazzle anybody with her understanding," says Zen priest and cookbook author Edward Espe Brown. "She was simply intent on awakening others to what was already theirs."

In February 1990, Maurine Stuart Roshi passed away from cancer. Her last words were "Wonderful peace. Nobody there."

There Are No Repetitions

WHAT IS THE condition of our minds right now? How are our hearts? This moment is all we have—so at this moment, how creative are we, how in touch with the source are we?

We need courage to be creative. To be sensitive and aware requires great courage. This word *courage* comes from the same root as the French word *coeur*, which means heart. So please have the courage to listen to your heart, to your body, your *hara*, not just to your head. You will discover new ways to experience your life.

We are always at the beginning. It is always the very first time. Truly, there are no repetitions. When I play the piano, I often come to a repeat sign. Can that passage be repeated? If I am teaching a piano student and we see a repeat sign, I tell the student that there are no repeats. We return to the beginning of a certain passage, but it's never the same. It's always fresh. Someone asked me, "Don't you get tired of answering the same questions day after day—what is Zen, how do we practice?" Never! It's never the same question, because it's always coming from a different person, in a different moment; and each person asks the question from his or her own state of mind. The words may sound alike, but each time they are coming from somewhere unique.

What is *zazen*? Hui-neng defined zazen this way: "In the midst of all good and evil, not a thought is aroused in the mind. This is called 'za.' Seeing into one's self-nature and not being moved at all, this is called 'zen.'" We sometimes say za is just to sit cross-legged, but it means more than that; it means to sit with no discriminating consciousness, no dualistic activity. And *zen* is to wake up to our fundamental self, not to be disturbed by anything—just letting it come, letting it go; in breath, out breath; just here. Allowing the calm, deep breath to penetrate every part of the body, allowing the hara to fill up, we let go of all fixed notions. We let go of "I." We let it all fall off. We are here to discover a way of relating to one another rather than to expound a set of doctrines. With this attitude, our sitting is receptive, alert, awake, open, so that we can hear what the silence has to say. We are letting ourselves be the vehicle for whatever teaching may come our way, not forcing or grabbing at anything.

Because I consider myself an artist, I tend to think in terms of poetry and music, but above all, it is the art of our own life that we are engaged in. The greatness of a poem or a painting is not that it portrays a certain scene or experience but that it shows the artist's vision of his or her own meeting with reality. Hence each thing, each time, is fresh and new. It is never the same place. There are no repetitions. It is not the head or the hand that paints the picture or performs the sonata. One of my teachers gave me a wonderful koan: "Play the piano without using your hands." When we are empty and free, then the brush or the notes move by themselves. This is the source, whether or not we call it Zen, that we are in touch with. Is it done by heaven, or is it our doing? Our doing is heaven's. Our movements are heaven's. If the artist interferes, or if we as artists of our lives interfere with this source through some self-conscious preoccupation, what happens? What is to be expressed gets lost, becomes hard, constrained; there is no true expression. When mind and heart are open, empty, when there is no selfish motivation, then all of one's actions are one with heaven. The spirit flows freely, and we have a heavenly dance.

On loan to us at the Cambridge Buddhist Association for a while was a most extraordinary calligraphy by Soen Nakagawa Roshi. The top character, *human,* was very still. The bottom character was a wonderful swirling energetic character: *heaven-dance.* This heaven-dance comes through all of us when we let go of all of our ego stuff, when we melt down the ego and let this source move freely through us.

In Japanese culture, the creative process is described by words like *ki,* vital energy; *kan,* transcendent intuition; and *myo,* wondrous action. When energy strikes intuition, a wondrous sound emerges. *Myo* also refers to a certain artistic quality not only in works of art but in anything in our lives, in nature. This myo is something original, creative, growing out of one's own consciousness, one's own experience: spontaneous and personal creativity.

We speak of the wonders of nature. Nature is full of myo. Nature is always showing this unfathomable, absolutely inexhaustible myo, and there are many wonderful poets who express this to us. Basho, who was the role model for Soen Nakagawa, who in turn was the great inspiration for my life, wrote wonderful poems of nature, but they are not just nature poems; they richly convey this myo. Here are two examples:

Stillness
penetrates the rocks
cicadas chirp

The temple bell dies away
but the fragrance of flowers resounds—
evening

Such elegance! By the way, this word *elegance* is also used by physicists to describe their discoveries. Basho has given us a glimpse of the source. To come to such elegance, to come to such feeling, doesn't happen by taking some pill or some magic potion but through strong discipline. This is true not only of Zen practitioners but of all great artists. How many times did Beethoven write, rewrite, tear up, sort out all the things that came to his mind, day by day, week by week, month by month, until he finally distilled everything down to the wonderful sound we hear at this point! How many times do artists draw, draw again, over and over again, perfecting their technique so that they can work freely and directly from this source. We can speak very easily about how we should be free, how we should empty our minds, how we should open our hearts, but to do this, we need strong practice. As musicians we practice hour after hour perfecting a phrase so that we may have some freedom of expression when it comes time to give it to someone else. As Zen practitioners we sit in zazen, hour after hour, day after day, year after year, refining our minds and spirits, to come to this elegance, to come to this place where we can be what Rinzai called the true person of no rank, or what Dogen called the primordial person: one who has freely dropped off the ego-self. Basho described this condition in another haiku:

Along this road
goes no one
this autumn evening

We are the no-person person, and at the same time, we are doing what needs to be done, completely, fully, absolutely, concentratedly.

We must be completely present with whatever we are doing—so completely present that there is no separation between it and us. Sitting on the cushion is relatively easy. To take it into everyday life, to be completely mindful of what we are doing, this is more difficult—and essential. We must make our base very strong, like the Daruma doll—no matter how many times he's knocked down, he pops right up again. We are doing mindfulness practice to nourish this fundamental source of our being.

We have this source within us, but we must do our practice over and over and over; sit over and over, do whatever tasks we are engaged in over and over. Yet nothing is repeated. It's hard to keep wide awake, to keep vividly present in the midst of endless repetition. But look at this! Taste this! We may have drunk a million cups of tea, but we have never tasted this one before.

Joan Sutherland

JOAN SUTHERLAND lives in the high desert of northern New Mexico, where from time out of mind, humans have lived by the cycle of wet and dry—the seasons of desiccation punctuated by winter snows and monsoon rains. So even in this modern era, with reservoirs and sewer lines, there is a constant awareness of the presence and absence of water.

Like water, awakening is everywhere, says Sutherland. It's "as sudden and complete as the crash of thunder on a summer afternoon, as promising as a distant smudge of cottonwoods, revealing the presence of water." Yet, she continues, "there are times of drought, too, when the very idea of awakening seems to have dried up under an unrelenting sky. We might think of awakening as something that happens inside us, but, as with a landscape, we also happen inside of it. . . . The fundamental promise of Buddhism is that any of us can awaken. As Buddhism has evolved, it has become clear that awakening is not just an individual matter. We are all in this world together, and we are all awakening together."

Sutherland is the founder of the Awakened Life community, which forms the center of the Open Source, a collaborative network of Zen communities and practitioners in the western United States. She is also a translator from Chinese and Japanese and one of the founders of the Pacific Zen School, a koan school with an innovative, contemporary approach.

Before becoming a Zen teacher, Sutherland worked for nonprofit organizations in the feminist-antiviolence and environmental movements and as a scholar and teacher in the field of archaeomythology.

Given Sutherland's background, it's unsurprising that her teachings have hints of the logic and dense language of academia, but their more predominant flavor is richly lyrical, as evident in the teaching that follows.

Through the Dharma Gate

As I THINK about the shapes and forms that meditative practices take, I keep returning to the afternoon before the fateful night in which a man named Siddhartha would sit under a tree and, at the rising of the morning star, become the Buddha. On that long afternoon, Siddhartha took a bowl, went down to the river, and made a vow: "If this bowl floats upstream, I'll become enlightened before tomorrow dawns." He threw the bowl into the river and bent all of his intention on its journey against the current, against the unceasing tumble of being and doing and becoming, making and unmaking, birth and growth and decay and death—against the unrelenting torrent of stuff and matter, of thought and feeling and sensation, to the source of it all, in its stillness and eternity.

That is the same intention we set as we take up a meditative practice: we throw our bowls into the river, hoping to find its source. And yet we set this intention as embodied beings, in an embodied world of shapes, colors, sounds, tastes, and smells. We begin practice with bodily acts— breathing, postures, gestures, sounds, offerings, rituals. These are accompanied by acts at a subtler level of embodiment, acts of the heart-mind: the stilling of thoughts, mindfulness of sensation and emotion, the contemplation of a koan, visualization, prayer. We trust that the world's radiant, eternal aspect is not outside our experience but an enlargement of it, and so it is with eyes and skin and hearts that we go out to meet it.

The bowl Siddhartha flung into the river did float upstream, but he chose to follow it by turning back toward the world. He bathed in the river, and then he went to sit under a tree. The world came to meet him, to offer its support: he encountered a grass cutter, arms full of soft, fragrant green, who offered him some grass as a cushion.

On that first afternoon there was no formal Buddhist practice yet; there was only Siddhartha's brilliant improvisation in a landscape of river and grass and tree. But over millennia we've added a gate to the landscape: we've created an edifice of meditation made of an architecture of methods. Rather than examine its individual stones, let's look at the gate in its original setting, there by the tree. Let's look at what it's like to sit in its shade, at the place where things come in and out and meet each other.

There is the gate, always in the same place, enduring, unmoving, and yet with an opening that invites things to pass through it. There is the person who comes to sit at the gate, different every time, agreeing to stay put so that those things moving in and out of the gate can find her. The location of the gate—the forms of meditation—is fixed and known, but what will happen there can never be known ahead of time. The experience of sitting at the gate is made up, inseparably, of both what is repeated and what is spontaneous—what can happen only in this moment, in this place, amid these circumstances with what we bring to the gate and what comes through it.

We sit down and gather ourselves. We are creatures of habit, using habit—a particular sitting posture, the smell of incense, the sound of a chant repeated many times—for our benefit, to bring body, heart, and mind together. In gathering ourselves we make ourselves available to be acted upon, to be marked by the worlds, visible and invisible, in which we sit. Available to what comes through the gate.

We're making an offering of ourselves. We're announcing our desire for the deepest meeting of all, the one between the vastness and the individual, between what is without form and what exists as form. We offer ourselves as the place where these two great realities might meet and mix and create something new.

Fortunately for us, people have been making this offering for thousands of years and have developed some good ways to do it. The constancy of forms and their repetition makes a field that holds us until we can hold ourselves. At the very least, we can fall back on forms, just do them no matter how we're feeling, in the same way we can fall back on courtesy when our natural instincts fail us. We can consent to a form and surrender for a while. The poet Adam Zagajewski writes about how the things of the world agree to every minute of the year, every change in season or the weather, so that they can go on living. In meditation each of us acknowledges that we too are things of the world.

Just as the postures of meditation are a way of holding the body still long enough for something to happen, our consent is a way of holding the heart-mind still, creating an opportunity for something to find us and strike up a conversation. For a while, at least, we are saying that we won't turn anything away; we won't jump to categorize or assign value to things. We'll just listen. For this little while we agree not to know and to follow where the form takes us.

Through the gate come our subjective experiences—our inner narratives, moods, and physical sensations. After a while, meditation also shows us what it's like before the shaping power of thoughts and feelings kicks in. We consent to giving the usual cognitive and emotional filters a rest so that meditative forms can influence us at deeper levels. Over time they change how we perceive and feel about things, how our intuition works, and even how we respond somatically, before cognition. We are allowing the long, slow waveforms of tradition and practice to act upon the spiky graph of our moment-by-moment experience.

This can be hard work, and it takes some trust, so it's helpful that we discover pretty quickly how not alone we are. There's the tradition and the ancestors; we're sitting with everyone who has ever sat. The gate is an address the ancestors recognize, and through it they come, bearing their encouraging and their disorienting advice. Through the gate come intimations of the vastness and of the source of the river of being. The vastness doesn't need an address to home in on since it's already everywhere, but we need to be able to receive it. It's one of the beautiful paradoxes of meditative practice that consenting to occupy a particular, small location in a very particular way—body arranged like this, heart-mind like that—actually opens us to the unbounded, immeasurable aspect of reality. What exists as form meets what is without form.

As these various aspects of the world begin to meet up in the field of our meditation, sometimes things flow together easily and the field effortlessly expands. We discover ways to harmonize with the rhythms of the Earth and eternity. We realize that we're becoming the place where the teachings take on actual, embodied life. When we practice together, our individual, introverted practices connect us with others and we become part of an even larger field.

Sometimes there's tension. Perhaps the most important aspect of our consent is the willingness to stay put, and even to be interested, when the things that come through the gate seem to jostle each other and argue with us or provoke us to argue with them. Sometimes becoming intimate with the realm of thoughts and feelings is tremendously painful. Sometimes the ancestral voices seem not just inscrutable but crazy or wrong. Sometimes the vastness is overwhelming and frightening. The conversation at the gate becomes colored with complaint, mistrust, or fear.

That's when it's good to feel solid stone at your back, something you can lean against when the field starts to spin. To stay with a form when things get dicey is simply to choose the ground upon which to meet the disturbance. Since we focus so much on meditation's stilling and expansive qualities, it might seem surprising that one of the intentions of meditation is to put us in a state of tension. The steadiness of meditative forms allows apparent dualities to emerge, and the invitation is not to smooth over their differences or choose between them. Doing either is settling prematurely; it's settling before unsettling tension can become creative. For example, meditation might go along quite deeply and peacefully for a while, and then one day it's filled with agitation and rumination. Has something gone wrong? Was there good meditation and now there's bad? Here's a tension. If we refuse to choose a label and we widen the perspective a little, we might notice a couple of things. The external form remains the same; we're sitting the way we always have. Is there something internally that also remains the same, something underneath states of either peace or agitation? Perhaps we discover that the field of meditation is constant, and it's just a matter of different qualities and states arising in it. This is how a tension between apparent dualities becomes creative, pointing us to a third thing that includes both and is bigger than either. To the extent that we can shift our allegiance from the transitory states to the constant field, we begin to create a new possibility, a new way of living.

If we stay put long enough, we'll confront the largest tension of all: that we and everything else are formed and formless at the same time. As we learn to see the creative potential of the smaller-scale tensions in our meditation, we experience for ourselves how the apparent tension between form and formlessness resolves itself over and over again to produce the manifest world.

All helpful forms eventually have to blow themselves up. Everything has its shadow, and the danger in having a static relationship with meditative forms is when we focus primarily on getting them right. When we do this, correct form is no longer a beautiful means of discipline and surrender but the goal itself. Instead of providing a liberating experience of the largeness of things at the intersection of form and emptiness, the forms of practice can become constricting and self-centered affectations. Eventually we have to break free of the idea that a particular state of heart-mind is dependent on a particular meditative form. What we experience by sitting at the gate has to roll out in a kind of slow-motion explosion to affect the rest of our lives. The original form doesn't necessarily disappear; we might continue to practice it. But it becomes something less bounded and more fluid, present in more of our lives, taking the form of whatever we're doing.

This is the final tension: that which is between formal discipline and the formless permeation of meditation throughout our lives. As we hold the tension, we might notice that a remarkable transformation is taking place. The gate has begun to impress itself on us, and we are taking it in. The gate made of stones is becoming flesh and blood, hands and eyes; it is becoming a part of us wherever we are. The decision to sit down at the stone gate in that ancient landscape is made by individuals, one by one, but there are no limitations on who and what can be affected by a gate made flesh, carried into the world.

Bonnie Myotai Treace

FOR ALMOST twenty years, Bonnie Myotai Treace was vice-abbess of Zen Mountain Monastery, one of the largest Zen monasteries in the West. She also established the Zen Center of New York City and served as its first abbess. She has led more than five hundred retreats, conferences, and workshops and is particularly known for her work in women's spirituality, poetry, water conservation, and koan study. She has advanced degrees in literature and hydromechanics and holds current EPA Watershed Management certification.

In 2004 Treace founded Hermitage Heart, a training program that is primarily Zen in flavor and that puts a special emphasis on home practice. The retreat house of Hermitage Heart is Gristmill Hermitage in Garrison, New York, where Treace lives and writes.

In order for women to see ourselves clearly and walk in awareness, we need other women, she has said. "Receiving the legacy of our grandmothers and mothers helps us. So does knowing that our sisters are beside us—even as they are different from us—and recognizing that we are here to make a better world for our daughters and granddaughters."

In "We Cannot Stop the Hail, but We Can Be Awake," Treace delves into the poetry and spiritual path of Rengetsu, a nineteenth-century Japanese nun.

We Cannot Stop the Hail,
but We Can Be Awake

A SCENT of wood smoke and incense, wind wrapping itself around a small hut, the quiet presence of a settled, generous spiritual friend: to sit with the poems of the Buddhist nun Rengetsu is to allow a teacher into the depths of one's mind. Over the winter, this has been my practice, taking up a few of Rengetsu's winter-inspired verses from the John Stevens translation *Lotus Moon* and staying with them, committing myself to let them inform whatever teaching happens during this time.

Keeping that commitment open hasn't always been easy. Some of Rengetsu's writing is so strong that it is immediately engaging and stirs the sense of trust and humility that comes so naturally when excellence takes hold of one's attention. Nothing truer or finer beckons; restlessness slips away. But some of her verses, like many of the classic koans in the collections used in Zen training, lie a little flat initially and take more work to open up. Since commitment to any practice means not moving to something easier when it gets difficult, the challenge has been to stay with them and give even her harder-to-appreciate poems time to work on the heart and soften the impulse to reject them and move on.

Born in the late eighteenth century, Rengetsu lived what could easily have become a tragic life. She was the daughter of a courtesan and a samurai, but her natural father had her adopted by a lay priest serving at Chionji, Japan's head temple of the Pure Land sect of Buddhism. Rengetsu's adopted father, Teruhisa, seems to have been devoted to her. He taught her martial arts, calligraphy, and an appreciation for art and literature that later—in a certain way—would save her life. For several years she served as an attendant to the lord of Kameoka, a city near Kyoto, and was fortunate in being able to continue her classical education while there. Stevens writes, charmingly, "Rengetsu was just as capable of dismantling intruders and subduing annoying drunks as she was at making poetry and performing the tea ceremony."

But then the challenges began to roll in: she was married off, had three children who died in early infancy, and separated from a husband who abused her and who also died shortly thereafter. She married again, and while she was pregnant with their second child, her husband became ill and passed away. Try to imagine, if you will, this woman's life: thirty-three years old, with two small children, having experienced more heartbreak and loss than most of us will know in a lifetime. If ever there was an excuse for feeling overwhelmed and depressed, her life certainly offered one.

One pleasure of discovering the lives and teachings of the rare women we find in the history of Buddhism is seeing how they take up the tragedies in their lives and transform them. They remind us of the freedom no circumstances can take from us. Because their stories are generally less accessible—and because the luxury of serious religious training was less available to them—finding someone like Rengetsu is a great gift. She faced this moment in her life when despair could have taken hold, when impermanence had pretty much whipped her to the bone, and somehow her heart sparked. She was ordained, taking her children with her to live on the grounds of Chionji with Teruhisa, and practiced in earnest. Still, death kept coming, and by the time she was forty-one, her remaining children and the adoptive father she had loved since childhood were all gone. Not allowed to remain at Chionji, she then had to find her way alone.

She walked into a world that attempted to limit her on the basis of her gender. It's said she considered whether she could make a living as a teacher of the game of Go, at which she excelled, but recognized that few male students would be able to muster student mind with a female teacher. She soon realized that art would be her path and began making pottery as a kind of moving meditation, inscribing each piece with a bit of poetry.

Over time her work became immensely popular, so much so that she found it necessary to never stay long in any one place, or crowds would begin to gather around her. Likening herself to a drifting cloud, she was still incredibly prolific, with her work becoming one of the most generous, sustained offerings of deep spiritual practice in Buddhist history. Reputedly, she was able to raise large sums of money for disaster victims because of her ability to be as at ease intermingling with statesmen and great artists of her day as she was meditating or making pottery alone in her hut. When she died in 1875 at the age of eighty-four, she left a legacy of more than fifty thousand pieces of pottery, calligraphy, paintings, and poetry. She is remembered not as a tragic figure but as one of those rare human beings who draw from a seemingly bottomless well of strength and love.

The three Rengetsu winter poems that I'd like to introduce to you have a straightforward, unadorned quality, as does most of her writing. And although she did not organize them into the sequence in which they appear in Stevens's book, their progression struck me as expressing a spiritual journey itself.

Winter Confinement in Shigaraki Village

Last night's storm was fierce
As I can see by this morning's
Thick blanket of snow:
I rise to kindle wood chips
In lonely Shigaraki Village.

Shigaraki Village is where Rengetsu would go to get the clay for her pottery. This is such a beautifully simple poem—a woman enters a hut, she's come some distance, she's worked all day. Darkness comes. At dawn she sees snow blanketing the hills and knows that there must have been a fierce storm in the night. She kindles the fire. In its thusness, it is just thus.

But as we stay with the poem, we might find ourselves reflecting on the journey we make to find the clay for our own vessel. We might begin to wonder about leaving home and coming to dwell alone. During our *ango*—our spring training period—at the temple, each of us, for instance, is asked to leave our familiar patterns and intensify practice: to dwell peacefully in each moment's sufficiency, making our home there. When monastics ordain, it's the same deal: we become *unsui,* "clouds and water," letting go of the activities in our life that are self-securing and giving ourselves to the journey that is itself our home. So when the poet makes her pilgrimage to Shigaraki, to go with her is to take that journey as well. Will we go, gather the clay for our real work, and settle into the moment?

In Shigaraki village, the poet is waking up. She's inferring from the evidence the realities of a night's storm. It's interesting that in the Buddhist tradition, night is often used to point to total intimacy, the reality of oneness, of not separating the self from things. In the night, or "darkness," there is no distinction, no separation between seer and seen. In the words of the Heart Sutra, it is the time of "no eye, ear, nose, tongue, body, mind." What is that night? Of course, when many of us begin to sense the "fierce storm" of night in spiritual life, we may yearn for nothing but to be elsewhere. On the edge of it, we pull back, trying to hold on to something of ourselves.

Haven't you felt the resistance that thrives right on the cusp of breaking through? There, on the edge, most of us have some kind of argument. "I can't sit another minute," we say. Or "I can't see this koan." Or "I don't know how to love this person." The poem points to a kind of sweet constancy, the kindling of the fire. Just take care of the moment. Stoke the flame when it falters. The poet stirs the wood chips; we stir our life to find the warm center of things. What is that center?

Master Dogen writes, "When the dharma does not fill your whole body and mind, you think it's already sufficient. When the dharma fills your body and mind, you understand something is missing." What is needed? The world has never depended more than it does now on those who will genuinely ask that question. Always encourage each other to go deeply into that inquiry. How might you serve? What remains to be seen?

Dogen continues, "To study the Buddha way is to study the self. To study the self is to forget the self. To forget the self is to be confirmed by the ten thousand things. To be confirmed by the ten thousand things is to cast off body and mind of self as well as that of others. No trace of realization remains, and this no trace is continued endlessly."

The fire of our freedom will always warm the hut, but somehow we won't feel it unless we kindle it. And that kindling of the fire continues. It's not on the clock, like a workday we can't wait to see end. It's loving and essentially timeless. Practically, getting this point means we're relieved of feeling we're behind or progressing too slowly in our training, or that we're spiritually talented and should set our sights on becoming teachers. It's just time to kindle the wood chips: get over yourself.

In the hut where she's come to make the vessel, responsible for the fire, awake to the night's storm as it was revealed only in the light, the poet faces the day.

A Day of Hail

Will the paper
On my makeshift
Little window
Withstand the assault
Of the hailstones?

A poem in which a woman, alone in a hut, wonders if her small window made of fragile paper will be strong enough not to be ripped apart by a long day of pelting hail. Simple enough: the sound of heavy stones of solid water hitting and hitting and hitting, the paper window pocking with each hit, quivering, providing such a thin barrier against the storm.

What is this makeshift window—this temporary point of view, if you will? The poet takes us into a day in which the essential vulnerability of our position is a visceral reality. She invites us to feel and hear and taste the aliveness of right now. How do we live with impermanence? By adding another layer to the window? By praying for sunnier days? We cannot stop the hail, Rengetsu seems to whisper, but we can be awake. Awake and at peace.

How do you find that peace?

Be yourself. Be yourself, and live that boundless reality intimately, generously, freely. Usually, if you ask someone who they are, you're likely to get the list: "I went to this college, I'm married to this person, I know how to make soup, I'm good at this, I'm bad at that, I can do this, I can do that." We list all the aggregates, all the things that change, all the makeshift identities. But what is the real nature of the self? Noticing the thinness of the seeming barrier between inside and out, just experience that permeability. What are we protecting?

A monk asked Master Dongshan, "When cold and heat come, how can we avoid them?" How do we live in this world of trouble, of suffering, of horror, of change, where we can't hold on to what's pleasant or completely get away from what's unpleasant? How can we avoid the heat and cold? Dongshan replied, "Go to where there is no heat or cold."

The monk then implored, "But how do I get to that place where there is no heat or cold?" Dongshan said, "When it's cold, the cold kills you. When it's hot, the heat kills you." In other words, kill the separation. Quit living in fear of what might be and dwell in this.

But what about the assault of the hailstones? When what hits is not just weather but something that arrives with intent to harm, what then? I find it inspiring that Rengetsu spends none of the precious moments in her poem cursing the sky or dissecting the cause of precipitation.

Why are so many people trying to kill so many people? Why is there such enormous greed? Why is there evil? Why did this happen to me? We should consider how a day of hail might be simply, utterly that: a day of hail. Not to be denied, not feared, not hidden from.

There's a story told about an old fisherman out on a very foggy day. Suddenly, this other boat comes and crashes into him. He spends the next couple of hours battening down his own boat where it's leaking and cursing about how this sailor, who shouldn't even be on the water, ruined his day, ruined his catch, ruined his family's meal and his livelihood. Enraged, he works through the morning cursing as, gradually, the fog begins to lift.

Suddenly he sees that what hit him wasn't another boat—it was a rock. All at once, he regrets the hours wasted in such anger, the birds he didn't hear, the enjoyment he didn't feel.

Mountain Retreat in Winter

The little persimmons drying outside
Under the eaves
Of my hermitage—
Are they freezing tonight
In the winter storm?

This last of our three poems brings us into the hermitage again, with a feeling of the life under its eaves. Entering the hermitage, in a sense we enter the heart of Buddhism. We stop waiting for company. We stop needing others to show us what's normal, to know what we should do. We sit alone. That's the first teaching gesture of the Buddha: he stopped deferring and referring and looking for an authority. He just sat down— in his own life, in his own mind, in his own condition, with his own karma—and aloneness was transformed. The whole world wasn't excluded; when he sat, the dividing wall between his life, mind, condition, and karma and that of the world was dropped. This is the hermitage heart that beats in each of us. We just need to stop being too afraid to trust it.

Practice is the journey to that trust. It begins when we stop waiting for someone to say: here's the plan; here's the right thing to do; here's the act of courage, of attention, of kindness, of wisdom that you can make. Each of us has that wisdom. Each of us, in fact, *is* that wisdom. Each of us can leap thoroughly into that hermitage heart and get on with it. We don't need another life, a different condition, a greater wisdom, a better personality. We just need to take care of the life under the eaves of this measureless hermitage.

How? In asking, we begin the journey home.

Credits

Karen Maezen Miller, "Waking Up Alone." From the September 2011 issue of the *Shambhala Sun*.

―――――, "Sanitize Option: What Children Do Not Require." Excerpted from the book *Hand Wash Cold: Care Instructions for an Ordinary Life* © 2010 by Karen Maezen Miller. Printed with permission of New World Library, Novato, Calif. www.newworldlibrary.com

Pat Enkyo O'Hara, "Include Everything." From Villagezendo.org.

Toni Packer, "What Is the Me?" From *The Wonder of Presence*, © 2002 by Toni Packer. Reprinted by arrangement with Shambhala Publications Inc., Boston, Mass. www.shambhala.com.

―――――, "Images in Relationship." From *The Light of Discovery*, © 1995 by Toni Packer. Reprinted by arrangement with Shambhala Publications Inc., Boston, Mass. www.shambhala.com.

Tenzin Palmo, "Vajrayana." From *Reflections on a Mountain Lake: Teachings on Practical Buddhism*, © 2002 by Tenzin Palmo. Reprinted by arrangement with Shambhala Publications Inc., Boston, Mass. www .shambhala.com.

Sharon Salzberg, "The Journey of Faith." From *Faith: Trusting Your Own Deepest Experience*, by Sharon Salzberg, copyright © 2001 by Sharon Salzberg. Used by permission of Riverhead Books, an imprint of Penguin Group (USA) LLC.

―――――, "Living Our Love." From *Loving-Kindness: The Revolutionary Art of Happiness*, © 1995 by Sharon Salzberg. Reprinted by arrangement with Shambhala Publications Inc., Boston, Mass. www .shambhala.com.

About the Editor

ANDREA MILLER is deputy editor of *Shambhala Sun* magazine and the editor of the anthology *Right Here with You: Bringing Mindful Awareness into Our Relationships*. She holds an MFA in creative writing from the University of British Columbia, and her writing has appeared in various publications, including *The Best Women's Travel Writing* series, *The Best Buddhist Writing* series, and *Buddhadharma: The Practitioner's Quarterly*. Miller practices in the Plum Village tradition.